ADRIFT

ADRIFT

A TRUE STORY *of* TRAGEDY *in the* ICY ATLANTIC—
and the ONE WHO LIVED *to* TELL ABOUT IT

BRIAN MURPHY

with **TOULA VLAHOU**

DA CAPO PRESS

Da Capo Press
Hachette Book Group
1290 Avenue of the Americas, New York, NY 10104
dacapopress.com
@DaCapoPress, @DaCapoPR

Printed in the United States of America

First Edition: September 2018

Published by Da Capo Press, an imprint of Perseus Books, LLC, a subsidiary of Hachette Book Group, Inc. The Da Capo Press name and logo is a trademark of the Hachette Book Group.

The Hachette Speakers Bureau provides a wide range of authors for speaking events. To find out more, go to www.hachettespeakersbureau.com or call (866) 376-6591.

The publisher is not responsible for websites (or their content) that are not owned by the publisher.

Illustrations © by Terry Kole

Print book interior design by Trish Wilkinson

Library of Congress Cataloging-in-Publication Data has been applied for.

ISBNs: 978-0-306-90200-0 (hardcover), 978-0-306-90199-7 (ebook)

LSC-C

10 9 8 7 6 5 4 3 2 1

For Zoe, as always.
And to all the immigrants, refugees, and sojourners,
past and present, who shape and enrich the world.

Contents

Author's Note

When my daughter was young, she and I enjoyed hunting for sea glass on beaches around Greece. For years, we filled containers and bottles with the sea-scrubbed nuggets. These castaway bits—different shapes, different textures and colors—gradually built a story. A layer of sea glass in a small cup might represent one week attached to one specific memory. A fat jam jar filled to the brim might be the remembrances of a full season.

This book is a lot like that.

I came across the first stray fragment of the story in a basement on Cape Cod, where a local historical museum had assembled a wonderful exhibit on shipwrecks. From there, and for the next three years, I collected more pieces wherever I could find them. They turned up in places such as the old waterfront in Liverpool on the River Mersey, the side streets of Fairhaven on Buzzards Bay, and the archives at Mystic Seaport on tidewaters pulled toward Long Island Sound.

Like the sea glass, the scattered shards of this story, waiting to be gathered and brought together, added up to a moment in time. This one took place far out in the cold Atlantic more than a century and a half ago.

This is a work of nonfiction. All the events occurred. I did my best with what I found, making every effort to portray, with accuracy and precision, the arc of the story and the people involved. The narrative comes together from an array of sources that include published material, family archives, civil and church records, shipping ledgers, and interviews conducted in Europe and the United States.

That was the easy part.

The more challenging task was properly conveying the thoughts, emotions, and dialogue of the people involved.

There is, of course, no way to know the exact words exchanged on the *John Rutledge* or among those huddled in an open lifeboat adrift in the North Atlantic. Even harder to discern are characters' inner voices and fears. On both fronts, I relied heavily on the only person who could know: the sole survivor of the wreck. Fortunately, just after rescue he gave detailed statements to various newspapers. He also offered recollections decades later and his accounts did not vary in any significant ways. Most important, they were highly consistent in describing how those on the lifeboat interacted, battled for life, and, ultimately, died. The various retellings, however, do include some minor discrepancies, mainly in the order of events aboard the lifeboat. None of these variations change the story in any fundamental manner.

To further enhance the dialogue, I consulted experts in mid-nineteenth-century linguistics and speech patterns in New England, Ireland, and Britain.

I mention all this for an important reason:

To ask for a small indulgence. Do not look on the dialogue as verbatim. Rather, view it as a carefully considered approximation based on research. I put quotation marks around only the passages that appear in logs, newspapers, and other sources. The rest of the dialogue—exchanges among the crew and so forth—does not carry quotation marks because I don't want to suggest that these are the exact words spoken. Instead, they are a literary reflection of what is known about how the various figures in the story interacted.

I try to recount this story in its full sweep and attempt to explore the souls and sensibilities of those involved. This is, I believe, my duty as a storyteller. I also have an obligation as a journalist. I can never turn my back on facts. I have endeavored to keep every aspect of this book aligned with what is known or what can be surmised with strong confidence.

The vagaries of recordkeeping and newspaper reporting in that era forced some decisions. A few names appear in records with different spellings. I added footnotes to further explain the choices I made. In every case, I selected the spelling most widely used in the accounts or confirmed through further documentation.

One final point of context: although this book keeps a tight focus on one tragedy in the age of sail, it strives for a greater reach. Scores of ships—carrying tens of thousands of passengers and crew—met a similar fate in the Atlantic before twentieth-century advances in communications technology enabled better notice on looming ice fields and approaching storms. The names of some lost ships are remembered. So are a few of the prominent figures who perished at sea.

But almost totally forgotten are the others who went down with them: emigrants, seamen, travelers, merchants, and envoys. Entire families. Young men and women striking out for a new life. Children too young to grasp the dangers of an Atlantic crossing.

They are the anonymous dead.

The sea is good at swallowing lives without a trace.

This is my belated elegy for them all and the risks they faced on the North Atlantic.

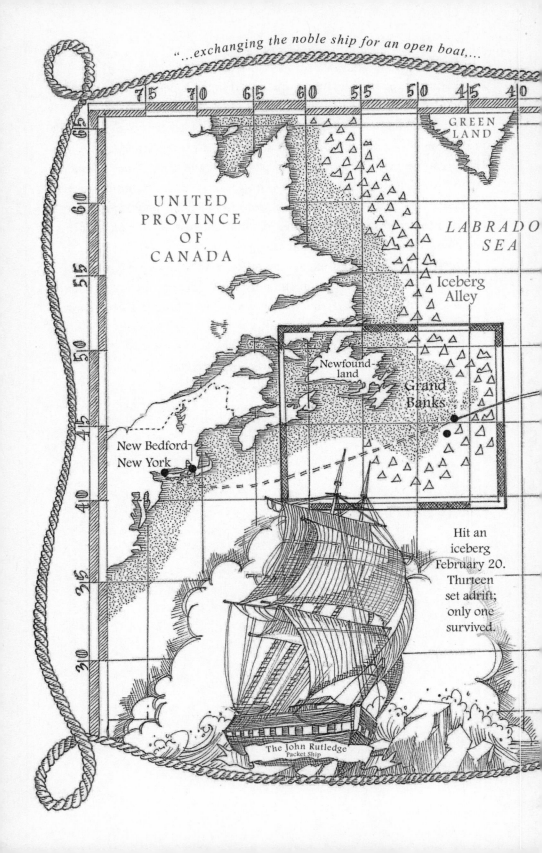

"...exchanging the noble ship for an open boat,..."

GREEN LAND

UNITED PROVINCE OF CANADA

LABRADO SEA

Iceberg Alley

Newfoundland

Grand Banks

New Bedford
New York

Hit an
iceberg
February 20.
Thirteen
set adrift;
only one
survived.

The John Rutledge
Packet Ship

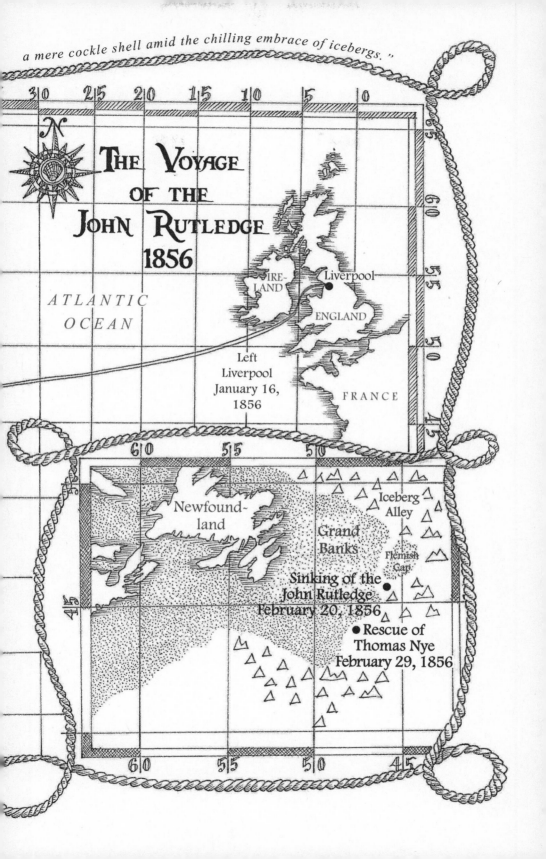

a mere cockle shell amid the chilling embrace of icebergs. "

The Voyage of the John Rutledge 1856

N

ATLANTIC OCEAN

IRELAND

Liverpool

ENGLAND

FRANCE

Left Liverpool January 16, 1856

Newfoundland

Grand Banks

Iceberg Alley

Flemish Cap

Sinking of the John Rutledge February 20, 1856

Rescue of Thomas Nye February 29, 1856

The Ice

The North Atlantic ice obeys its own rhythms.

Some years, the ice is sparse and sporadic. Jagged castaways drift down from the Greenland ice sheets, but not in great numbers. The next year, however, the ice can flake away from the glaciers, thick and dangerous—as if the Arctic is shrugging off its frozen skin. When the vectors of wind, currents, and other elements take over, they can, under the right circumstances, keep most of the ice safely in the far north. Or they can carry the ice floes farther south into the main sea routes between Europe and North American ports, from Newfoundland to Baltimore. In the era before satellites, radar, and mobile communication, these years of thick southern ice frightened even the most hardened sailors.

The year 1856 was a time of North Atlantic ice like few others.

Starting in January, seamen arrived in New York, Boston, and other Eastern ports bearing alarming reports. No one had seen ice this dreadful in ages. They weren't just sighting huge icebergs—some wider than the plans for Central Park or taller than the Westminster Palace clock tower being built in London. The worries about the ice in 1856 were a culmination of everything that made mariners shudder. The bergs were bigger, the pack ice denser, and the ice field's edges more southerly than many could recall.

"Old and experienced sea captains state that they never saw the ocean so much obstructed with ice," said a dispatch in the *New York Times*.

One clever wordsmith coined the phrase "ice armada."

The steamship *Arago*, en route from the French port of Le Havre to New York, was forced to take a two-hundred-mile southern detour to stay clear of the ice. The steamship *Baltic* reported treacherous ice as far south as 43 degrees, 30 minutes, about the same latitude as southern Maine. Other ships sighted bergs in the North Atlantic approaching the forty-second parallel, about as far south as Cape Cod Bay.

Off Newfoundland, the crew on the ship *Henry Reed* passed icebergs three hundred feet tall. These titans carried so much mass below the surface that they ran aground on the seamounts of the Grand Banks. In early 1856 at least a half-dozen ships arrived in American and European ports with ice damage or tales of being held tight for days in ice-locked seas.

They were the lucky ones.

Before the first three months of 1856 were out, nearly 830 passengers and crew went missing in the North Atlantic. The packet ship *John Rutledge* was torn open by ice and sunk. This was the presumed fate of at least three more vessels that vanished somewhere between England and New York. Meanwhile, other ships, carrying dozens more people, sailed or steamed into the Atlantic that cursed winter.

They, too, were never heard from again.

. . . souls gone down in the great deep, without leaving a ripple on the surface of the ocean, or causing a ripple on the great surface of society. A cool announcement is made that they are lost, and that is all. Who can estimate the long protracted agony of surviving friends, who waited from day to day for the arrival of the missing ships, until hope faded away into despair! So passeth the world.

—*Pittsburgh Gazette,* August 1856

The most amazing wonder of the deep is its unfathomable cruelty.

—Joseph Conrad, "The Mirror of the Sea"

Prologue

FEBRUARY 29, 1856.

Sir, you are wanted on deck. It's urgent. We believe we see something, the second mate added quickly, the words tumbling out.

First mate of the *Germania,* Charles Hervey Townsend, looked up from his logbook. It was just before three in the afternoon on Leap Year day. He had just recorded a somewhat uneventful shift. That was always good for February in the North Atlantic. They were thirty days out from France and bound for New York with forty-seven passengers. For the past twenty-four hours, light winds rolled in from the west-southwest to accompany the moderate swells and steady snow. Nothing alarming. Best of all, the sea ice had eased. A day earlier it had surrounded the ship, and the captain was forced to haul in the sails. And then they waited and prayed the ice would not grow thicker.

Everyone familiar with those waters knew well how quickly the ice could change from a bothersome obstacle to a lethal danger. Even a modest iceberg could easily rip open a hull. Pack ice could crush the sturdiest vessel like a walnut. They were lucky this time. The ship had slipped through a corridor of dense ice without damage. But the angry winter weather kept the crew on guard. For days, howling gales and towering waves had roared in from the general direction of the Canadian Maritimes—it was the kind of weather that pushed the Greenland sea ice toward the Atlantic shipping lanes. But that morning the storms had finally taken a breather.

This respite on the last day of February gave Townsend a chance to look ahead. With favorable winds, the *Germania* could clear the most dangerous stretch through the ice fields off Newfoundland. Once safely

I

to the south, they would then set their final course for New York, and possibly tie up before the next full moon, in late March.

Good fortune was required to pass southeast of Newfoundland, one of the busiest shipping corridors in the western Atlantic. It was impossible to predict when the ice giants would appear. About eighteen months earlier, the master of the British brig *Queen* reported a berg five miles around and three hundred feet tall. This monster was spotted just about where the *Germania* now sailed: some three hundred fifty miles southeast of Newfoundland on the eastern edge of the Grand Banks.

And there was the fog to contend with. It churned up thick and sudden along the seams where the warmer Gulf Stream brushed against the Arctic-chilled currents from the north. These were some of the densest and most persistent fog zones in the world. The *Germania* had been passing in and out of fog banks for days.

Townsend, in his cramped script, jotted down the ship's coordinates. Latitude: 44 degrees, 11 minutes north. Longitude: 47 degrees, 34 minutes west.

Sir? Please hurry, the second mate urged. You are needed.

Well, what is it? Townsend asked.

Some of the crew—the ones fixing the outer jib—they think they spotted a small boat with a distress flag, sir. And . . .

Survivors? Townsend interrupted.

Maybe, said the mate. We think maybe.

Townsend went quickly to the deck. All he could think about was the puzzling incident from a few nights earlier. He had spoken to no one about it, but he knew the crew would be talking. That night, the helmsman swore he heard a voice crying out from the sea. The crew on deck thought they might have come across shipwreck survivors somewhere out there in the darkness. Townsend dismissed the noises as nothing more than the wind and ordered the ship to sail on.

Now this.

Keep an open mind, he told himself. It could be debris that looks like a boat. The North Atlantic was full of such flotsam.

On deck, Townsend walked along paths cleared of the more than six inches of snow that had fallen since morning. He climbed into the rigging on the foremast near the bow. Even though snow still fluttered down, the flat winter light was good, casting a nice contrast between the water and anything on it. Townsend adjusted his spyglass, a fine mariners' model built back home in New Haven.

There it was, just as the mate had said. This was no hunk of shipwreck. There was no doubt it was a lifeboat. But what was that in the stern? It looked like a figure. A man perhaps. But alive or dead? The figure didn't offer any clues. It sat rigid. Townsend wondered whether it was just a lifeless body rocking in the sea.

Signal flags flapped along a pole and line on the boat. Was that an oar propped upright? And what was on the line running from the oar to the stern? Were they shirts?

Townsend moved the spyglass lens slightly. Mounds of something were scattered about the tiny boat. Possibly more people. No, wait. Something was odd. Townsend studied the unnatural angles of their arms and heads and then drew a sharp breath. Could they be frozen bodies?

But hold on. The man sitting stiffly in the lifeboat seemed to stir. It looked like he was moving.

The man raised a weak arm to signal the *Germania*.

Townsend, hesitantly, waved back.

Chapter One

Call it a premonition.

Or perhaps a husband's protective reflex. Then again, maybe the impulse arose from something far more obvious: an ambitious ship captain wanting to concentrate on a hard trip across the Atlantic without any distractions. Such as his wife on board.

She was fine with any of these explanations. Each one offered some comfort. At the very least, they were something to hang on to.

The way it turned out, however, was the worst of all possible outcomes for Captain Alexander Kelley's wife. She would never know the real reason she was left behind in Liverpool that January. Later court documents never offered a clue. And she cared not to talk about it much. What was the point of revisiting a painful mystery? All she was sure about was the peculiar way the matter was decided. The captain—her husband of eight years—was unusually insistent. He had made up his mind. Almost to the point of being unreasonable.

She would stay in Liverpool, he said. And that was that.

This was a side of her husband that Irene Snow Kelley hadn't seen before. He could, at sea, be iron-willed. She expected that and so did his crew. All ship captains had a bit of an imperious streak. But Irene never had it directed at her in any meaningful way. She considered herself more his partner and helpmate, in the model of many captains' wives. Their bond had grown even stronger on their last trip, a December sail from New York to Liverpool.

Then, her husband made it clear she would not be making the return crossing. At least not yet. Not in winter. Irene said nothing and let him talk. She looked for a hole in his argument or a flaw in his logic. He gave her little to work with. Well then, she thought. Let's look at this from his perspective. She couldn't be blamed for his decision to leave her behind. She had done nothing wrong to anger him or the crew, either on the voyage over or while they were docked in Liverpool. So it must be something about the coming trip itself. There was no doubt he was caught up in the pressures of his new command.

This was a big one for him.

It was Kelley's first transatlantic circuit—New York to Liverpool and back—as captain of the *John Rutledge,* a fine specimen of a packet ship with less than five years of service under its belt. The new responsibilities must be weighing on him. Why else would he want to leave her in a strange port?

He justified his case.

There was simply no reason for her to endure a winter crossing back to New York. The weather would be rough the entire way.

Wait here, Kelley said. Enjoy Liverpool. Maybe go to London. I will be back in the spring, he added, and we can return to New York together.

She thought it over.

True, she would not be lonely. Even though they were new to Liverpool, the couple already had a wide circle of acquaintances and others angling for the captain's attention. All ship captains in the Atlantic packet business were instantly included in a network on shore as old as Liverpool's shipping trade, made up of portside gentry, businessmen of all stripes, royal contacts, self-styled dandies, diplomatic liaisons, and various hangers-on. A constant hum of invitations occupied ship captains—and their wives, of course, if they were along—in northern England's main port.

And Irene could not argue with her husband's premise: setting out on the North Atlantic in mid-January—westbound, with the wind in your teeth—was guaranteed to be a nasty affair. The seas could be monstrous and the ice could close in like a pack of hungry wolves.

He would be back in the spring on the next sail of the *John Rutledge,* she told herself.

If nothing else, she could count on the regularity of the Atlantic packet ship fleet, which included the *Rutledge* and hundreds of other sailing vessels and paddle-wheel steamers. They were in constant motion: back and forth across the Atlantic on a demanding schedule carrying passengers, freight, and mail. It certainly would be more pleasant to stay in England. She could sail home in May and arrive in time for the lovely first day of summer.

So, my dear, are we in agreement? Captain Kelley said this more as a statement than a question.

Fine, she consented. But promise me one thing. Promise me you will be safe.

She knew it was an empty appeal. The sea and ice dictated the terms of the crossings, not the captains or crew. Still, it made her feel better to hear him pledge to take extra care.

I promise, he said.

Irene Kelley then let the whole thing rest.

She didn't want to quarrel with him two days before his thirty-second birthday, which they planned to celebrate at the Waterloo Hotel, one of Liverpool's finest. At the Waterloo, you might just bump into the American consul Nathaniel Hawthorne, who was always happy to chat with a fellow New Englander, that is, so long as they met his rather pretentious standards. Ship captains made the cut. Normal seaman, middling merchants, and average working stiffs most certainly did not merit his attention. Hawthorne liked the good life and the exclusive company who could afford it or who were welcomed in by benefactors.

Irene understood that her husband had a lot resting on his shoulders just to prepare the *John Rutledge* for sea. The ship was scheduled to set sail in a little more than a week and there was much left to do. The Liverpool agent was still soliciting cargo. And Kelley needed to round out the crew.

After shedding some deck hands to Liverpool's many temptations and traps, the *Rutledge* was a few men short, and a ship needed a full complement in winter. There was always the chance of losing one or two crewmen along the way: swept overboard or subject to a ghastly accident. All it took was a rogue wave or a misplaced step on the rigging.

Besides that, the crew would have to deal with an unexpectedly full passenger list. Though many emigrants preferred to wait for spring, more than a hundred had booked tickets for steerage, the gloomy compartment below the main deck that would serve as their place to sleep, eat, wash, worry, battle seasickness, stave off disease, and generally hold on until the ship reached American shores. To some of the poorest folks heading to America, the hardships of a winter crossing didn't matter all that much. Being cold and miserable at sea was not much different from being cold and miserable on land.

The steerage passengers booked on the *John Rutledge* were mostly Irish. No surprise there. It was once assumed the flood of Irish to America would ease up once the potato blight ran its course in Ireland. But that wasn't proving true at all. Even though potato crops started to rebound by the mid-1850s, the number of Irish emigrants did not decrease. Irishmen with jobs in the States were like homing beacons for relatives and friends. Some dreamed of setting out for America's western frontier, maybe making it all the way to California with the other strike-it-rich dreamers and homesteaders. The island was emptying at a frightful clip. Packet ships such as the *John Rutledge* crowded them in and sailed them over if they had the fare.

Spring will be here before you know it, Kelley said. You are really the lucky one, my dear. You can stay in Liverpool. I must get this ship to New York.

That evening, just before five, a strange light appeared in the southern sky.

It cut ruler-straight across the last blushes of twilight—a glowing scar of aqua blue and silver that angled down into a cloudy haze on the horizon. The streak in the heavens held there for minutes before the last shimmer was gone.

The learned classes in Liverpool knew immediately what it was. Why, a meteor was giving an uncommonly fiery farewell. "Very similar," wrote one observer in a Royal Astronomical Society journal, "to the trace that is left by a Roman candle on a dark night." But many common deck hands in Liverpool, hard-wired to recognize omens and specters, didn't like it. Not one bit. This was not a promising sign for those about to head out to sea.

The compendium of sailors' superstitions is as vast as it is baffling. It covered everything from specific days not to set sail—all Fridays included—to special seagoing curses, including ones brought on by crewmates with flat feet or ginger hair.

Seamen had no trouble interpreting a weird flash in the sky as bad juju. About a century earlier, the Scottish poet William Falconer, a seafarer who was lost rounding the Cape of Good Hope, wrote of "portentous meteors" cutting through the gloom in his epic "The Shipwreck." The average shipmate probably never heard of Falconer, let alone delved into his work. They might not have been able to read at all. But Falconer was attuned to what set sailors' knees knocking. And that definitely included strange lights of all kinds.

One young seaman, a thin and soft-spoken American with coal-black eyes and not much of a beard, didn't go in for such foolishness. Thomas W. Nye was firmly rooted in a world he could see and measure and explain. The sea was complicated and dangerous enough, he figured. Why add hocus-pocus to make it more frightening?

Nye was not yet twenty-two, but he felt like he'd been partnered with the sea forever. In one sense, he was right. His education in all things nautical went back to as early as he could remember. It was part of being a New Englander of the Nye clan, which extended far and wide from its roots on Cape Cod. His pedigree included an impressive assortment of ship captains, whaling shipowners, and merchant sailors. There was always a Nye heading out to sea, returning from sea, tallying up how much he was making off the sea, or mourning someone lost at sea. Understanding the rewards and the risks of life offshore was all part of being a Nye.

The rest of Thomas's upbringing came in the form of basic, but solid, schooling. It was the kind drilled in by no-nonsense Quaker schoolmarms along Buzzards Bay on Massachusetts's southern coast. The classes included reading, writing, civics, and enough etiquette to get him by and spare him some embarrassments—nothing close to the polishing offered by prestigious schools to the north, like Boston Latin or Phillips Academy. Yet it was a far sight better than the spotty schooling of many of his crewmates. Nye was no scholar. He was no simpleton either.

He tried to tell his fellow seamen on the *John Rutledge* that the thing in the sky was just a meteor. Same as a shooting star, he said. You see those all the time, right? But this one was bigger and closer. That's all. No harbinger. No sign from sea nymphs or Davy Jones. Simple, old science, my friends.

Some listened. Some scoffed. Nye didn't push it.

He didn't want to get a reputation as a nag or know-it-all. He had to live and work with these men—a stitched-together crew of Yanks, Scots, and Irish. They had come over from New York together on the *Rutledge,* sorting out their personalities and peculiarities along the way. It wasn't a bad mix of gents. There were no big fights or smoldering tensions crossing from New York to Liverpool. But that leg was a smooth, twenty-one-day milk run, riding a nice late-fall tailwind and relatively easy seas. They all knew the trip back would be a far greater test. The season was later, the water colder, and the winds brasher, slamming into their faces rather than caressing their backs.

The *John Rutledge* had arrived in Liverpool on Christmas Eve. The weather had warmed a bit, and that brought smiles after a wicked cold snap had covered the port in a thick varnish of ice. The city's markets, decorated by festive gaslights, weren't slowed by any weather. Holiday geese and slabs of beef and extravagant seasonal delights such as hot chocolate packed sellers' stalls for those who could afford them, and plenty could in Liverpool.

This was one of the world's busiest ports. With ships came money. That meant a few coins for the lowly dockhands, but piles of cash for the traders and shippers at the highest reaches of the port city pyramid. Still, not everyone was boosted by Liverpool's rise. Those who were sick, disabled, widowed, or orphaned and numbers of others struggled in Liverpool, like they did in any Victorian-era city on both sides of the Atlantic. The rules of the sea transposed onto land: you stayed afloat or you went under. No one was going to help you.

But once in a while, often at Christmas, guilt made an appearance. Those with means might toss a bit extra to those without. At one Liverpool workhouse, a last-chance haven for the destitute, the overseers decided that their charges should be "regaled" with roast beef and plum pudding on Christmas Day. By their own count, there were 372 more paupers this Christmas week compared with this Yuletide week in the previous year.

There was no holiday rest for the *Rutledge* crew. They were thrown into work the moment the ship reached port. They stowed the sails—first repairing any rips—checked the rigging, and scrubbed the deck. They took shifts keeping an eye on the Liverpool dock porters who unloaded the cargo, making sure nothing slipped into a pocket or slipped away in a sack. The crew preferred sailing for Liverpool for one important reason: usually the ship carried no passengers down in steerage on the eastbound voyage. That spared the sailors the unpleasant dockside task of cleaning and disinfecting the bunks and alcoves that acted as steerage passengers' makeshift urinals and places for the seasick to retch. It was horrid work. Sailors said it could be worse than slithering down into the head of a giant sperm whale to scoop up that last bucket of oil.

Word spread among the crew that the ship would have an unusually full manifest of emigrants for the westbound leg. That brought some groans, especially from the cook, who would have to keep the chow coming. The *Rutledge* crew expected a few dozen passengers down in steerage—not the one hundred or more who had already bought their tickets for New York. This was unusual. Sometimes, a winter sail back to America could carry as many passengers as crew. That didn't matter too much to the shipowners. The far more critical factor was keeping to the timetable and getting the mail and cargo across the Atlantic on schedule. This was where the real money was made. On its latest trip, the *Rutledge* had carried some of America's fall harvest bounty: 8,433 bushels of wheat, 12,738 bushels of corn, 977 bags of oats, and 177 bales of cotton. It was going back with iron rods, good English crockery, and salt.

Packet ships like the *John Rutledge* were the shuttles of the day.

The idea of the packets—born several decades earlier—was to impose predictability on the unpredictable seas. The concept was simple: if merchants and travelers knew a fixed date when a ship was leaving port, they could make their plans accordingly, saving time and limiting frustration. Before the advent of the packet lines, ocean travel and trade were largely loose affairs. Ships left when they had enough goods in the hold to make it worth their while, or simply when the captain was in the mood.

The packet lines changed all that.

They advertised specific departure dates and schedules so that, say, shopkeepers in Philadelphia would know when crates of British silver or guns could be expected to arrive from London and correspondents in Boston would know when their letters bound for Le Havre or Bremen were leaving. Finally, the flow of commerce, travel, news, and mail had some order and structure. And, in the years before the transatlantic telegraph, fortunes could swing on the timing of a packet ship's arrival, especially those carrying news from Liverpool.

The city was then the world's biggest cotton market—a key destination for loom-ready bales from the American South. If cotton prices in Liverpool were up even slightly, an American trader in New York or Boston could get that news straight from the docks and telegraph orders to the South. Those who were quick could buy cotton at a lower asking price—before Southern cotton brokers got wise to the demand—and book the cargo on the next packet to Britain to catch the higher price. Tens of thousands of dollars could hang in the balance.

The packets represented a powerful change in how the world traveled and conducted business.

But something else profound was unfolding in 1856. It was clear for all to see along the Liverpool quays. More and more steamships berthed there. Sea travel was in fast transition from one age to the next. Bigger and better steamers crossed the Atlantic faster and in more style than the sailing ships or even the sleek tall ship clippers could. Steamers had come onto the scene a few decades earlier as noisy, belching novelties. By the early 1840s, ships with a combination of steam and sail were common. At the end of that decade, powerful sidewheel steamers featured regularly in packet ports from Scandinavia to New Orleans. And by the mid-1850s, steamships were considered the speedsters of the seas; the press covered their advances with breathless prose as transatlantic speed records fell.

In the summer of 1854, the American wooden sidewheel steamer *Baltic* made the Liverpool–New York run in a once-unthinkable time of just under ten days. In early 1856, the *Baltic* possessed—for the moment—the coveted Blue Riband, the unofficial title of the fastest Atlantic crossing. The rival Cunard Line of Britain desperately wanted the Riband prize back in its hands. Cunard set its engine designers to work on ratcheting up horsepower and finding other ways to coax higher knots from its vessels.

Speed came in some very handsome packages. The new steamers were loaded with luxuries that would make a sultan blush: heavy velvets, gleaming leathers, aromatic rosewood and mother-of-pearl inlays. Even the handbills and newspaper ads for steamers dripped with snob appeal: "The owners of these ships will not be accountable for gold, silver, bullion, specie, jewelry, precious stones or metals unless bills of lading are signed therefor, and the value thereof therein expressed" read the standard disclaimer. For the packets, the situation was a lot more down-to-earth; they advised their passengers: keep an eye on your money and hand luggage.

The steamship lines were all about marketing. They knew people would pay for speed and fine trappings. The faster the vessels and the more lavish the amenities, the higher the ticket price to be leveraged. Passenger fares sometimes hit stratospheric sums such as $130 each for a first-class cabin and $325—about the annual salary of a well-paid American craftsman—for an extra-size stateroom. Let the packets tote the cargo and the immigrants, the steamship lines reasoned. We will cater to the better classes, who care to zip along under coal power and be happy paying for the privilege, thank you very much.

The snooty strategy worked well. It even swayed people who were still sinking their money into sailing ships.

While the *John Rutledge* was in port in Liverpool, so was one of its owners.

James Lawrence Ridgway, a fifty-one-year-old New York moneyman with a taste for the maritime inherited from his sea captain father, was half of Howland & Ridgway, the shipping line that had added the *Rutledge* to its stable of packets a few years earlier. In Liverpool, Ridgway was meeting with the shipping agents and port officials who kept things humming for the packet line on that side of the Atlantic. But it was time he thought about getting back to New York, where his wife and children were still a bit peeved that he had scheduled this trip to Liverpool over the holidays.

Just one cabin passenger was booked on the *Rutledge,* a fellow described as a Philadelphia businessman named C. J. Gale, so Ridgway could have picked any accommodation he wanted on his own ship. But he desired to return to New York in more elegant surroundings.

He booked passage on the *Pacific,* a sidewheel steamer like the *Baltic* and a past winner of the Blue Riband for the eastbound voyage.

Young Thomas W. Nye,* seaman on the *Rutledge,* had made a point of getting a closer look at the *Pacific.* He'd been hearing about the very same steamship from proud relatives for quite a while.

A distant uncle from his family's Cape Cod branch, Ezra Nye, had been captain of the *Pacific* for more than five years. Recently, Ezra had entered a kind of celebrity retirement, giving lectures, offering Old Salt observations to newspaper reporters, and, in banquet halls and salons from Boston to Philadelphia, using his sea chest of stories as a meal ticket. Ezra's career embodied the fast-moving times at sea. He had spent more than a decade as master of the fine sailing ship *Independence,* which he pushed in 1836 to an astonishing New York–Liverpool run of fourteen days, twelve hours, throwing down a new speed mark. He then moved up to the *Clay,* a sailing ship considered so luxurious that British aristocracy toured its accommodations during port calls in Liverpool.

In 1850, Ezra embraced the advancing technology of steam and took command of the stunning *Pacific,* which offered such hotel-style graces as steam heating and the service of a maître de cuisine from France. On one of his first runs, he just missed breaking the ten-day barrier for an Atlantic crossing to New York.

Not many ship captains' names were recognized instantly. But anyone who knew even a little about transatlantic shipping knew Ezra Nye, and

---

*Logic suggests that Thomas Nye's middle name was William, the name of one of his uncles (his father's brother) and others in the extended family. But available records—census logs, marriage and death certificates—note him only as Thomas W. Nye. This leaves open the possibility that Thomas could have had a different middle name or was given only an initial, which was done rarely in the nineteenth century but was still an option for parents.

he looked the part as well. He kept his beard cropped into mutton chops, as was the fashion for New England seafarers. He seemed always at the right place at the right time. In 1852, six days out of Liverpool on the *Pacific,* Captain Nye came across the British bark *Jessie Stephens* being pummeled by a gale that nearly sank it. Nye managed to rescue all aboard, and for the act, he was presented with a gold chronometer by Queen Victoria. The Liverpool Shipwreck and Humane Society later commissioned a gold medallion in Captain Ezra Nye's honor.

A widely read nautical publication, *The Sailor's Magazine and Naval Journal,* helped further fan the Ezra Nye mystique. It ran a piece describing him as something of a Good Samaritan of the high seas. "It might be readily supposed, from the rivalry existing between the companies which are contended for supremacy of the Atlantic, it was no light matter for Captain Nye to turn aside from his course. Of course we do not mean to say that as a man of proper feeling there was any alternative open to him but that of saving his perishing fellow creatures at all reasonable hazard at whatever commercial risk. There is, however, such a thing as cheerful and such a thing as reluctant aid."

As Ezra was fond of saying: a good name is better than precious ointment.

The seaman Thomas Nye paid attention.

As Thomas walked along the Liverpool waterfront, he passed more of the steam giants of the day.

There was the *Arabia,* a pride of the Cunard Line, with a hybrid design of sails and huge boilers that cranked out 950 horsepower—and burned up to 120 tons of coal a day—for its three-story-tall sidewheel. Nearby was its brand-new sister ship, *Persia,* being readied for its maiden voyage. The *Persia* was the biggest steamer of the day, 390 feet of wave-flattening power on a frame of twenty-one thousand tons of iron. A "leviathan vessel," wrote the *Illustrated London News,* which gushed about its "ponderous metal welded, jointed and riveted into each other with exceeding deftness." Here lay Cunard's new hope to get back the fastest-crossing crown.

It didn't take a nautical scholar to see where money and energy were being spent. But it took a while to get it right with the steamers. The early years of steam travel were shambolic. Boilers exploded, pipes sprung leaks with scalding jets, pistons ruptured, and crank shafts literally shook apart. In 1852 alone—just before US reforms were enacted to improve steamship safety—at least eighteen major explosions on steamships claimed 395 lives, according to a congressional report. The new safety measures didn't mean an end to the risks. On the California coast, in late January 1855, a boiler rupture blew apart the sidewheel steamer *Pearl* at the mouth of the American River, the same river where a chance discovery had set off the California gold rush. More than seventy people died on the *Pearl*.

Tragedies occurred. But no one doubted that steam power was the future.

Thomas Nye did not disagree.

He could sense the inevitable like any seaman. The new industrial age was rewriting everything. Steam trains drove out horse-drawn carriages, and bolt-action rifles leapfrogged over muskets. Yet Nye wasn't ready to make the jump to steamships. He was born into a family—and a town and region, for that matter—shaped by wind and sail. That was not an easy heritage to abandon. Something about the ethos of the glitzy steam packets didn't sit right with him. To Nye, and many others, including report writers in Congress, the steamers' emphasis on speed seemed to come with a sacrifice of safety. It didn't seem acceptable to put passengers and crew in extra peril just to trim time from a voyage. He also felt at odds with the trends toward high-society opulence on the Atlantic steamers. They clashed with his upbringing: Quaker egalitarianism at school and Methodist-Yankee abolitionist fire at home.

But Nye wasn't prepared to turn his back on the sea even if sailing vessels were falling by the wayside. He liked the fact his family tree was full of renowned and successful seamen. What would he do on shore anyway? A factory job had zero appeal. He wasn't drawn to any of the trades such as blacksmith or builder. No, Nye was happy just where he was. He figured he would stay in the packet trade as long as he could handle the deck work. And then, who knew? Maybe move up to be one of the mates. And from there, possibly cast an eye toward becoming a captain. Why not? He came from the same stock as Uncle Ezra and dozens of seagoing Nyes, who found a heaving deck preferable to a stable shore.

What troubled young Nye was how fast the packet world was changing in the age of steam. Sea travel was breaking into two camps: the high-end steamers that would get all the attention from owners and investors, and the rest of the sailing vessels, like the *John Rutledge,* that would limp along until they ended up dismantled for scrap. Nye was right, of course. The era of sail, which had been very good to the Nye family, was indeed coming to an end. But not just yet. The great sailing ships had still many years ahead. It was his duty to stick with the canvas and rigging as long as he could.

Nye looked over the shipping schedule printed in one of the Liverpool newspapers. The steamer *Pacific* was set to leave exactly a week after the *Rutledge.* That would still put the *Pacific* in New York weeks before the *Rutledge,* given the clear speed advantage of steam over sail. But any predictions, of course, had to take the Atlantic into account. Never assume anything at any time of the year, but especially in winter.

Nye put down the paper. He had no particular place to go until he was needed back on board. He liked to wander Liverpool's jigsaw of streets and alleys, which climb a gentle hill from the port. He always made sure to keep to the better parts of town, and he could afford to. He was good with his money and usually had a few dollars to spend, which was not always the case for many of his shipmates. They could easily burn through their pay on drink and women and gambling—and whatever else they fancied. Some wrapped up a hitch from New York to Europe and back with less money than when they started. Newspapers of the day were fond of running hectoring little truisms. One went: "More are drowned in the wine cup than in the ocean."

Nye's cautious habits gave him more options, including securing a reasonable room in one of the many hostels along the docks that catered to seamen. This was a big step up from the rank-and-file flophouses—infested with both fleas and thieves—and the dank sleeping berths on the *John Rutledge.*

☙

Nye learned the ways of Liverpool's urban jungle.

Grifters, flimflam artists, pimps, and pickpockets prowled, and seamen were high on their list of prime prey. Nye was better prepared than most because he knew the tricks of their trade.

He grew up exploring and observing every inch of the waterfront in Fairhaven and later cut his teeth in the bigger and grittier docklands of New Bedford, home port of the world's largest whaling fleet. All manners of crime and conniving went on there, but that was American-level scheming.

Liverpool was in another league. Its underworld had a few centuries' jump on honing scams of every dimension. The city had seen it all. The courts tried a nonstop parade of petty larceny, shakedowns, and sinister acts, both big and small. Often a female accomplice was used as bait. One American seaman, an unlucky chap named Peter Dodd, came across a man on King Street promising private female companionship. Indeed, as advertised, four women waited nearby. What Dodd soon discovered was that it was an ambush that left him twenty pounds lighter. Another crook in petticoats was the comely Fanny Williams, who heisted a tidy sum in jewelry from sailors and others beguiled by her charms. "She looked as mild as a moonbeam," a constable marveled.

Sailors weren't always the victims, though. While the *Rutledge* was in port, police were looking for a seaman named George Lamb from the Boston ship *Chariot of Fame*. He was charged with serial bigamy—marrying one woman in Liverpool in 1845, another in New York in 1848, and a third in Liverpool in 1855.

Some of the most notorious—and colorful—bad apples in Liverpool were an outlaw bunch known as crimps. In other ports, they were called Shanghai men, as in, *you've been shanghaied*. As in, *you've been waylaid*. A Liverpool crimp had one aim: finding crew members for ship captains and first mates who needed extra hands and who did not care, or ask, where the new crew members came from. The *John Rutledge* was just one of many ships short a few crew members. No one knew where they went, but being waylaid by crimps was high on the list.

Crimps were paid in cash for delivering a new man. Whether the new deck hand was willing or not was immaterial. The crimps also padded their income with whatever they could steal off the hapless mark in the process. They had a rich playbook to net a sailor, including straight-up threats and kidnapping. More than a few seamen were knocked unconscious only to awake as an unwitting crew member on board a ship heading out of port.

Crimps' favorite places to stalk were the many low-end boardinghouses for sailors—the type of places that Nye had the money to avoid. A notorious crimp-friendly landlady known as Ma Smyrden was said to have once tried to trick a crimp into taking away a corpse from her boardinghouse on Pitt Street. She claimed the poor dead chap was just passed out, and demanded an advance cut from the crimp as a finder's fee.

But Liverpool crimps employed other, less thuggish techniques, too. These almost always involved alcohol. Groups of crimps would board inbound boats in the River Mersey with cases of booze and persuade sailors to jump ship for the promise of more booze and better pay on another vessel. Some did. Some drowned in the process.

One Cape Cod–born captain, Alexander Holway, described a close escape when he was a young and green seaman exploring Liverpool. Two men approached him saying they had some "Canton silk handkerchiefs" they would sell cheaply because they had been smuggled ashore. Holway made the mistake of expressing interest. He was led to the back room of a saloon and beers were ordered. "I soon became conscious that they were professed robbers," Holway wrote in his diary. He saw their plan: get him drunk or slip something into his drink. "They had no hopes of stupefying me," he wrote. "So after an hour or so, I managed to leave them by paying their price for the handkerchiefs. They were real villains."

The cops and crimps were in a running battle of wits. In 1850, Liverpool opened the Sailor's Home on Canning Street with the promise it would be a crimp-free sanctuary—copying similar safe-zone projects for seamen in American ports. The Liverpool crimps simply added another twist, pretending to be the caring representatives of the Sailor's Home and directing the seamen to their own flophouses where more crimps awaited.

The writer-turned-diplomat Nathaniel Hawthorne didn't spare his fellow Americans his class-conscious mutterings. His journal held unkind words for the American seamen who sought the consulate's help after run-ins with Liverpool's lowlifes. The "most rascally set of sailors that ever were seen—dirty, desperate, and altogether pirate-like in aspect," Hawthorne wrote.

A verse in a popular sea shanty was part warning about the crimps' reach and part homage to their cunning:

> Them boarding-house masters was out in a trice
> A-smiling and promising all that was nice
> And one fat old crimp took a liking to me
> Says he, "You're a fool, lad, to follow the sea."

Nye was schooled enough in portside plots to steer clear of the lowlife side of Liverpool. It wasn't just self-preservation. As his distant uncle Ezra Nye had urged, Thomas Nye felt a responsibility to his family name.

It carried distinction in Fairhaven and, across the briny Acushnet River, in New Bedford, too. The big Nye clan had a knack for making sound choices. In the 1830s his New Bedford uncles sensed the shift in the whaling world from Nantucket and moved quickly to get their own whaling ships out to sea ahead of others. The Nyes stood firmly on the right side of history on the slavery question, too, offering support and money to the abolitionist cause, whose leaders in New Bedford included an eloquent escaped slave who took the name Frederick Douglass. Other Nyes included merchants in China, a diplomat in Canton, and a far-sighted entrepreneur, William Foster Nye, who found new and profitable uses for whale oil—even if he was a black sheep among the straight-arrow Nyes with his passion for spiritualism and belief in reaching across the great divide to communicate with the dead. William founded Nye Lubricants, a company that became a world-leading supplier of whale oil for clocks and precision machinery and, later, sold the petroleum products that replaced whale oil.

Thomas Nye had no intention of soiling the family name with some kind of scandal in Liverpool of being shanghaied or robbed by a prostitute. To prepare for the return crossing, he kept to a simple routine when not on board the *John Rutledge*. He picked a few taverns where he felt comfortable and read whatever books and newspapers he could get his hands on.

One recurring story line in the Liverpool papers caught his eye.

Ships coming into port were giving accounts of terrible ice encountered in crossing the Atlantic. Some called it the worst in decades—rivers of thick pack ice and huge sawtooth bergs. British steamers out of London were delaying their passage because of it. A few American shipping lines planned more southerly routes to skirt the ice.

Nonetheless, the *John Rutledge* would stick to its schedule. Captain Kelley made that abundantly clear to the crew, even as rumors leaked out about him leaving his wife behind for some unknown reason.

The ship, Kelley said, is set to sail on January 16.

Nothing was going to change that.

Chapter Two

William Henderson counted out the cash. It was exciting and staggering at the same time. He had never had such a sum. And now he was paying it out all at once.

Seven, eight, nine . . . The pile grew of one-pound sovereigns with the visage of Queen Victoria, who was one year short of marking her twentieth year on the throne. Then came the gray Bank of England notes in denominations of five pounds. They, too, were counted out atop a desk in the office of George Saul, the agent in Liverpool for the *John Rutledge*.

Thousands of similar transactions—with money ceremoniously doled out by nervous soon-to-be emigrants—unfolded every day in places just like this around Liverpool. For years, Henderson had socked away spare money from his pay as a railway laborer pounding spikes and laying roadbed. He was proud of his work. It seemed more important, more tied to progress, than the ditch-digging or slaughterhouse work that employed many fellow Irishmen who crossed to England after the potato famine took hold. But the British economy was cooling. And so were English attitudes toward the Irish. In a classic turnabout during hard times, the Irish went from being regarded as low-level job fillers to unwelcome job stealers. Henderson and his wife, Margaret, hadn't planned on joining the emigrant wave to America. If things had worked out in England, they would have been happy to stay. But now, with the English starting to turn against the Irish, leaving seemed the only sound choice.

Henderson surely walked briskly that morning to Saul's office at 36 Waterloo Road, a few miles from the docks where the *Rutledge* and scores of other ships were tied up. As he threaded through the crowds, he kept his hand shoved deep in his pocket, covering his money like a crypt slab sealing a grave. Anyone who had spent more than a few hours on Liverpool's docks knew it was foolish to take chances with the city's prying eyes and sticky fingers. An Irish bloke walking toward a shipping office was a tempting mark. He was likely carrying the fare to buy passage to North America or possibly all the way to Australia.

Henderson finished laying out the money. Around thirty pounds—the equivalent of nearly $150, or many months' pay for a good factory job in New York—bought steerage compartment passage on the *John Rutledge* for Henderson and his family, including his sister and her infant daughter. They were lucky, in one sense. Ticket prices for the sailing packets had recently dropped as a result of competition from some of the hungrier steamship lines. Steamers that couldn't compete with the glitz of rivals such as the *Pacific* dabbled in third-class, steerage-style barracks.

Henderson dictated the names and ages of his family to a clerk. That was easier than writing them out himself in his scratchy, unschooled hand.

William, 39. Margaret, wife, 37. Robert, son, 16. Margaret, daughter, 14. Mary, daughter, 9. James, son, 5. Eliza, niece, 1. Elizabeth, 32, sister and Eliza's mother.[*]

Destination? the clerk asked, as he did with every emigrant.
Well, America, Henderson replied with a bit of cheek.
No, do you plan to stay in New York?
Ah, no, said William. We are on our way to Boston.
The clerked noted it.
American officials weren't meticulous with the paperwork so long as new arrivals weren't oozing disease, mentally unhinged, or clearly up to no good. Simply too many newcomers showed up every day on ships from England, Germany, Norway, and elsewhere. But it never hurt, the clerk

---

[*]The ages cited for the Hendersons are based on England's 1851 census. The ages listed on the ship's manifest are slightly different. But recordkeeping by the shipping companies for emigrants in steerage often was highly imprecise.

told Henderson, to give the American gatekeepers some idea of where you intended to start your new life.

Henderson nodded politely. He knew that already. This is what the immigrant guidebooks advised, too. Henderson and tens of thousands of others pored over these guides like code breakers. They were the oracles of the day, offering tips such as how to survive the rigors of steerage, what to bring and what to leave behind, and how to make a good first impression on the American officials: Look decisive. Answer questions clearly and succinctly. And, whatever you do, don't come across like a deadbeat without a plan.

With the tickets in his pocket, William headed back to the lodging house where his family had crowded themselves in a single room since arriving a week before from the other side of England.

Room after room in the lodging house was the same. These Liverpool dives—offering nothing more than a bare board for bring-your-own blankets—were depressing but important waystations in one of the epic migrations of the century. From the flophouses, the next stop on the emigration trail was the Merseyside piers to get tickets on a ship heading out. Provided, of course, you didn't get robbed. Or fall critically sick. Or find yourself with a knife in your belly over some silly fight in a pub or at the hands of a thief in a back alley. Liverpool was a good dress rehearsal for the capricious sea journey ahead. Anything could happen.

You have the tickets? William's children asked excitedly as soon as he entered the room.

I do, he said. We leave in six days' time. We should be in America in time for spring.

More than a million departing Irish emigrants had passed through Liverpool before the Henderson family waited its turn in January 1856. Hundreds of thousands more would follow in the generations to come.

This migration started about a decade earlier. Potatoes with strange mottled skin and blackened insides began appearing in one field, then the next. Diseases had hit Ireland's crucial potato crops before, and in those

cases, the rot had been isolated and soon ran its course. But nothing was
seen previously like the happenings of 1845. This blight came from the
air, it seemed. It invaded the plants through the leaves and reached the
tubers belowground. When the potatoes were harvested, the haywire sug-
ars and starches began to do their damage, shriveling the potatoes with a
sour-smelling decay.

The British prime minister, Sir Robert Peel, mobilized the era's top
scientific minds to figure out what was occurring. The best they could do
was debunk some of the hysteria. No, it wasn't caused by subterranean
vapors. No, it wasn't the result of smoke from steamships and locomotives
wafting over from Britain. The commission wisely sidestepped comment
on the most popular Irish folk myth—that the blight was divine retri-
bution for sins. In the end, the British report did little to explain what
was happening to Ireland's potatoes. But it did contain some depressing predictions about the scope of the disease, which it called "wet rot."
More than half of Ireland's potato crop might perish. That amounted to
a death sentence for many Irish families, whose diets depended heavily on
the potato—which had more to do with England's tough-minded grain
export policies than Ireland's taste for spuds. The Britain-grown exports
that could have fed Ireland—corn and other crops—were just too costly
for many Irish residents to afford.

Yet even the potato blight wasn't enough to persuade London to leg-
islate some compassion. The prime minister tried. He proposed ending
protectionist laws that propped up the price of English grains. For a time,
England's powerful land-owning aristocracy refused to budge because
they strongly opposed losing what amounted to a built-in windfall each
year with the artificially high grain prices. It took years of negotiations to
finally roll back the laws. Yet even when lower-cost corn and wheat became available in Ireland in the late 1840s, huge obstacles existed. Ireland
didn't have enough mills to grind the grains into flour.

By this time, it was already too late for much of the island. Villages
were emptying at a frightful rate.

Nature didn't help either. A hard winter in Ireland followed the first
sightings of potato rot. Decisions had to be made. The poorest and hun-
griest were among the first to make a move. They escaped to England or

Scotland, and from there many chose to continue across the Atlantic. The irony of this migration wouldn't be clear until years later: the pathogen that caused the blight was an airborne fungus that had hitched a ride from North America in the holds of the same ships that would carry the emigrant wave back across the Atlantic.

The Hendersons were among the first families to pull up stakes in County Tyrone, a vast wedge of peatlands and hedgerows west of Belfast and across the far shores of the sprawling Lough Neagh, home to myths of ancient giants and mystic horsemen. They bounced around northeast England for nearly a decade, having two of their children on English soil. But the Hendersons, like most Irish wayfarers and strugglers, understood the limits on the English side of the Irish Sea. They were welcome as long as work was plentiful and they didn't siphon anything from the English system. In the iron-making town of Bedlington—not far from where the Hendersons had their first English-born child—Irish men found work easily at first, when the forges were going strong. Then richer iron ore deposits were found elsewhere. The Bedlington ironworks scaled back and the Irish men got the message, subtly or from broadsheet missives or by being at the receiving end of a fist or foot in an English mob: move on.

By 1848, the potato crops were in full collapse. Irish ports, meanwhile, were in full bloom. They were often so packed with people waiting for a Liverpool-bound boat to make the 150-mile crossing that makeshift camps sprung up on the quays in Dublin and smaller ports. To the north, Belfast also was jammed with families seeking to make the short hop over to Scotland.

The Atlantic packet lines from Liverpool were more than happy to pack the Irish emigrants into steerage. At the beginning of the famine, one journalist began calling the vessels leaving Ireland and Liverpool "coffin ships." The name stuck, and for good reason: it was very apt. A first-class passenger named Robert Whyte peeked into steerage on a crossing from Liverpool to Quebec in 1847. From below, a passenger noticed the well-dressed Whyte and sensed he had a receptive ear. He let loose, bemoaning his decision to leave Ireland despite the famine. "For sure, supposin' we were dyin' of starvation or the sickness overtuk us," the passenger in Whyte's account said. "We had a chance of a doctor, and if he could do no good for our bodies, sure the priest could for our souls. And then we'd be buried along wid our own people, in the ould churchyard with the green sod over us; instead of dying like rotten sheep thrown into a pit, and the minit the breath is out of our bodies, flung into the sea to be eaten up by them horrid sharks."

There was plenty of desperation and exploitation to go around on every step of the migrant route. Typhus fever and other sicknesses ravaged ships, claiming the lives of up to half the passengers in steerage and then spreading to the crew. When the immigrant ship *Virginius* docked in Quebec's main quarantine station at Grosse Isle in the middle of the Saint Lawrence River in August 1847, nearly half the ship was stricken by the fever. Close to a third of the 476 passengers had died in the crossing. Some crew members, too, were dead, including the first and second mates. "A few that were able to come on deck were ghastly yellow looking specters, unshaven and hollow cheeked, and without exception the worst-looking passengers I have ever seen," wrote the medical superintendent for the station.

"The graves are walking," penned William Butler Yeats as one of the opening lines in his famine-set play *The Countess Cathleen*. A great psychological shift was also taking place among the Irish emigrants. A bond with their homeland had been broken. A popular view was that God had somehow forsaken the island and set the people to roam. With exile, however, comes hope, the optimists said. Many believed that, maybe, like the Hebrews out of Egypt, they were heading for a better place. They just need to push through the hardships in front of them.

The hemorrhaging was stunning. The 1841 census counted 8.17 million people on the island. By 1851, the population was down to 6.33 million, a decrease of nearly 20 percent.

By the time the Hendersons had their tickets for the *John Rutledge*, the worst was over in Ireland. The potato crop had come back and some of the gloom had lifted. But there was nothing left for the Hendersons even if they nursed any last-minute ideas of going home. William and Margaret had already made an emotional break with Tyrone. They were not going back. For many Irish people who took to sea, their home county was like a gossamer strand: shiny and special in the benevolent glow of memory. Ireland, though, could barely stand even one more tug of bad luck.

So it was on to Boston for the Hendersons. William certainly knew some good lads from Tyrone who had set themselves up there. They had their bearings in America, he presumed, and could maybe vouch for him for some kind of job. Imagine, the couple thought, our little James probably won't remember much of this. He will only know America.

⌘

Their last night in Liverpool, William and his older son, Robert, spent a long time walking the docks.

William must have wanted the boy to have a good look. He thought it was important to show him the *John Rutledge,* their home for the next month or more. But he also hoped to give the boy an idea why they were all getting on that ship the next morning. No stronger message could be sent than by the sad collection of men and lads working as mules at the lowest rungs of the portside food chain.

This won't be you, William promised his son, hoping he was right. You'll have a much better go of it in America.

Many of the dock haulers were no older than sixteen-year-old Robert. The corn porters, known as bushellers and lumpers, struggled to remove huge sacks from the holds of ships cloudy with the crippling grain dust, which eventually left many young men wheezing from damaged lungs and unable to work. Near the steamships, the junior stevedores hauled the cargo and trunks of the cabin passengers. They were mostly Irish, but the bottom-of-the-heap workers were called, for some reason, "Grecians." English and Scottish dockworkers might make up to six shillings, or about a dollar twenty-five, for a twelve-hour day. The Irish, however, were offered the take-it-or-leave-it proposition of two shillings a day. And don't think about complaining. The foreman could blackball any worker for any reason. One hulking lumper told the *Liverpool Journal:* "I have often been so tired in an evening that I could not lift my hand to my head."

William Henderson had done all right for himself. His railroad pay was enough to cover rent on a flat big enough for his growing family on Ropery Lane in Sunderland, a sooty laborer's town that fanned out from the docks and shipyards on the North Sea in England's northeast. Sunderland had a bit of seaport cosmopolitan flair—like Liverpool—which made it a slight step up from some of the other dreary factory spots along the Irish migrant trail through England's coal country. Daughter Mary was born in 1847 in Morpeth, an old market town well to the north. Their youngest son, James, came into the world in 1850 in Sunderland.

William and Margaret congratulated themselves on how they managed to claw up a bit as they shifted around. Ropery Lane, a little spit off High Street, by even modest standards was a dismal little enclave. But at least it was not in one of the unsavory Irish ghettos that had sprouted in other cities. There was even room enough for William's sister, Elizabeth, and her little daughter, Eliza. Elizabeth's husband was gone. By death or desertion or early emigration to await his family—she never told anyone outside the family. But County Tyrone was no place for a mother alone. She found a spot on a ferry and made her way to Sunderland to join her brother's family, which was planning for America.

On nice days in Sunderland, the Hendersons could walk across High Street to the banks of the River Wear and watch the passing coal barges and ferries. This was no small thing. Life wasn't too bad by comparison. In Newcastle, Irish coal miners and their families crammed themselves into single rooms in the slums on Sandgate Street. In 1851, a medical officer in the English town of Darlington described an Irish colony as a sad collection of "low, crowded and ill-ventilated hovels." His report was kind enough not to get personal. Other English inspectors minced no words with their contempt: "English dogs were cleaner than Irish people," said one 1854 report that was requoted in the *Sunderland Herald,* a paper the Hendersons might have read. And, if so, William and Margaret might have taken it as less of an offense and more of an acknowledgment that they had done all right. Their flat was at least warm and didn't leak.

And I'm going to turn forty next year, William reminded himself as he and Robert roamed the docks. Well, I can still swing a spike-driving hammer with the best of them, if that's what it comes to. Yet that won't last for too many more years.

Maybe, he hoped, he could parlay his rail experience in England into a job in America that required more brains and less brawn. He had already done his homework. When he could, he got his hands on American papers brought over by the Boston packets. He combed them for references to the rail line and any new ones being built. He likely memorized some of the new routes under way: the Boston & Maine Railroad expanding from Portland to Bangor; the Boston and Providence Railroad adding new branches in Rhode Island and Fall River.

Sure, back-breaking jobs exist on the other side of the ocean, William told himself. But there must be other paths, too. The youngest boy can finish school. Teenage Robert might find an apprenticeship and learn a good trade like carpentry or tailoring. They can have options I didn't have. That's a big country over there. It might also be a good reinvention for the girls, he thought.

The Irish migration gave a swift kick to some very stale ideas about women. Being on the move—and all the improvisation it entailed—often put the competence and confidence of women at center stage. Men might have cobbled together the money, but it was the women who held the whole enterprise of migration together. They had no time for the silly drinking and jaw-boning of the men. If men were the financial lifeblood of the immigrant world, the women were the backbone. "The women especially were brave," the *New York Times* wrote in an 1856 essay on the immigrants. "They always are in trying circumstances."

A few even struck out on their own. It was shocking at first for young and unmarried Irish women to set off for America seeking work, many as domestic help for wealthy families. Gradually, though, the priests and morality blowhards stopped yammering about it as a Jezebel dishonor. Every Irish woman could sense the changes, even if they were small and spotty. Popular newspaper clippings tucked into the handbags of some emigrants included bits about the new fashion of billowy "Turkish" pantaloons instead of dresses. On a more serious note, they also followed the latest vote-for-women campaigns after a groundbreaking suffragette meeting in New York's Finger Lakes at Seneca Falls.

On a damp, drizzly morning, the Hendersons took their place in line to board the *John Rutledge*.

A steady wind blew across the Mersey. The coal fires were already roaring in flats and shops, giving the air a slightly oily smell that mingled with the sharpness of fresh horse manure. The docks were busy. Porters lugged cargo for dozens of ships either coming or going. Street hawkers—peddling everything from bowls of thin soup to stacks of well-used luggage—tried to out-yell each other. Pickpockets wended through the crowds, bumping into victims with a mumbled "pardon me." Crimps put their arms around baffled sailors as if they were long-lost friends.

The emigrants in line with the Hendersons carried essential items for the trip. For the time being, there were no greater treasures: blankets and bedding for the wooden berths in steerage, or between decks, as it was sometimes called; washing soap and pots and bowls for food. A new American law imposing stricter regulations on shipping companies required cooked meals for passengers, but there was no guarantee there would be enough dishware to go around. Better to bring your own, the guidebooks advised. The women were probably the most thankful for these reforms. Before, though many ships provided staples, women in steerage had to jockey for spots in the small galleys to cook their own meals.

The third mate on the *Rutledge* checked tickets. All was in order.

The Henderson family walked toward the stern and the stairs leading down to steerage. Elizabeth followed, carrying little Eliza. The only real rule in steerage was a bit of Victorian segregation: single men in one section, women and children (and the few single women) in another, and the rest for families and couples. The wood still had the sharp smell of vinegar and chloride of lime from its last big mop-up in New York. The crew had given steerage only a quick once-over in Liverpool. Whale oil lamps burned, but the compartment was more in shadows than in light. The wooden berths were stacked two high. The expectation was one family per berth, but the *Rutledge* was built to carry many more steerage passengers than were making this crossing. There was room for the Hendersons to take two berths. Some people—probably on the advice of relatives or the handy guidebooks—strung up laundry lines. Even simple tasks like this would be hard once the ship was out in the Atlantic. The high berths went first. Every guidebook emphasized—over and over—the benefits of being on top. When people got seasick—and they would *definitely* get seasick—the spew dripped down, not up.

Some men were already sleeping off the previous night's bender.

Liverpool's Irish population had developed its own version of the American wake. It was a tradition born back home. A night of drinking and feasting—with whatever could be scraped together during the famine times—was held in honor of those about to leave. Calling it a wake was a sobering reference to the finality of migration. Everyone knew that those who set off would probably never return to Ireland. This was their forever goodbye.

In Liverpool, the wake consisted of pint after farewell pint in the cheapest pub in port. No praying or preaching in this bunch. These were hardscrabble men who, by and large, were wondering what the church had done for them lately. No doubt any number of private Catholic aid societies offered help. But who hadn't noticed that parishes gobbled up abandoned land during the worst years of the famine and were more than willing to usher members of their flock to a workhouse or debtors' lockup? To be fair, Ireland's clergy were in a bind. Many of England's most powerful figures—from as high as the chancellor of the exchequer to members of the stuffy hierarchy of the Church of England—saw Ireland's priests as a sort of fifth column of anti-English sentiment. If the Irish people needed help, the hardliners said, let them and their church pay for it. Irish property must pay for Irish poverty was an often-repeated sneer.

Still, many of the *John Rutledge* passengers didn't want to completely break with what they knew. For all its warts and flaws and betrayals, the Roman Catholic Church was theirs and they would hang on to it. In Liverpool, perhaps no saint was more popular than Brendan the Navigator, the patron of sea travel. With their bags packed and tickets in hand, many Irish emigrants lit a candle in his name.

The *Rutledge* would not leave port for several hours yet.

William Henderson joined others on deck in a well-worn tradition of bidding farewell to Europe and having a last look at dry land for weeks to come. All the second-guessing and worrying were finally over. There was no turning back now.

Everyone was gabbing and joking and looking ahead to the biggest move of their lives. Henderson looked down the docks toward the buildings of Liverpool. No one else seemed to take much notice of the *John Rutledge*. It was just another ship heading out for America with more poor migrants aboard.

However, one person was watching the ship closely. A woman standing to the side of the quay waved to someone on board, trying to get his attention. It was considered bad luck for a wife to wave goodbye to her sailor once he was out the door for a voyage. If Irene Kelley knew this, she didn't care. She didn't want to miss a last chance to see her husband—even from a distance—before the ship set off.

Irene may have hoped for a sudden and romantic change of heart by her husband. Maybe he would realize that it was a mistake to leave her in Liverpool and call her aboard. She could have someone run down and pick up her belongings.

But Captain Alexander Kelley's attention was no longer on shore. He turned his back on Liverpool as he readied the *John Rutledge* to sail.

Chapter Three

The *John Rutledge* crew hauled in the lines the dock riggers freed from Waterloo Dock. The ropes slithered past the squat capstans and slimmer bollards used to tie up ships.

Lines clear, first mate Samuel Atkinson yelled to Captain Kelley.

The captain nodded.

It took all hands to bring in the dock ropes, a blend of sturdy hemp and supple manila fiber. Anyone shipping aboard a big square-rigger like the *Rutledge* had better have outfitted himself with a good pair of gloves or learn to live with chewed-up hands—and the risk of potentially deadly infections. Rope was everywhere: bull ropes for the heaviest jobs on the masts, halyards for hoisting sails, yard horses for sailors to stand on the yard arms, piles of coiled rope known as quails, and dozens of other special rigs. There were miles of rope in the rigging alone, much of it treated with pine tar and other concoctions to ward off rot. And the lines were in constant motion from the moment the ship set off to when the last knot was secured at the next port.

Under way, cried Atkinson.

Kelley checked his chronometer and marked the time.

The *John Rutledge* was pulled from the dock—known as being warped out—into a wider area known as Prince's Basin. A small steam tug was then made fast to the ship and, at high tide, towed her out into the River Mersey. The *Rutledge* rudder was set hard to starboard to swing the ship's bow north to point downriver and, from there, out to sea.

Irene Kelley watched from the Prince's Basin pierhead. Waterloo and Prince's were tucked amid a series of heavily used docks on the waterfront,

which added more berths and anchorages every year to keep up with ship
traffic. On any day, the Mersey was a forest of masts—like a strand of
barren winter trees—that stretched for nearly two miles. At the hub was
the decade-old Albert Dock and its fine stone- and iron-beam warehouses,
which provided extra fire protection for exotic fare such as ivory and sugar.
Plans for another set of massive grain warehouses at Waterloo were on the
drawing boards. This dock had one distinction above all others: it was the
site of a weather and astronomical observatory that gave meteorological
forecasts and provided accurate time for shipboard chronometers, vital
tools for figuring out longitude. From Waterloo, the sky watchers had the
best seat in Liverpool for the meteor blaze more than a week before.

From time to time, Irene caught glimpses of her husband through the
scurry of crew and swinging ropes. She was already looking ahead to the
John Rutledge's return in May, wondering whether the ship would again
dock at Waterloo and she would stand in the same spot waiting to catch
sight of her man. She would certainly find ways to pass the winter in Liverpool. That did not weigh on her mind. But time away from her husband
was, to put it bluntly, more missed opportunities. She was twenty-six.
They hadn't yet had a child. In her mind—and those of her gossipy and
anxious in-laws—time was fast running out. "This branch of the Kelleys
was hanging by a thread, and everyone knew it," said a historian from the
captain's hometown on Cape Cod. Sibling after sibling in the big Kelley
family had died of disease or was lost at sea. Only Kelley and an older
brother were left.

Irene may have wanted to yell out a farewell to Alexander. But one
voice was no match for the clamor of a ship leaving port. She knew the
first mate Atkinson and the other officers from the trip from New York.
There could have been a twitch of jealousy when she saw Atkinson's wife,
who was heading back to New York on the *Rutledge*.

A few sails were set, just enough canvas to move the ship along. The tug's
towline was slipped free. The *John Rutledge*'s bow rose slightly as the sails
caught the wind. The ship gave a groan of rope and wood as it began

to move under its own power. The tide helped carry it seaward. Next stop was New York, about thirty-four hundred nautical miles on the best-planned route, and hundreds more if storms or ice forced the course to be rewritten.

Irene was already in a covered coach heading back to the center of Liverpool along Bath Street and onto the Strand, which was packed with horse carts and all manner of sailors, porters, dock haulers, and, of course, emigrants. The low January sun cast weak, web-like shadows from the ships' rigging, with an occasional darker spot from unfurled sails hung out to dry. The portside breeze cleared away much of the coal-dust smog that hung over the city. At least the *Rutledge* didn't have to set off in sloppy weather.

Slowly—and with extreme care—the *John Rutledge* moved down the Mersey, with the northern edge of Liverpool passing on the right. The best shops and hotels didn't make it out this far. But the city was expanding in every direction, and it was only a matter of time before sprawl gobbled up more of the Mersey's banks. To the north, former marshlands had been transformed into collections of smoky pubs warmed by coal embers and outdoor markets that lured customers with delicious smells of fried winter flounder. The *Rutledge* passed another series of docks and lock systems built side by side: Victoria Dock, Trafalgar Dock, Clarence Half-Tide Basin. Farther on, in the northern docklands, a maze of newer berths, jetties, and break walls swelled to keep pace with the nonstop arrivals and departures of ships and steamers.

The *Rutledge* passed the wide entrance to the Sandon Basin. Then it moved past the newly opened Huskisson Dock, where the mighty steamer *Persia* was being prepared for its first transatlantic run.

Finally, it passed the narrow channel leading to the planned Canada Dock, being dug out of the Merseyside loam by Irish laborers who perhaps wished they were instead on a ship heading out. At the water's edge, like a stone cliff, stood the bow-shaped North Fort with its cannons fixed toward the mouth of the Mersey. The guard on duty gave a stiff salute to the passing ship.

The helmsman on the *Rutledge* returned the gesture. He was a Liverpool man, too. He deeply respected the fort's role as the city's unblinking sentinel, even though the threat of a major naval invasion by French or Norse forces seemed rather quaint and remote. A few passengers mingled on deck but kept well clear of the crew working the sails and rigging. When passengers got too close, they received a sharp glace or a few choice words from seamen, who had no trouble hurling salty language.

The *John Rutledge,* from the time it left its berth at Waterloo Dock, was in the hands of a Liverpool pilot—a specialist who knew every sand bar, every skeleton of a wreck, every eddy, every tricky sweep of the waters from Liverpool to where the coastal shallows dropped off into the Irish Sea. If all went well, he would be home for supper after turning the ship over to the command of Captain Kelley at the river's mouth.

And so it went every day on the Mersey. Each vessel arriving or departing Liverpool was placed under the temporary command of a pilot service, whose expert navigators patrolled the waters ready to board inbound ships or waited at the pilot office to take the wheel of outgoing vessels. The pilot office, tucked into the courtyard of the brownstone Saint Nicholas Church, just a few minutes' walk from Prince's Dock, was built to accommodate the growing presence of ocean steamers. It was a welcome upgrade for pilots. For decades, the pilot office shared space in the Liverpool Jail, which was situated next to a giant dung pile that smelled ripe in summer. Pilots were picked strictly in order. Whoever was next on the list took the next ship. No favoritism, no special requests from ship captains.

As much as any captain might chafe at taking a supporting role, he knew it was necessary. Many major ports employed pilots to navigate ships safely through local waters. The goals were the same, even if the rules were still a bit loose. In New York, it was often a free-for-all for the incoming ships. Whichever pilot made it to a vessel's deck first got the job. In Sydney, pilots sometimes set up camps and had boats at the ready to sail out to arriving ships. An 1841 census noted a tent camp consisting of six seamen described as "Mahomedans and pagans"—probably Indonesians, Maoris, or Polynesians—working the pilot boats.

Every port has its own particular perils. Few places, however, were as unforgiving as Liverpool.

The Mersey has a language all its own, and the pilots are among the few that could understand it fluently. Navigating these waters—especially in the age of sail—required mastering timing the tides and judging the winds. The difference between the right call and a mistake was often brutal. Scores of ships were run aground on sandbanks or flung against the coastal rocks with just one miscalculation. No pilot wanted the ultimate shame of losing someone else's vessel.

At certain times of the year, the tide difference at the Mersey's mouth could be more than thirty feet. A channel that offered a comfortable twenty-foot clearance at high tide became the knoll of a sandbank sticking ten feet above sea level at low tide six hours later. This was all part of an ever-changing sandy kingdom that stretched more than sixty square miles and bore ominous names like Half-Tide Swash and Beggar's Patch. The nautical maps were only as good as the last major storm. A gale could rearrange the Mersey's sand and silt into new and unpredictable patterns, crucially redrawing the edges of banks and flats, advancing in some places and receding in others. What was an off-limit sandbar just days ago could have a new deep-water cut right through its middle. Pilots did their best to keep up. They made constant depth soundings with a lead line and traded notes to keep their knowledge of the Mersey one step ahead of the weather.

A nineteenth-century maritime engineering study of the Mersey put an official government stamp on what the pilots already knew: "The scouring action of the tides in the channel which pass through the sand beds is constant and continuous . . . the [sand bank] sides and bottom are of a mobile character." The first Mersey sea chart was produced in 1689. It has been in continual revision and refinement ever since.

It wasn't just the puzzle below the surface that challenged pilots. The winds played head games, too. The prevailing winds cut perpendicularly across the mouth of the Mersey. Inbound ships had to make sure they weren't showing too much canvas because gusts could easily push a ship onto the shore.

Heading out of the Mersey on a sailing ship—as the *John Rutledge* was—required pinpoint timing. Too much of a tack into the wind could land the ship on one of the Mersey's sandy graveyards such as the Great Burbo Bank or the Jordan Flats. A ship clearing the shallows at the wrong angle could miss one of the three main channels out to open sea. It was no wonder the sailing shipmasters—in private, of course—mocked their steamship colleagues as glorified coach drivers who no longer had to contend with the tricky winds. They simply had to point their vessels in the right direction.

Captain Kelley kept a respectful distance from the pilot. Every captain did. They often thought it amusing how ordinary these extraordinary Liverpool seamen appeared. Their attire looked like they had just strolled in from inspecting livestock at a fair: a regular wool suit, rubber boots, and a cap with a small badge. When the weather was rotten—which was often in northwest England—pilots tossed on oilskins or heavy coats, just like everyone else. But the *John Rutledge* was lucky this time, having got under way in a moment of easy weather. The winds were light, coming from the west-southwest.

Thomas Nye and the other deck crew tweaked the rigging as the pilot commanded. Kelley kept a sharp eye on them. If the *Rutledge* went aground outside his command, he wanted to know exactly where to point the finger.

The ship approached the Crosby Floating Light, something of a cross between a lighthouse and a signal ship. It was part of the constellation of lightships, lighthouses, and beacons sprinkled along the Mersey. To portside was the Great Burbo Bank and to starboard, Taylors Bank. At high tide the Crosby Lightship anchored in more than forty feet of water. This was where the winds started to drive crossways over a ship's bow. The *Rutledge* pilot steered as close to the Crosby as possible.

The ebb tide was running strongly, carrying them seaward. The *Rutledge* turned more into the wind, which still blew from a kindly direction over the portside. The pilot made sure every turn of the wheel was the right one. The Burbo's maze of bars and low-tide islands was legendary, the maritime equivalent of a spider's web. Once a ship was caught, it was very hard for it to wriggle out. Veteran pilots in 1856 were old enough to remember a disastrous summer night when they were boys. In August 1821, the Dublin-bound *Earl Moria* plowed into the Burbo during a severe gale. The ship broke apart, leaving dozens to die within sight of shore, where their screams were loud and plain. Other ships had met similar fates. But evidence of wrecks did not remain for long. Scavengers and salvagers saw to that, picking wrecks clean at low tide—sometimes before all the bodies were recovered or washed out to sea. If a plank or pane of glass could be grabbed, it was gone. Same went for every bit of the foundered ship, from the yard arms to the keel wood.

After the Crosby light, the *John Rutledge* followed the buoyed channel to the next beacon, the red-hulled Formby Lightship, which stood at a literal crossroads. At night, the onboard caretaker of the Formby shone a brilliant lantern from the lightship's single mast. During the day, a large black ball was raised as its signature identifying mark. Three channels fanned out from the Formby. For outbound ships, to the left was Victoria Channel. It was the deepest—close to forty feet at high tide—but also the narrowest.

Straight ahead of Formby light was Queen's Channel, wider but shallower, and to the right was Zebra Channel, which skirted the Jordan Flats. As far back as the 1820s, debates were waged about how to dredge out the channels. Decades later, an engineer proposed an ambitious plan to build barriers to create something of a saltwater lake-and-dike system that would offer a calm backdoor into the Mersey. People talked and ideas were drafted. But in 1856, the Mersey—apart from the lightships and beacons—looked pretty much the same as it had for centuries.

Captain Kelley watched the pilot's moves closely. Here was a chance to learn some seacraft that could one day come in very handy if—for an unforeseen reason—he was forced to thread his way out of the Mersey. The pilot pointed out telltale clues in the water. The channels revealed themselves to be a shade darker and less choppy than the dangerous banks around them. The pilot eased the *Rutledge* down Victoria Channel. Black cormorants and their smaller kin, known as shags, perched on the buoys.

The pilot didn't talk much to Kelley. Pilots everywhere were, for the most part, a flinty breed while on the water. They lived by economy and precision, with no time for the braggadocio and story swapping of long-haul seamen. They could do all that back at the pilots office or the taverns they favored, such as the old Pig & Whistle or the Slaughter House on

Fenwick Street. But with a ship's wheel in their hands, they were all business. Every nudge of the rudder was important. An odd-looking line of
waves, overlooked by ordinary sailors, could mean a shift in a sandbar that
no one else had yet noticed. Pilots had to know every ripple.

⤬

The *John Rutledge* safely cleared the channel.

So far, so good. The last maneuver was to get the pilot off to one of
the waiting schooners, which in Liverpool tradition were two-mast vessels
with a flat bow and plenty of deck space. They were built for the job they
served and rode the seas with authority—despite the slightly disparaging
remarks of a brash young cabin boy and aspiring writer named Herman
Melville. He saw them as lumbering cousins to the "little gull of a schooner" that took away the pilot that guided ships out of New York to Sandy
Hook. Melville, in fact, seemed more taken with the look of the Liverpool
pilot crews. "Fellows with shaggy brows, and muffled in shaggy coats, who
sat grouped together on deck like a fire-side of bears, wintering in Aroos-
took," Melville wrote in 1849 in *Redburn: His First Voyage*.

The *Rutledge* crew pulled the rigging ropes to let loose the sails, preparing for open water.

But the winds and sea presented one last riddle. The Mersey's reach
stretched miles from its mouth. At high tide, the river currents inter-
weaved with the wash of the Irish Sea in a kind of crazy quilt. One patch
could be a churning mess where the outflowing Mersey ran against the
incoming tide of the sea. Yet a neighboring stretch of water could be pond
smooth. The pilot picked his way through. He guided the *John Rutledge*
about twelve miles out. This was where the nearest pilot boats patrolled,
waiting to take pilots off the ships outbound on the tide. Farther seaward
more pilot schooners were on the lookout for inbound ships and steamers.

Getting the pilot off forced one more decision. When the weather was
kind, it was a simple matter of tossing over a rope ladder for him to scam-
per down into a waiting boat. But in a gale, it might be nothing short of
a commando operation. Sometimes pilots were tied to a line from the
ship's yardarm and swung out onto a waiting schooner. If conditions were

too violent, pilots couldn't attempt to get off at all and found themselves as surprise new members of the crew. In pilot jargon, they were "carried away." Sometimes all the way to the Americas. One pilot spent weeks on a ship until it reached Brazil, where he was put on a Europe-bound ship. If a carried-away pilot was lucky, on his way out he might shout or signal a schooner in hopes a crewman would break the news to his family that he wouldn't be home for a long while.

The Mersey didn't pose any problems that day. Conditions were about as good as they got in mid-January. The pilot turned to Kelley and spoke more words to him than he had since leaving the dock in Liverpool.

Have a good voyage, Captain.

Kelley signed the pilot's chit, a receipt for services rendered.

Thank you, sir. Maybe I'll see you this spring.

I look forward to it, answered the pilot.

With that, the pilot was down the rope ladder with speed. He'd done it countless times. A small leap put him in the pilot punt. He gave Kelley a farewell wave as he was rowed to the waiting pilot schooner. The schooner veered away from the *John Rutledge* as it headed steadily seaward on the fast-flowing ebb.

Kelley looked at his chronometer. He wanted to note the precise time in his captain's log. He liked that kind of detail, and it didn't go unnoticed by the *Rutledge's* owners. One of whom, Williams Howland, a former sea master of some renown, was now waiting in New York for the arrival of the *Rutledge* and of his partner Ridgway on the steamship *Pacific*.

Stations to set main sails, Kelley told the first mate, who passed the order.

Nye and the others up in the rigging lowered the main sails. Then came word to bring down the topsail gallant, the smaller canvas just above the main sails.

T'gallant set, sir, they cried when done.

Starboard, forty-five degrees, Mr. Atkinson.

The ship's bow tipped lower into the sea as the wind billowed the sails. The planks and boards and ringbolts on the *John Rutledge* groaned and clicked. Kelley enjoyed these sounds after the fussy commercial chatter and lazy lapping of the Mersey in port.

He still couldn't fully let down his guard. Drifting too close to the coast could snag a ship in the banks that stretched for miles. In October 1854, the *Rutledge,* under its former captain, ran aground in the East Hoyle bank southeast of the Mersey's mouth. It waited more than a week—the captain prayed no hull-wrecking squalls would kick up—for the tides to lift the ship clear.

Steady ahead, Mr. Atkinson, Kelley said. Here we go.

More sails were set. In steerage, the passengers could feel the change in the ship as she heeled. Pots clattered and children were roused from sleep as the wind grabbed the sails. The ship's timbers creaked as the *Rutledge* rose and fell in the seaway. They could hear the regular swish and bump of the waves breaking against the hull.

The captain set a course that packets had been following for decades. Tight around the isle of Anglesey, which sticks out like a fist from the Welsh coastline. A prudent distance from the notorious rocky Skerries. Past Holyhead and south through Saint George's Channel, with gentle Rosslare Harbour on the Irish side and the wind-scrubbed coast of Pembrokeshire on the Welsh shore. A day later, around Cape Clear off southern Ireland.

Then the open Atlantic, dead ahead.

Chapter Four

The crew quickly fell back into the cliques that had formed on the voyage over from New York. It always happened this way.

The Irish banded together, led by the boatswain William Ryan, mostly by virtue of his rank. A bos'n served as something of a taskmaster for the taskmasters. He made sure the rigging, anchor lines, and deck were kept in order. The goal was to keep the chief mates happy and off the backs of the crew. For his troubles, a boatswain earned a few extra dollars pay and some small privileges. Best of all, he was generally excluded from the nightly watch for ice and brewing storms—both depressingly common in the North Atlantic.

The Scots kept their own little group, too. They had a new man under their wing on this trip. The greenhorn John Daley* couldn't have been more than twenty years old but claimed he was older. No one really cared about such things in the packet trade if a man could do the work. Aliases, fake ages, fabricated life stories, and every kind of untruth, big and small, were part of the seamen's world. If a young man was looking to reinvent himself—or just plain escape from his past life—it was as easy as seeking work on a ship looking for a hand. In Liverpool, the *John Rutledge* needed sailors and Daley needed a ship. As simple as that. A new seaman who made the cut could put down any name and hometown. If it was fictitious, so be it. The rule aboard ship, especially on the American packet

---

* Daley was cited as *Daly* in several published crew lists for the *John Rutledge*. British merchant marine records and most press accounts in 1856 spelled his name as *Daley*.

lines, was don't ask too many questions and you won't be pressed for details about your past.

There was always some chap in New York or Liverpool ready to sign the crew list. Even if that meant taking the worst possible jobs, such as burning oil rags in the ship's latrines when the stench became too foul. This was Daley's lot on the *John Rutledge*. He was among three members of the lowest caste, ordinary seamen. Daley's Scottish mates probably told him not to worry. A bit of bottom-of-the-barrel work on this trip and he'd be promoted to able seaman in no time—with a bit of extra coin in his pocket.

The national rivalries aboard ship were mostly good-natured.

The Scots tried their best to goad the Irish with songs about the poor Paddies, and the Irish ribbed the Scots about their impenetrable street slang and the swill that passed as Highland ale. Don't push it, though. Everyone tried to keep it light. A fight on board was the worst of all possible scenarios: no place to run, lots of potential weapons, and the wrath of the captain to face afterward.

Captains had incredibly wide discretion to deal with renegade crew. Flogging rarely occurred in the American merchant fleet but was still a last resort in the captain's rule book. Kelley was a new figure and seemed pleasant enough. Whereas some captains spoke only to the first mate and ship's doctor, Kelley chatted with the crew in his Cape Cod accent—saying *storm* as *stahm* and *weather* as *whetha,* which provided private comic fodder for the Irish and Scots. But all in good fun. Kelley gave the impression that he wanted to be respected, but not feared. Still, no one wanted to test his preferred methods of discipline by getting into a brawl.

Americans held the biggest bloc of the *John Rutledge* crew.

In those days, that wasn't always the case, even on packet ships flying the Stars and Stripes. There were too many options for those bent on going to sea. You could sign on to a whaling ship bound for the Pacific grounds or find a spot on a noble clipper setting off for the California territory. And then there were the tugs and pilot boats and coastal packets, the types Captain Kelley had worked on for years as he climbed the ranks.

Able seaman Thomas W. Nye, handy with all tasks, from rigging to lashing down cargo, could have easily fallen in tight with his Yankee ship-mates. He was considered a New Bedford sailor. It didn't matter that he grew up next door in Fairhaven—it was all the same for most outside Buzzards Bay. Having that New Bedford stamp meant a lot. Among 1850s seafarers, there was no bigger name to drop than that of New Bedford.

The city was the superpower of the whaling world and, by extension, a crucible for seagoing culture and innovations. It was perhaps, for a time, the world's richest city per capita, an incubator for ideas and experiments of all kinds. Most of the brain power, though, was dedicated to finding craftier ways to hunt, kill, and process whales for their valuable oil or, with some species such as the humpback, their stiff, krill-straining baleen, which was used for corsets, horse whips, skirt hoops, and other items. Patents and plans constantly rolled out. New sail designs were tested. Super-efficient winches that saved seconds in lowering the whaleboats were crafted. Harpoons and harpoon guns were tweaked and retweaked to improve their deadly efficiency. Products to keep New Bedford whalemen on top dominated newspapers ads: an "improved bomb lance for killing whales"; extra-sharp spyglasses for spotting spouts; nautical charts for waters as far away as New Zealand. New Bedford women were told how "lucky" they were to squeeze into the world's most waist-cinching corsets, which might be needed given New Bedford's rich and eclectic cuisine. Local cookbooks included recipes for delights that were mysteries just a few miles inland: gumbos, curries, and peppery stews made with spices brought in from all corners of the globe. From a New Bedford kitchen might waft the tangy smells of a South Asian kedgeree with a New England twist: three hard-boiled eggs, peeled; a handful of basmati rice; butter; onions; smoked haddock; cup of milk; curry powder; cardamom pods; and bay leaves.

Towns such as New Bedford and Fairhaven were doorways to the wider world in an age when many Americans never wandered far from the place they were born. It was all very intoxicating for anyone looking for a nibble of adventure or a break from hometown drudgery. The price, however, was years of unending work on the whaleboats punctuated by stretches of nightmarish slaughter and processing as the whales were carved up and cooked down at sea, their oil stowed in tightly sealed casks in the hold. It was a deal some were willing to make. In January 1841, when Nye was just a boy, the new crop of aspiring whalemen included Herman Melville, who walked down Water Street in Fairhaven to sign on with the *Acushnet,* bound for the Pacific.

Multitudes of young men would join him before the decline of the whaling world. Even so-called landsmen—from such places as Vermont's Green Mountains and the Berkshires in western Massachusetts—set out for New Bedford, ready to ship off from the only shores they ever knew. Something else awaited them, however, something impossible to prepare for: how deeply life at sea could change a person. There's a reason Shakespeare popularized the phrase *sea change.* After a long whaling voyage, more than a few men found life on dry land not what they remembered, and themselves no longer fit to live it. In a legal dispute over a seaman's wages in 1856, a lawyer made a pithy dig at the aggrieved sailor: "He went out a gentleman, and came home a seaman." The responsibilities of debts and jobs were too complex; the demands of relationships with women and families too nuanced after experiencing the strange all-male microsociety aboard ship. There was just something about the escapist clarity of the sea. Fortunately, there was always another whaling ship or packet heading out. For a while, the sister docks of New Bedford and Fairhaven were probably responsible for more rash decisions, divorces, flings, and fights than any other port in the world.

New Bedford's whalers and merchant seamen were, in effect, some of America's first globalists. It's doubtful many saw it that way at the time. They were, a whaler might say, just simple hunters looking to fill their barrels with oil and get home. All true. But that is like calling the Silk Road traders traveling salesmen or the Renaissance merchants of Venice ordinary shopkeepers. Nothing is ever the same when cultures rub shoulders. The New Bedford whalers were no exception. Along with their tattoos and trinkets, they brought back a new perspective on the world and America's place in it as the industrial age began.

Think of New Bedford at the apex of whaling in the 1850s as a cross between the innovative spirt of Silicon Valley and the single-minded economic drive of Wall Street, with the global crossroads vibe of Dubai.

The captains—several being Nye's relatives—were New Bedford royalty. Their houses were big and sturdy like their ships, and their salons, decorated with knickknacks from the faraway Pacific, lent themselves to grand discussions. Even the austere Quakers, patriarchs of the whaling trade since the early Nantucket days, found their concepts of Christianity shaped by the pastiche of humanity on their ships: oarsmen from Cape Verde, riggers from Haiti, adventurers from the South Seas—real-life versions of Melville's famous harpooner Queequeg. Black seamen served on whaling ships since before the American Revolution. Among them was Crispus Attucks, who was killed in the Boston Massacre. Some black whalemen rose to become master harpooners or captains. A New Bedford blacksmith named Lewis Temple, born into slavery in Virginia, developed a toggle-tipped harpoon that became the preferred lance on nearly every whaling ship. Fewer black whalemen found places on board when European immigrants began seeking the jobs in the 1840s. But the image of whaling ships as a place for all was set in the public's mind.

Nye could have parlayed his roots into a nice niche among his crewmates.

Merchant seamen never seemed to tire of tales about New Bedford whalemen and the sea giants they stalked. Nye would have had a rapt audience. On shore, hardly a day went by without newspapers making some reference to the whereabouts of a New Bedford whaling ship, whether it was far north in Russia's Kamchatka subarctic or cruising the tropic doldrums.

Some of those globe-wandering vessels flew the Nye flag, a blue banner with "NYE" in white letters. While the *John Rutledge* was making its way west of Ireland, the whaling ship *Nye* was finishing up a disappointing two-year hunt in the South Atlantic that yielded a modest 412 barrels of sperm oil. The *Desdemona*, another whaling ship under the Nye flag, stalked the Pacific on a nearly five-year-long voyage that would be counted among its most successful. Known by whalers as a "greasy luck" trip, it stored 1,712 barrels in its hold.

This was precisely why Nye kept quiet on board the *Rutledge*. A privileged piker—some kind of dilettante out to sea to collect fireside-and-brandy stories for later—was among the lowest forms of life among a crew, excepting maybe the cook when the grub wasn't up to snuff. Though this wasn't even close to the reality for Nye, he felt it would take far too much energy to explain that he wasn't a silver spooner.

His family name was grand, but his personal story was less so.

Nye was born in 1834 into a backwater of the family's milieu: the more rural northern part of Fairhaven that would later be incorporated into a town named Acushnet. His father, James, billed himself as a ship captain but appeared to have an uneven career and, for a long time, convalesced from a malady loosely described as "sunstroke." James was neither poor nor wealthy. The family was in comfortable middle ground. They were solid citizens and Methodists in good standing among the elders. This was not a bad place to be compared to the struggling deck hands, fishermen, and dock haulers of Fairhaven. Yet it couldn't have escaped notice in the wider Nye family that James never quite made his mark. James's father, Thomas Nye Sr. (Thomas W. Nye's grandfather), was a celebrated shipowner, and James's brother, Thomas Jr., amassed a fortune as a shipping merchant with a taste for life's more rarified pleasures. His artistic patronage included such talents as the German-born landscape painter Albert Bierstadt, who spent his youth in New Bedford before heading west into the American frontier. Thomas W. Nye's mother, Harriet Stevens, also came from a well-connected clan. But she appeared to have been in step with her husband's approach of having enough and evading the risks at sea needed to strive for more.

Fairhaven didn't set any limits, though. During Nye's boyhood, the port was rich with possibilities. The short walk from Acushnet to the waterfront took Thomas past one of the region's most prosperous farms. Off Main Street was a thumb of land undeservedly dubbed Poverty Point, after a new bridge to New Bedford in the 1790s cut its shipyards off from the sea. By the 1840s, however, it had rebounded as a favored enclave for ship captains and prominent merchants. In town were the impressive homes of Nye's uncles and other local muckety-mucks, including the Delano family, whose line would one day famously merge with that of the Roosevelts of Hyde Park, New York.

On Washington Street, the Union Meeting House threw open its doors to speakers roaring about the issues of the day—none given more attention than the abolitionist movement that counted Fairhaven as one of its strongholds. Nearby was the gothic First Congregational Church and its astonishing one-hundred-foot wooden spire—so tall and prominent that it was used as a navigational aid for ships heading in to Fairhaven and New Bedford.

The real action took place a few blocks over on the docks. Nye was in his teens when he first set off on runs with local packets, making trips down the coast or over to Martha's Vineyard. He didn't mind the deck work. It felt good to earn his keep on a crew and learn a bit more with each trip. He didn't have to endure an ordinary apprenticeship like this. He chose it. He didn't feel right asking his powerful relatives for a cushy job. It would have been too easy and, in his mind, a bit unfair. A different person might have jumped at the chance. Nye's clan had the connections and clout to smooth out anyone's career at sea. In fact, it was hard to talk about anything without bumping into a reference to the expansive Nye clan.

Nyes were officers and foot soldiers in the Revolutionary War. In the War of 1812, a regiment from Sandwich, the Cape Cod town where the Nyes first set down roots, included seventeen privates named Nye. A Nye was among the prominent American merchants in China. In California's Yuba valley, when it was part of Mexico, a Nye fought on the Mexican side against Anglo rebels and later married a member of the disaster-haunted Donner Party.

Thomas W.'s great-grandfather, Captain Obed Nye, launched some of the first New Bedford trading ships. His grandmother, the former Hannah Hathaway, had a family tree that included the old Nantucket whaling clan the Starbucks and the island's Quaker sage "Great" Mary Coffin.

Among the Nye family's Cape Cod whalemen was the remarkable Peleg Nye, who first shipped aboard a New Bedford whaler when he was a teenager. Later, in 1864, at the venerable age of forty-seven, he found himself on the Provincetown whaler *George W. Lewis* off the Cape Verde islands. A sperm whale was spotted and boats were launched. As the story goes, Peleg was seized in the jaws of the dying whale, which carried him under before releasing him. His legs were permanently damaged, leaving him in chronic pain, but he also earned an impressive nickname for his troubles: Jonah of Cape Cod.

Nye kept all this to himself on the *Rutledge*.

Captain Kelley, however, must have recognized the Nye name as soon as he saw it on the crew list. Any Cape Cod sailor knew of the Nyes. If nothing else, the great Ezra Nye of *Pacific* steamship fame was something of a legend in his own time. A story making the rounds was that Ezra once visited an elderly woman in Marshfield up the coast of Cape Cod Bay. She looked him over and declared: "Nye! I always wished my name was Nye for then I would be sure of getting on in the world."

Kelley was discreet, though. He didn't want to single out the young man. It wouldn't be good for either of them. It could hurt Nye's standing with his crewmates if he was perceived as a favored soul. And it could tarnish the captain's reputation as even-handed. Maybe they could chat after they arrived in New York, Kelley decided.

The *John Rutledge,* now out in the open Atlantic, moved toward the point where westbound ships cross the Gulf Stream as it bends along the western Irish coast. Ice was not a danger yet, but anything was possible once they were on the other side of the Stream. For the next few weeks, the *Rutledge* would still be far from Ice Alley, the waters southeast of Newfoundland where more ships collided with icebergs than in the rest of the North Atlantic. Captain Kelley took no chances. Watches were set. Nye was among the first group to scan the sea for ice.

On the French side of the English Channel, the *Germania* was just getting under way from Le Havre. It, too, was bound for New York.

Chapter Five

Captain Kelley was finally getting a good feel for the *John Rutledge*. It took a westbound trip on the Atlantic—sailing directly into the wind and weather—to really figure out what a ship was all about. How it tacked, how it handled heavy seas, whether the hull responded sluggishly or sprightly.

In New York, Kelley had had a chance to talk with the ship's former master, Captain William A. Sands, a Rhode Island seafarer who had been with the *Rutledge* on packet runs since 1853 and knew her as well as anyone. Sands considered her a fine ship. Newspapers described the *Rutledge* as masterfully built and very seaworthy. But don't push her too hard, Sands warned. This is the kind of ship that runs better under gentle persuasion rather than straining sails. The word was, according to shipping reports, the *John Rutledge* was "not a favorite" of insurance underwriters because of some perceived design flaws. The *New Bedford Mercury* said the ship's high poop deck in the aft "hampered her badly when sailing on the wind"—meaning wind blowing straight at the bow, which occurred with nearly every crossing from Europe to America.

Advice from former captains and critiques from shipping reporters were just part of the picture. Kelley knew the only real test would be out in the blue-water deep with nothing between him and oblivion but the masts, sails, hull, and his capabilities as a mariner. For Captain Alexander Kelley, a sturdy-built man with thick legs and a close-cropped beard in the Cape Cod fashion, there was a new element to contend with on this trip. The *John Rutledge* was a far bigger ship than the packets Kelley had previously commanded. The *Rutledge* had about twenty-five thousand square feet of canvas when every sail was unfurled. That's more than a half-acre of pulling power, glorious when the wind was at your back. When sailing into the wind, however, a captain needed to be surgical. The spars on the three main masts didn't offer much adjustment to catch oncoming winds and—in a ballet of torque, bow direction, hull angle, and rudder pressure—drive the ship forward on a tack. Captains of the big square-rigged vessels often had to rely on smaller, and more maneuverable, jib sails at the bow. It wasn't easy to line up the sails with the correct angle. And every calculation for Kelley was now magnified, with more sail over-head and more ship under his boots.

Kelley never shared his thoughts about why he demanded his wife Irene stay in Liverpool. At least his reasoning never made it into the logbook the first mate Samuel Atkinson kept. But, just as Irene liked to think, it's a logical guess to suppose that Kelley wanted full concentration on his first westbound trip in charge of the *John Rutledge*. It's also not a stretch to wonder whether the first mate had second thoughts about bringing his wife on this winter leg to New York. Nye, steeped in by-the-book sea-manship from his family, likely felt it a bit impertinent that the first mate didn't automatically copy the captain's decisions, right down to whether his wife would accompany him. But, naturally, Nye kept those thoughts to himself. There was no reason to risk getting on the bad side of the two men most in control of his life until the ship reached port.

Kelley had a lot on the line. The *Rutledge* had crossed these waters more than twenty times before Kelley took command. He hoped to add many more trips to the list. He wanted his first roundtrip with the *John Rutledge* to be flawless.

So far, so good. The trip over from New York was textbook—fast and clean. But it was becoming clear that the return leg was not going to be so smooth. The seas and wind fought the *Rutledge* every mile since they rounded Ireland. Harsher winds and more ferocious storms likely lay ahead, Kelley knew. And don't forget the ice. The ship had to make it through the dreaded Ice Alley before tacking toward home.

❧

The *John Rutledge* was christened in Baltimore less than five years earlier, in the summer of 1851, and joined the fleet operated by the Ravenel family out of Charleston, South Carolina. The Ravenels were Charleston aristocracy, with all its Southern antebellum honors and horrors: homes along the stately East Battery corniche staffed by slaves, plantations worked by slaves, children cared for by nannies who, of course, were slaves. "The Ravenel house is at the center of the Battery," wrote one of the children, Rose, in her diary. "There is nothing between us and the Canary Islands, save Fort Sumter." The ship's owner, William Ravenel, planned to use the *Rutledge* to haul cotton to Europe and pad the family's already substantial fortunes and holdings, which included some of the most prestigious properties in Charleston.

The Ravenels, perhaps by design, never made public who they were acknowledging with the ship's name. Most assumed it was the John Rutledge of Revolution fame, who was South Carolina's top political leader opposing George III during the war. He was later a delegate to the Continental Congress and then went on to replace the retiring John Jay to serve a brief and stormy stint as the new nation's chief justice of the Supreme Court. Rutledge was picked by President George Washington while Congress was in recess, but lawmakers had the final say and rejected Rutledge's nomination as a result of South Carolina's criticism of the so-called Jay Treaty, which helped solidify peace after the Revolutionary War. Rutledge's rejection was a rare congressional slap-down of Washington and an unceremonious rebuke for Rutledge, who was once considered presidential material. In 1788, Rutledge received six electoral votes for president—two more than John Hancock.

There was a lot to support the idea that the Ravenels looked back to the John Rutledge of Founding Father days for the name of their ship. But with the tension between North and South in the 1850s, many Northerners, like Kelley, interpreted the ship's name as indirect homage to another member of the Rutledge line: a former Navy captain and rabble-rousing secessionist also named John Rutledge.

In July 1851, just as a Baltimore shipyard put the finishing touches on the *John Rutledge,* the incendiary rebel Rutledge led a North-bashing meeting in Charleston. Many at the gathering backed his call for an immediate break with the Union. It was clear the country was in jeopardy and John Rutledge was trying to hasten along the crisis.

A month later, in August 1851, work on the *John Rutledge* was finished. The ship was the pride of the J. J. Abrahams shipyard, which was situated at the foot of Caroline Street on the Inner Harbor. At the time, the *Rutledge* was one of the biggest merchant vessels launched into the Chesapeake: 175 feet long, a beam of 37 feet across at the water line, and 1,108 tons burthen, which was based on an old-time formula to gauge cargo capacity. A twenty-five-cent ticket—half price for children—allowed you to walk the deck of the *John Rutledge* as part of the celebration at its launch, which included singalong tunes by an outfit known as the Lilliputian Brass Band.

So impressed were the Baltimore newspapers that one scribe waxed biblical in the *Sun:* the *John Rutledge* "will be hard to beat anywhere, in any port since the day old Father Noah made harbor on the summit of Ararat." The reports went on about the ship's sturdy build. Its floor timbers were a foot wide and held in place by one-inch iron bolts. The keel was reinforced with a spine comprising seven feet of solid timber. The hull was up to eight inches of Southern yellow pine, a strong and durable wood favored by shipwrights. There was never any mention of North Atlantic ice when the shipyard was showing off its latest masterwork. But there was no need. Everyone knew it was out there.

It was not uncommon for captains to have an ownership stake in ships. This was true for the *John Rutledge*. Its first master, Captain E. C. Wambersie, was a well-known civic figure in Baltimore who kept watch over the *Rutledge* construction every step of the way. He was also a veteran of the Liverpool packet runs and knew just what the Atlantic could throw at a vessel. The previous year, in 1850, he had made a Liverpool-to-Philadelphia sail on another of the Ravenel ships, the *John Ravenel,* with fifteen Irish and English emigrants aboard. It was a harrowing crossing. They barely managed to slip through the pack ice, which tightened like a vise around anything afloat. The ship right behind them, the *Oriental,* was not so lucky. It was stuck in the ice for eleven days. At the same time, another ship in the area with at least eighty people on board bound for Quebec City was lost. The *Oriental,* when it was finally free, passed right through the tragic remnants of the other vessel, whose name was never confirmed. "A great many bodies were seen intermingled with the ice, together with some portions of the cargo," said one account. William Ravenel didn't need any convincing of the sea's cruelty. His eleven-year-old niece was among four children swept away by the surf three years earlier off Sullivan's Island near Charleston.

A week after the *John Rutledge* slid into the Chesapeake, the men who built her were treated to a feast at White Hall, a famed tavern on Bank Street. The pub made a potent version of a popular drink known as sangarees, with red wine, brandy, lemon, nutmeg, and cinnamon. The sangarees flowed that night. The party ran into the wee hours.

Just about the same time, down the coast, Captain Wambersie took the *John Rutledge* south to Charleston. Waiting there on the brick-and-marble Vanderhorst wharf was Ravenel, anxious to place another ship into service. South Carolina had cotton that Europe wanted and was willing to pay top price for. One of his biggest payoffs came each spring when his ship unloaded cotton in Saint Petersburg and then filled its hold in Sweden with top-grade iron. Builders in South Carolina and Georgia would rather deal with a fellow Southerner than negotiate for iron with the Yankee foundries. Ravenel also shipped low-country South Carolina rice to Europe and his ships returned with all manner of European goods and textiles. Especially prized in Charleston was a rugged wool cloth known as Welsh plain, used for slaves' clothing.

The *John Rutledge* was put to work directly. It was soon off to Liverpool with thousands of bales of quality Sea Island and Upland cotton and other goods such as palmetto and cigars. Liverpool was Europe's gateway to American cotton, and the city's merchant class wanted nothing to disrupt the flow. Southern sympathies were clear. As the Civil War loomed, Liverpool was often derided or applauded—depending on which side you backed—as a foothold of the Confederacy on the other side of the pond.

On its first trip from Liverpool, the *Rutledge* returned with kitchen goods, salt, and other items in high demand. In September 1852, Ewbank, Stone & Co. of Charleston proudly announced it would showcase the latest European cargo coming off the *John Rutledge:* "Hardware, Cutlery, Guns, Pistols" priced on "liberal terms." At the time, there was one thing the *John Rutledge* wouldn't take back from Liverpool: steerage passengers.

The Ravenels didn't want to get into that mess. They were happy to accommodate a few better-heeled cabin passengers, though, which they lured on with puffed-up ads about the ship's speed and appointments, including a spacious ice room that cut down the need for canned vegetables and salted meats.

That all changed when the Ravenels—suffering a bit of a cash pinch—sold the *John Rutledge* to a New York shipping concern. The ship was soon sold again to an investment group that included the wheeler-dealer James Ridgway, who was trying to break into the big leagues on his own. The shipping business was—and still is—a complex tangle of revenue-sharing deals, temporary partnerships, and licensing pacts. At times, it could require a maritime lawyer just to cut through the legal brambles to figure out who owned what.

This is where Ridgway shone. He had a knack for piecing together deals, courting investors, and keeping silent partners happily silent. Ridgway's plan was to cut leasing agreements for the *John Rutledge* with the serious players of the day, such as the Black Ball Line, the Swallow Tail Line, and the fleets of shipping impresario Edward Knight Collins. In Ridgway's view, immigrants were just as good as cargo. Heck, they even loaded themselves on board. The *John Rutledge* entered the frantic game of Liverpool emigration.

Captain Sands was at the helm in 1853 when the *John Rutledge* started to take on more and more passengers. Three years later, on his westward run to New York in the winter of 1856, Captain Kelley carried one of the vessel's biggest lists so far. Accepting command of the *Rutledge* gave him a front-row seat to how the world was being reshaped and his small part in it.

The Howland & Ridgway offices were on Wall Street, not far from the main packet ship piers. From there, from week to week, Kelley could see how the waves of immigrants were changing New York. He certainly appreciated the dynamism of cities fueled by trade and migration. Otherwise, he would have abandoned the packet trade long ago.

A new order was taking shape—industrial, modern, forward looking. But Kelley wasn't an urban man at heart. He was a Cape Codder, which he saw as a badge of honor even if his ambitions had grown larger than could be satisfied on that thin cape of sand and lichen-speckled pines sticking out into the Atlantic.

When Kelley turned thirty-two, Centerville, a small village in the town of Barnstable just uphill from a sandy sweep along Nantucket Sound and the tidal inlets that brimmed with striped bass and horseshoe crabs, hadn't changed much. It was essentially the same place as in his boyhood. Elm-shaded Main Street, a wide path of sand and crushed clamshells, was lined with the homes of one sea captain after another. Everything in Centerville was about the sea. Like those in any town along the New England coast, the villagers knew well what the sea gave as well as what it took. And beating in the hearts of those sea town inhabitants was something ancient and primal that ran right to the core. They feared the sea and its raw power, yet were inexorably drawn to it in ways that couldn't be fully explained. No doubt there was money to be made at sea. But it was something more. The sea was their birthright. No dangers, no funerals would keep them from it.

Hardly a year went by without a gathering at Centerville's white clapboard South Congregational Church to mourn someone lost at sea. In a storm in 1843, when Kelley was nineteen, a shipwreck took the lives of three Centerville seamen. Still, there was no shortage of others willing to ship out on the next vessel. Options on shore—jobs at the saltworks down by the tidal flats or mucking around the clammy water of the cranberry bogs—just did not tempt them. The most daring souls joined lifeboat rescue crews, which splashed out into the harshest seas to reach ships foundering off the coast.

As a boy, Kelley had little doubt that he would end up at sea.

One of his hometown heroes was a former Cape Cod sea captain, Russell Marston, who had begun his seafaring days as a cabin boy at age nine (along the way, he learned to make a fancy dessert known as a plum duff). In 1847, after a long career at sea, Marston sailed his ship to Boston with a broom tied to the mast, a signal that the vessel was for sale. Marston used the sale money to start a food shack open to all races, with no segregation, that later grew into a prestigious restaurant.

Kelley's grandfather, Levi Kelley—who reworked his birth name of O'Killey—took part in naval campaigns in the Revolutionary War and helped found the Congregational Church in Centerville. Levi had an audacious streak, too. In 1822, he was ostracized by the Congregational flock, according to church records, after he declared he had reached a "state of sinless perfection." That didn't stop the Kelley clan from spreading far and wide around Barnstable County. Levi and his wife, Abigail, had a dozen children. One of them, David, married a woman named Patience from the Bearse family, another well-known shipping clan on the south shore of the cape.

Yet even in a time when many lives were routinely cut short by disease or infection, David and Patience weathered a heaping dose of misfortune. Only two of their ten children lived past their teens: David Newton Kelley and his younger brother, Alexander. Both grew up to be sea captains. David became a father in 1854,* which may have helped take a bit of the pressure off Alexander and Irene to get moving with their family.

It was a short walk from the Kelley household to the cemetery behind the South Congregational Church. Many family graves were grouped in patches. The Kelley family was front and center through the graveyard gate. All but one of the brothers' siblings were there. Their younger brother Francis Kiriathian Kelley was lost in 1850 on the schooner *Juliet* in the Connecticut River. He was just fifteen years old.

In 1839, a Harvard professor, John G. Palfrey, came to mark Barnstable's bicentennial. He could not dream of offering remarks to a crowd from Centerville and other Barnstable villages without heavily referencing the sea.

"The duck does not take to water with a surer instinct than the Barnstable boy," said Palfrey. "It is but a bound from the mother's lap to the masthead. He boxes the compass in his infant soliloquies. He can hand, reef and steer by the time he flies a kite."

---

*Carleton Francis Kelley, the son of David Kelley and Abigail Howland, had one son, Nowell Carleton Kelley. Nowell did not have children, according to public records.

That was all true. But some wanted to keep their kin on dry land. One Centerville man, so upset his grandson intended to go to sea, devised a "cure" by making sure the boy signed on to the most problem-plagued boat with the most ornery captain. It worked. The grandson retreated inland to New Hampshire.

Alexander Kelley was just a teenager when the professor delivered his address, and he proved the good professor's point. He had a few runs under his belt as a cabin boy on the schooners out to Martha's Vineyard and along the Nantucket Sound waters from Falmouth to Chatham, where the cape's arm turns north to get pounded by the Atlantic. It's hard to go half a mile along this part of the coast without sailing near some wreck. The bones of ships and men have been piling up along the cape's Atlantic side for centuries: warships, merchant vessels, pirates, fishermen, and whoever else was caught in the wrong place at the wrong time.

Yet the open Atlantic pulled at Kelley.

Not that Centerville didn't offer him all it could. He could have stayed put and enjoyed the prestige of being a master mariner on cape waters. The Kelley name was local gold. The family had made its mark in nearly every corner of the mid-cape. Banks had Kelleys. Businesses had Kelleys. So did taverns and, of course, ships. Even a pleasantly eccentric Kelley, Captain James Delap Kelley, who plied local waters as a skipper and fisherman, walked through Centerville, rain or shine, under the canopy of a big black umbrella to keep himself from getting soaked and sunburned.

But Alexander Kelley wanted grander ships and more famous ports than Cape Cod. It wasn't just wanderlust. If that was the case, he could have easily sailed down the coast to New Bedford, signed up on a whaling ship, and never looked back. Kelley had always seen himself as a leader. He moved right up the ladder, from deck hand to mate to skipper. He figured it was time to try the packets, and not the ones hopping down the Atlantic seaboard. His mind was set on the big Liverpool packets out of Boston and New York.

He talked it over with his wife, Irene. She was fine with his goals. And perhaps the change would do them good. At least no one in New York would give one plug nickel whether they had a child or not.

Still, leaving the cape was a big leap for both of them.

If Kelley was a marquee name on the cape, the name of Irene's family line, Hatch, carried even more weight.

It went back to the Massachusetts Bay Colony in the 1630s, when Boston was just a cluster of houses around a little tidal inlet. A generation later, the Hatch line spread to the southwest corner of Cape Cod and helped found the town of Falmouth. Jonathan Hatch, the first to arrive, purchased prime bay-front land from the Wampanoag tribe. The settlement became known as Hatchville. By the time Irene Hatch was born in 1829, Falmouth was an important stop on the packet runs up the coast from New Bedford. And one of those ships might have brought Alexander Kelley to town for their first meeting.

On the deck of the *Rutledge* heading west from Liverpool, Kelley was perhaps the farthest away from Irene since they were wed. He calculated a few more weeks of ice-free sailing before the ship reached the dangerous edges of the Grand Banks. Kelley had seen the papers in Liverpool reporting the first signs of heavy ice. But ice fields and bergs could shift hugely from week to week. All he could do was hope for the best, keep the watchers vigilant, and press westward. The sooner he got to New York, the sooner he could turn back around to Liverpool and Irene.

Chapter Six

She hated most the long stretches of darkness. She hadn't left her little corner in steerage for days. No one had. And she guessed it could be days more before she might see daylight again.

The North Atlantic slammed the *John Rutledge* for the better part of a week. It was the longest stretch of unbroken storms since they had left Liverpool. The hatches on the deck were battened tight, including the opening leading to steerage. A handful of swaying oil lamps provided the only light down below, casting a soupy yellow glow through their thick glass. The sleeping nooks remained in perpetual grayness.

As a steerage passenger, Jane Black learned to steady herself as the ship pitched and rolled. This was another trick explained in the emigrant guidebooks and passed from passenger to passenger. She first wedged herself into the back of the wooden berth, then used one hand to hold her young traveling companion, a girl named Betty Black, on her lap. She jammed her other hand against the ceiling. It was awkward. But at least it kept her from feeling those stomach-tingling drops as the ship's bow crested a wave and slid down the other side. It also seemed to help a little with her seasickness. Maybe it was the concentration needed to keep her arm in place that distracted her from her queasy stomach. The only thing she knew for sure was that her sense of time had been reordered since the *Rutledge* faced the nonstop mid-Atlantic winter storms, which made even the most frothing seas back near Ireland seem tame by comparison.

Jane no longer measured the pace of things by days, or by the next meal, or even by the hours. It was now just a question of pushing through the next jarring wave, the next swell that rolled as big as a hillock.

She tried not to think about what was on the other side of the hull. The more anyone imagined the sheer might of the sea, the more it unnerved them. The *Rutledge*—all ships, really—was a trespasser on the winter sea. For sure, the vessels were built with such weather in mind. But there was a great hubris about it all. Sailors and shipbuilders claimed to be masters of the deep. Nothing could be less true. These waters had the real power. They could snap a mast at any moment or tip a ship onto its side with an unruly wave.

In 1848, an Irish immigrant wrote to a friend in Dublin describing a frightful open-ocean maelstrom very much like the one the *John Rutledge* was in: "Ten o'clock, the scene below no light, the hatches nailed down, some praying, some crying some cursing and singing, the wife jawing the husband for bringing her into such danger, everything topsy turvy,— barrels, boxes, cans, berths, children rolling about with the swaying vessel, now and again might be heard the groan of a dying creature, and continually the deep moaning of the tempest."

Every vessel engages in a constant power struggle with the sea. Physics decides which side wins. It comes down to hydrodynamics and strength of design versus the immense power of water in motion.

A cubic meter of water weighs about one ton. Multiply that weight dozens of times over to calculate the mass behind even a modest wave striking a ship. Then add momentum to that great load of water. A wave pushed by strong winds packs enormous energy, capable of breaking any board and snapping any fitting on a ship. The main element in a ship's favor is that water flows around objects. The less area exposed to incoming water, the less the water's destructive potential. This is why every calculation, every turn of the ship's wheel, was meant to keep the bow pointed directly into the direction of the storm. Facing into the sea made the difference between a glancing slap and a body blow.

It was clear to every passenger between decks when the *Rutledge* was cutting properly into the storm because the consequences ran in straight lines through the compartment. The bow rose high and then fell quickly in gut-twisting drops. Over and over. That was bad enough. But a miscue by the helmsman or a sudden shift in the sea brought even more punishment when the waves struck the hull flat-on from the side. The ship would roll sideways in an out-of-control skid across the water. Those might be the most dangerous few seconds of any voyage.

Ships are built to naturally right themselves.

But only to a point.

A vessel tipped too far off center risks flopping into the drink, or being on its beam-ends, where the masts angle toward the water rather than point toward the sky. Ships are built to recover their equilibrium as the keel curve and ballast pull the ship right. But cargo and passenger load can alter that failsafe design. With packet ships, often filled to the gills with goods and people, the risks were amplified. An off-kilter ship risked having its cargo shift or dislodge and tumble downhill. That's when things got very scary, very quickly. The ship could very well be knocked past the point of no return.

When the sails dip in the water, it creates even more downward drag on the vessel. The ship is now flat on its side and unlikely to rock back upright on its own. The only choice, for some captains, was amputation—cutting away the masts to free the ship from being dragged down further or flipping completely in a disaster known as turtling, when the ship turned keel up, like a floating turtle. In the summer of 1847, the captain of the *Mamlouk,* bound for Liverpool from New York, ordered the crew to cut away the main and mizzen masts after their ship was knocked on its beam-ends by hurricane-force winds. The *Mamlouk* was righted. But a head count showed thirty-five steerage passengers and seven crew members had been swept overboard.

On the *Rutledge,* each sideswipe sent everything not tied down skittering across the wooden floor in steerage, including cooking pots and pails filled with the watery vomit of those who couldn't shake the heaves of seasickness. About the only thing that stayed put were the lice and fleas that burrowed into every possible place on the steerage passengers and their belongings. It wouldn't be wrong to imagine that many emigrants—with the Atlantic storms bearing down—wondered why they ever left home in the first place. Or maybe they cursed themselves for not waiting until summer to make the crossing.

⌁

Jane Black probably didn't consider going back. There wasn't much for her there now. America was her future for better or worse.

She was like many women in that era traveling without a husband or elder brother. She closely guarded her personal story. Always better, she felt, to be enigmatic than open. Where is the gain by sharing too much? It only attracted more questions.

It's unclear why Jane left only a vague paper trail from Scotland to Liverpool and onto the *Rutledge*. One reason might have been to discourage inquiries about the relationships of her little three-person group that included the girl Betty and a teenager named Samuel Black. Jane was born in Argyllshire, a spill of islands and inlets in western Scotland. She was part of a big clan of Blacks in that region. But options for women in Argyllshire were limited: marry a struggling farmer or marry a struggling fisherman. She chose neither. She followed work and opportunities to the nearest city, Glasgow. It teemed with Black relatives from back home. At least the Scots from the hinterlands didn't have to face the ethnic mocking many of the Irish endured. Jane didn't leave any clues about why she pulled up stakes in Glasgow, or even whether seven-year-old Betty and young Samuel Black were her children or kin traveling with her to America.* What did it really matter? She probably would never see any of her fellow steerage sojourners after they all went their separate ways. Still, it felt smarter to be discreet. An Atlantic crossing like this taught you a lot. For Jane, one important lesson was to mind her own business.

She hoped Samuel, now in his early teens and burning with the invincibility of youth, wouldn't take to the sea like the lads she saw on the *John Rutledge* crew. Now that she knew what sea travel was like, she could never rest if he was out there.

Samuel? Jane said.

Yes, he answered.

Do you know how many days we've been out?

Must be just short of a month. I've lost count. But it's more than three weeks. Must be getting toward a month.

---

* It is possible family archives in Scotland could shed further light on Jane Black and the two younger Blacks, Betty and Samuel, aboard the *John Rutledge*. This account is based on the public documents available.

Some of the young bloods sitting with Samuel agreed. The chaps got tossed around like ragdolls sometimes as the ship bucked and rolled. But, in their minds, it was better than hunkering down like frightened chattel in the berths like Jane and others.

Everyone expected the trip to be difficult. Steerage, after all, was as basic as it came. But it's doubtful anyone was prepared for the realities of life below deck even after reading every page in the guidebooks. No flop-house, no hovel—nothing they had known on shore—could match this. At least on land there was some light and air in even the most depressing situations. But on the ship when the storms hit and the hatches were sealed, so was most of the venting system.

The air in steerage was weirdly stagnant even as the winds howled just above. The stench quickly grew overpowering. The unmistakable acid-sweet smell of vomit infused every corner. If you couldn't get to the deck, the only place to retch was in your berth or onto the floor. Washing up was out of the question. The only way to do that was on deck with a bucket and some fat-and-lye soap. The two latrines—for more than 120 people—were simple holes that emptied into the bilge water, a horrific concoction of waste and runoff that sloshed in the hold below the steerage compartment. Rags soaked in vinegar were provided for common use as stand-ins for toilet paper. Once in a while, the first mate would send down an unlucky crew member with a hot iron poker dipped in tar. The acrid fumes were intended to mask the putrid odors in steerage.

People rode out the storms deep in their own thoughts. No one talked much anymore. The gabbing and excitement of the first days out from Liverpool had ceased. Mostly now, moans from the seasick and quiet words of encourage among families could be heard. We're one day closer, they would say. One day nearer to America.

William Smith, a steerage passenger on a ship crossing from Liverpool in the winter of 1847–1848, at the beginning of the Irish potato famine, wrote in his memoir that he would never forget the chaos and, of course, the smell.

Around midnight, a number of boxes and barrels broke loose and rolled from side to side, according to the motion of the ship, breaking the water cans and destroying everything capable of being destroyed by them. To fasten them was almost impossible, for we could not keep ourselves from sliding down without grasping something. In a few minutes, the boxes and barrels broke into atoms, scattering the contents in all directions—tea, coffee, sugar, potatoes, pork, shirts, trowsers, vests, coats, handkerchiefs &c., &c., were mingled in one confusing mass. The cries of the women and children were heart-rending; some praying, others weeping bitterly, as they saw their provisions and clothes (the only property they possessed) destroyed. The passengers being seasick, were vomiting in all parts of the vessel. The heat became intense in consequence of the hatchways being closed down, and the passengers, three hundred in number, being thus kept below, were unable to breath the pure air or see the light of heaven but a few hours at a time. The scent rising from the matter vomited up, and from other causes, became intolerable. When the weather finally cleared and the hatches opened, most of the passengers were so eager to get on deck that they pushed each other off the ladder.

Years later in 1909, an investigator for a US congressional report wrote, "The sleeping quarters were always a dismal, damp, dirty, and most unwholesome place. The air was heavy, foul and deadening to the spirit and mind." The sad conclusion of the report was that steerage conditions hadn't progressed much in more than fifty years despite laws and campaigns calling for reforms.

On the *John Rutledge,* life was marginally better for the lone cabin passenger, the Philadelphia merchant C. J. Gale. Cabin quarters on most sailing packets were little more than a closet and a commode, and just slightly less horrid than steerage. What Gale was provided, however, was some insulation from the illnesses that brewed in steerage like in a Petri dish.

Remarkably, the *Rutledge* had been spared a serious outbreak so far. Typhoid fever was what everyone feared the most. They had heard enough stories of plagued ships to know the basic symptoms: pounding headache, spiking fever, rash. But other killers were right around the corner. Cholera. Dysentery. Influenza. Any sickness could rampage through steerage with devastating effect, especially among the oldest and youngest. Few passengers on board were older than fifty, and just one infant made the trip. Betty Black was among about a half-dozen children under ten. Jane checked her constantly for signs of fever or malaise.

Jane was relieved the girl still had an appetite. It was a welcome sign that she hadn't fallen ill.

Let's see what we have, Jane said.

She steadied herself. All that was left was cold oatmeal, made a few days ago during a rare break in the heavy seas. Most people tried to stash little bits from the basic meals churned out by the *Rutledge* cook, a fellow named Lecrompt. It was never certain when he would be back in the galley. If the seas were too rough, cooked food was prioritized to go first to the captain, then officers, then crew, then the cabin passenger. Steerage passengers were, as always, at the bottom of the list.

In Ireland, which had by far the biggest stake in packet ship conditions, the press was far from silent. Irish accounts of the famine ships—and the exodus that continued even after—had a mix of melancholy and anger. There was a recognition that Ireland could no longer keep many of its native sons and daughters. But there was outrage at what awaited them 'tween decks.

At the beginning of the famine, many Irish newspapers set an activist tone by republishing the grim observations of an intrepid Anglo-Irish member of the British Parliament. Philanthropist Stephen de Vere rode in steerage from Liverpool to Canada in 1847 for a first-hand look at the conditions.

"Hundreds of poor people, men, women and children of all ages, from the driveling idiot of ninety to the babe just born," wrote de Vere, "huddled together without air, wallowing in filth and breathing a fetid atmosphere, sick in body, dispirited in heart . . . dying without voice of spiritual consolation, and buried in the deep without the rites of the church."

De Vere's letter was read aloud in the House of Lords by the 3rd Earl Grey, then secretary of the colonies of the empire (his father, the 2nd Earl Grey, is the namesake for the tea blend flavored with bergamot oil).

In Liverpool, some groups did what they could for those waiting to leave or stuck in limbo, simply too beaten down to pull together the steerage fare. One agency, the Domestic Mission Society, was something of a whirlwind in the Liverpool slums, dispensing assistance and advice that were well meaning if not just a bit pompous: "Day after day dealing with

the ignorant, the dissipated, and the debased portions of the human race,"
wrote the group's chief so-called minister for the poor in an 1856 report,
"to go down into the dark place of social life and work the lower strata of
the living world."

Still, there were some purported happy endings. One young woman—
a "wretched outcast"—who had turned to prostitution and thievery, was
somehow plucked from the streets and given a ticket to America. The
woman's caretakers later wrote back with an uplifting message—true or
not—that she was back on the straight and narrow.

By the mid-1850s, the public mood was shifting ever so slightly.

Maybe slums and tenements were too big a problem to tackle. But
companies making money off the poor were pushed to offer at least a bit
of dignity. The shipping operators bent to the will of public opinion. But
not by much. They upgraded the food on the ships, but not its quantity
or variety.

Shipboard diet could vary hugely from ship to ship, and season to
season. Generally, it consisted of oatmeal, potatoes, salted meat, and possibly tea. Many steerage passengers brought baskets of food to supplement
what was provided. But usually those provisions were quickly eaten—and
just as quickly tossed up when seasickness struck. On ships with many
first-class passengers, there was always a way to land tasty handouts from
sympathetic travelers. But on the *Rutledge,* the rough seas were keeping
the cook Lecrompt from attempting little beyond opening canned rations.

Almost four weeks out from Liverpool, the hatches hadn't been flung
open nor had the cookhouse fired up for days. The passengers had no idea
when the weather could break. Neither did the crew. Weather forecasting
at the time was a matter of studying the clouds and using experience to
guess what was coming next.

While riding through the angry ridge of weather, steerage passengers
had to make due with cold meals or whatever could be scrounged. Samuel
Black was getting good at the scrounging part. He had fallen in with some
boys. They ferreted out food and drink from every corner of the ship,
mostly cajoling friendly crew when the weather was good enough to visit
the deck. It was a useful talent. There was no telling how long the crossing
could take.

Captain Kelley had done some calculations. If the storms kept up, they could have up to three weeks of sailing ahead. Rumors soon spread among the passengers that rations could be reduced if the voyage was unusually long, meaning two months or more.

The *Rutledge* had left Liverpool just as the earliest reports of that year's huge ice fields began to reach port. Nye had noticed them in the English newspapers, and certainly Kelley did as well. But they were long gone from the Mersey when the ice reports published in English papers took a more worried tone. This wasn't just an average run of drift ice and bergs, they said. It was far more menacing. Ship captain after ship captain said the same thing: set a course farther to the south or take your chances, and God have mercy on your souls.

Not privy to the later reports, Kelley sailed directly into the ice fields. They would navigate only by what they could see from the bow. And that was starting to worry him.

Chapter Seven

First Mate Atkinson dipped the nib of his pen in the inkwell anchored in a hole in his small desk and marked the milestone in the ship's log: a month out from Liverpool.

The weeks had passed without too many mishaps. That was the good news. The troubling part was that they should be hundreds of miles closer to New York than they were. The Atlantic was not making this crossing easy. Storms continued to hit with almost clockwork regularity. Three, four, or more days of fearsome white caps roared down from the northwest—just the kind of storms that pushed icebergs south from the Labrador Sea. The winds had been so fierce that they ruffled the water's surface into what looked like corrugated metal or fish-scale armor. Then there might be a day or two of relief. Then another tempest. Atkinson was well aware of the added horrors for the steerage passengers, effectively locked below with the hatches closed. But there was nothing anyone could do until the weather eased.

It was now quite clear this would be one of the longest westward passages for the *John Rutledge*. Captain Kelley was not happy about that. Weather or no weather, ice or no ice, shipping lines tended to blame the captain for a slow crossing. Kelley had to be prepared to present his own defense.

He made sure to keep every detail sharp and verifiable in his personal diary, a separate account from the official ship's log kept by Atkinson. Kelley was sure the owners would want to see both when they arrived in New York—especially if they were weeks behind schedule. Any significant discrepancies in the two ledgers would demand an explanation, but consistency would go a long way in their defense, that they couldn't have pushed the ship any harder.

Kelley was disappointed he would not have a fast winter crossing to show everyone down the line—the owners, the shipping line, the merchants whose crates filled the hull—that he was the right man to put in charge of the *Rutledge*. Captains, with their big egos, had a special contempt for the weather. It was one of the few things out of their control. So instead of making his mark with speed this time, Kelley concentrated on skill. He wanted to bring in the *Rutledge* without even a galley pot or belaying pin out of place.

Kelley's logbook, like those of most captains, was a subjective account of the voyage that included impressions of the crew, how the ship performed, morale, and notes to himself for the next trip. The first mate's log was, in contrast, the pages of record. It was intended as a barebones fact sheet, or as close as any first mate could achieve. Both logs had their role. The shipping lines considered the captain's account an unimpeachable last word on decisions made during the voyage. The first mate's entries gave a general picture of what happened after the orders came down. Every scrap of detail was important to soothe angry merchants who wondered why their goods weren't in port on time or to provide an answer for a stingy insurance underwriter on a damage claim.

Kelley kept a closer eye on the crew than usual. As a new captain, he knew some of the veteran crew were watching him, too. There would be the inevitable comparisons made with the former master, William Sands. That was fine. But Kelley wanted to make sure no one would push it and test his authority. There had been nothing like that so far. Atkinson*

---

*Some newspaper accounts spell the first mate's name as *Aitchison* and there are other variations, but *Atkinson* is used in Nye's personal recollections, and the same spelling is used in shipping company records. Nye also described Atkinson as being "of Philadelphia." Existing records from that era did not turn up a merchant sailor from Philadelphia or nearby areas with the same name. A Philadelphia rope maker named Samuel Atkinson may have had some maritime experience, but his wife died in 1853 and it was unclear whether he remarried. Apart from the Philadelphia research, another interesting lead emerged. An 1843 affidavit for seamen's documents was drafted in New Orleans for a Samuel Aitchison, described as "mulatto" and a seemed to respect him as captain, which was crucial, because some first mates could be bitter if they were passed over for command. The crew, for the most part, was working well as a unit even with the loathsome weather.

That pleased him. Kelley was looking ahead to his return trip to Liverpool, where Irene waited. Any crew member who couldn't pull his weight during the lashing seas would be cut from the *Rutledge* when they reached New York. His predecessor, Sands, had made one big housekeeping sweep of deck hands in 1854. Five seamen who signed on for a New York–Liverpool run suddenly—and inexplicably—turned on Captain Sands as the ship was leaving port, forcing passengers to help hoist the anchor to get under way. The men then battled the rest of the crew. As the *John Rutledge* moved through New York harbor with a pilot at the helm, one of the mutineers threatened Sands. "[He] said he would blow my brains out," the captain told New York police after the ship returned to shore. All five were arrested.

On this trip, Captain Kelley was already down one deck hand.

Several days earlier, a crew member was blown from the jib boom, the spar that stuck out from the bow like a unicorn's horn. There might be no more dangerous place on a ship in a bad storm. A wave snatched away the shipmate in an instant as he worked the rigging. Another wave also took a passenger, who was washed overboard when he came topside during a break in the weather to help bring food down to steerage.

Atkinson recorded the deaths in the same matter-of-fact manner as he marked the wind speed or the spotting of an iceberg. Any death was sad, but not unexpected on a winter crossing.

The next day was Sunday. If the weather held, Kelley planned to mention the lost crew member and the passenger in a brief shipboard service. He wasn't much on prayers and formalities like that. The messy break of

---

"free person of colour." Aitchison appeared to be illiterate. He made the mark of an X instead of a signature. This makes it extremely unlikely that he could have been the first mate on the *John Rutledge* because the job required, among other skills, the ability to keep clear and cogent logs. It is possible, of course, that Aitchison learned to read and write in the thirteen years between the time the affidavit was signed and the 1856 sailing of the *Rutledge*. If so, it would bring an extraordinary element to the story. But without documents or other credible records, that remains nothing more than a fanciful scenario.

his grandfather with the Congregational Church in Centerville may have soured his taste for wind-baggery from the pulpit. Let everyone face their fears and faith in their own way, he thought. But if a few words during a Sunday service made others on board feel better, so be it. He could also use the moment to remind the crew to be mindful that the most dangerous Atlantic waters were still to come.

In 1843, a fellow Cape Codder, Captain Alexander H. Holway—the same former deck hand who wrote about falling in with the near-miss thieves in Liverpool—penned a homily for everyone who ever turned seaward:

"If any class of men need to pray, it is the seaman," Holway wrote in his diary, "for his life is one of constant peril and is in danger of being called to eternity almost any moment, either from falling from aloft or by sickness or by sudden shipwreck. No one can fully comprehend the hardships of a sailor unless he has had actually experienced as much."

Kelley would have likely agreed.

The packet trade for sailing ships in the Atlantic was built upon difficult promises.

One bad run could throw everything out of alignment.

Departure schedules were published in newspapers weeks in advance. The dates were calculated by predicting when a ship would arrive from its previous leg. A scheduled sailing date of, say, May 1 from New York for Liverpool depended on the ship arriving in port no later than April 15. And that arrival time depended on making it across from Liverpool without getting hung up by any of the many variables that stalked ships at sail—weather, ice, winds, problems with the sails, and whatever else the sea could churn up.

This was all easier to manage for steamships, which could generally power through the weather. Coastal packets, too, were usually on time because their routes were over less storm-tossed waters.

The North Atlantic sailing packets were far more of a wildcard.

One slow trip—like the *John Rutledge* was likely to clock this time— set in motion a domino effect. The next *Rutledge* departure to Liverpool would be delayed. This, in turn, would push back the return from Liverpool to New York and so on. The ripples would then reverberate through the ship's schedule for the rest of the year.

Even one fewer trip per year meant thousands of dollars in lost revenue and, perhaps much more hurtful, a black eye for the shipping line in the cutthroat packet world.

A reputation for chronic slow sailing was the last thing any shipping line or shipowner wanted. Captains were the most convenient scapegoats when ships were delayed seriously. And a history of slow crossings was enough to get a captain blackballed. A shipmaster could quickly find himself out of work as an ocean-going skipper and back in command of a modest sloop making day runs to Nantucket or bouncing around the sleepy ports in the Gulf of Mexico.

Image was king. Sticking to a timetable and building a reliable record of fast Atlantic crossings were a big part of building one. The American merchant fleet did everything it could to promote its swagger, particularly as the competition with the British packet lines heated up. As far back as 1829, one of the handbooks for emigrants gave the Americans high marks. The Yankee captains, it said, try to squeeze advantage from "every puff of wind."

"The ship will be no other than an American one if you wish for a *quick* and *safe* passage," says a passage in the *Emigrants' Guide*, which seemed to relish using italics for emphasis. "The Americans sail *faster* than others, owing to the greater *skill* and greater vigilance of the captains, and to their great sobriety."

After a month sailing and still not getting far past the midway mark, Captain Kelley knew it would be impossible to make it to New York in forty-five days unless the weather turned incredibly favorable. That was not likely. In fact, it probably would get worse before they could find protection off the Canadian Maritimes.

Forty-five days was, more or less, the outer range of a respectable Europe-to-America crossing in winter for a sailing ship. (The steamers routinely muscled through in well under two weeks.) Of course there had been much longer westbound voyages under sail. Some stretched three months or more in the worst cases.

And at least they got their ships to port rather than leaving them at the bottom of the sea. Kelley had been lucky so far. He had delivered intact every ship under his watch with the safe deposit of goods and passengers— well, at least those who didn't die by accident or illness en route. He was also pleased before taking command when he read the ship's papers.

The *Rutledge* was a fighter. Every veteran mariner tried to discern the cursed ships from the good—the ones that have gotten blasted by the sea and somehow refused to go down. The *John Rutledge* had had its share of close scrapes and had come through each time. Captains and others paid attention to such things.

In 1855, just a year earlier, the *Rutledge* struggled into Liverpool after being slammed by a storm just west of Ireland that broke loose the cargo and shifted tons of weight to one side, knocking the ship on its beam-ends. The crew had to heave off cargo just to right the ship, and the storm tore off its starboard anchor and many of its sails. Two crew members were lost. Still, owners Howland and Ridgway didn't dump Captain Sands when other owners might have done at the first sign of anything but a flawless voyage.

Kelley appreciated this, and it may have contributed to his decision to take the *Rutledge* when Sands moved on to a new ship. Back in Liverpool, Sands was now in charge of the *Caravan,* which was about to leave for New York with more than 450 Mormon converts aboard.

Kelley called Atkinson.

Aye, sir, said the first mate.

Make sure we are sharp on the watches, Kelley said. Use your best men. Tell them to sing out if they see anything. We've got ice ahead.

They had already encountered more pack ice than usual. This kind of floe was uncommon for February. Normally, the Arctic sent down its worst during the spring melts beginning in April.

Remind the crew, said Kelley as Atkinson turned to leave. This is not like any year I've seen. It's not average ice.

Aye, sir.

Down in steerage, the passengers took heart of the date. It was official. One month at sea. One month out meant that they might be closer to New York than to Liverpool. Just the idea that the ship had put half the Atlantic behind them was powerful medicine.

That same day, the American clipper ship *Driver* set sail from Liverpool for New York with 344 passengers and 28 crew. Another American clipper, the *Ocean Queen*, was a few days out from London for New York with 90 passengers and 33 crew. On February 15, on the Isle of Wight in the English Channel, the lighthouse keeper watched the *Ocean Queen* head west. The ship's bell chimed an "all's well." To the north, at the mouth of the Mersey, the Liverpool pilot handed over the helm to the captain of the *Driver,* and then the ship crossed over the horizon.

It was the last time either ship was seen by anyone, apart from those unfortunate souls on board.

Chapter Eight

FEBRUARY 18, 1856; SOUTHWEST OF THE FLEMISH CAP;
THIRTY-THREE DAYS OUT OF LIVERPOOL.

K elley and Atkinson finally started to mark their bearings by features of the distant Canadian shores, still hundreds of miles to the west. They also were running into their first brushes with the enormity of the ice. Though Kelley had read the early reports before leaving Liverpool from inbound ships, nothing prepared him for this. Fields of drift ice, dotted by small but very dangerous icebergs, seesawed in the great Atlantic swells.

It had been a week or more since the *Rutledge* had seen another ship. Most captains, it seemed, had shifted to a southern course as word spread of the North Atlantic's unusually icy grip.

The *Rutledge* sailed southwest of the Flemish Cap, an underwater rise warmed slightly by the Gulf Stream and teeming with cod, swordfish, and halibut. At that time, the area was so rich in catch crews took incredible risks to cast nets into its waters. Hardy schooners from as far away as Gloucester made the trip carrying a mini-fleet of one-person dories, essentially big row boats, which then set out to fish the Cap and bring the catch back to the mother ship for quick salting. Many dory crews never returned.

The *Rutledge* was too far south of the Flemish Cap to cross paths with any fishing vessels. Its bearing was set west-southwest, toward the Grand Banks. Beyond the Banks lay Newfoundland to the north and Nova Scotia to the south. But in between was the Atlantic's most deadly range of ice.

Atkinson wrote in his log:

Monday, 18th February. 8 a.m., the weather is thick, foggy with drizzly rain. In the latter part strong breezes and rainy. Passed several icebergs on both sides, passed one within ten feet of the weather side. Lat. D.R.,[*] 45. Deg, 34 min. N., lon. D.R. 46 deg. 56 min. W.

Each year, thousands of bergs and ice slabs break off the Greenland glaciers, a process known as calving. Bergs range from tabletop size to peaks of ice that stick up hundreds of feet above the surface. Seamen did not worry about the calving but about what happens after. If the ice stays to the north and out of the shipping routes, then all is fine. But some years, like 1856, a huge amount of ice roams south. The reasons are many: slight shifts in the Labrador Current running between Canada and Greenland, changes in the direction of the prevailing winds, and variations in water temperature. In the great age of sail, what made it worse was sailors' helplessness to figure it all out. They had no way to collect, transmit, and analyze the data from the Far North to forecast—before it was too late—whether the ice would float south.

Ice detection was strictly a contact sport in those days. Crews knew the ice was bad only when they or other vessels stumbled into it. Probably the only thing the Atlantic packet lines feared more than ice was a hurricane spinning up from the Caribbean or a supercharged nor'easter slamming in from the north. But at least the skies and the wind always gave some advance warning with storms. In mid-September 1855, a major hurricane pinwheeled up the middle of the Atlantic. The *John Rutledge* was just heading out of Liverpool for New York. But Captain Sands, seeing the barometer fall and sensing the shifting winds, put on the brakes. He pulled down the big sails and moved at a lazy pace for a few days until it seemed the storm had passed. It worked. The *Rutledge* missed the storm and reached New York without incident that fall, when command then shifted to Kelley.

Ships that encountered heavy ice immediately shared every detail once in port. Ice reports might have been the single most watched items in newspapers. Normally, the first word came from westbound ships, whose path took them through the heart of the North Atlantic ice zones. That

------

*The "D.R." noted in Atkinson's log refers to dead reckoning, a method of calculating position using average speed and time from a previously known location.

information—spread by the new technology of telegraph—was sent to American and Canadian ports for ships about to weigh anchor for Europe. But this wasn't any good for those ships setting sail from Liverpool, London, and Le Havre. The details wouldn't reach Europe until eastbound packet ships arrived, and by then the news was weeks old.

Years earlier, in the archive room of the Navy's Depot of Charts and Instruments, an enterprising lieutenant, Matthew Maury, had started a popular navigation-aid journal that compiled wind and current observations from ships around the world. It was a godsend for captains and first mates, especially those on new routes. Yet it could only offer conjecture on ice movements and nothing about where ice could be at any given time of year.

For years, there had been conferences and studies on laying a transatlantic telegraph cable. Few supported it more than the shipping lines, which would then have ice reports as soon as they were available. The first step, a line between Newfoundland and Nova Scotia, was just a work in progress in early 1856. A gale had kicked up in 1855 and scrapped the first effort. Another attempt was set for the summer of 1856, around the time when Kelley expected to return from Liverpool with Irene.

It wasn't until 1858, however, that the first dots and dashes flowed across the ocean on copper wire. But when the voltage was increased weeks later, the insulation failed and set back the whole project another six years.

Perhaps nothing in a ship's logs was more important than detailed and accurate accounts of the ice. To inform future trips, captains could then dissect the logs for patterns and timelines and clues on where and when the worst ice was encountered.

For the most part, first mates' logs on packet ships were studies in shipboard journalism—clear, factual, and rich with details about time and place.

But those hunting whales—who considered themselves a breed apart—were a bit more freewheeling with what they put to paper. Some logbooks on whaling ships doubled as a kind of scrapbook and diary of the first mate and whoever else he deemed worthy to add flourishes of his own. If packet ship logs were the fact sheets of the day, whaling ship logs were bawdy adventure novellas.

On the *Prudent*, a Long Island whaling bark that began a three-year trip about the same time the *John Rutledge* left Liverpool, the entries include sketches of Polynesian women, with emphasis, as expected, on their uncovered breasts. The *Sea Serpent*, out of New Bedford, carried a log festooned with newspaper clippings; drawings of rays, jellyfish, and other sea life curios; and poems that ran from racy to downright dark—a window on the frailty the crew felt amid the power of the sea. Tucked into the *Sea Serpent* log was a clipping from a portion of the "The Isle of Devils," a gloomy ode written in 1827 by the British-born novelist Matthew Lewis. His work peered into corners so creepy that Lord Byron once wondered what lay in the "deeper hell" of Lewis's mind.

> The morn to that Vessel no succour shall bring!
> Now high o'er the main-mast I hover:
> Now I plunge from the sky to the deck with a spring.
> And I shatter the mast with one flap of my wing—
> It cracks and it breaks, and goes over.
> Hew away, gallant sailors! fatigue never dread;
> You shall all rest at morn from your labours:
> The ocean's white mantle shall o'er you be spread.
> The white bones of Mariners pillow your head.
> And the whale and the shark be your neighbours.

On the Fairhaven whaling ship *Adeline Gibbs*, which Thomas W. Nye may have seen set off in 1853, the log had fine woodcut stamps to record each fluke seen and the variety of every whale taken. In September 1855, nearly two years out, in the North Pacific off the Kuril Islands, the *Adeline Gibbs* crossed paths with the *Faith*, a bark out of neighboring New Bedford. This might seem like a staggering improbability to shore people. But for the fraternity of New England whalemen, it was nothing more than a pleasant diversion. Remarkably, running across a familiar ship and crew fifteen thousand nautical miles from home was not unusual. The New Bedford whalers, and their harpooning cousins across the Acushnet

River in Fairhaven, spread everywhere over the main whaling grounds in the Pacific.

They rounded the howling Drake Strait and made resupply stops at Valparaiso, where pastel-colored homes rose up on hills from the docks. From there, the Pacific whaling grounds hugged the equator. Other ships headed north, skimming the shores of Japan and Russian-ruled Alaska. Along the way, they tasted breadfruit and coconut in the tropics, and walrus and salmon in the Arctic. If nothing else, it gave New England whalers and Atlantic packet ship men a crash course in the world's common humanity. These weren't the type of men who populated the salons and lyceums of the Victorian elite. That's a shame. What they had to say about parochial notions of Western cultural superiority and other tripe was a message that is important and timeless.

This was the cultural stew that bubbled around seaman Thomas Nye as a boy.

He would have heard sea tales of all kinds with all degrees of hyperbole. There was the good stuff that perked any lad's ears: glimpses of sea monsters and other briny imps real and imagined. More often, though, the spinnings of a story were about the real demons of the deep: the storms that snapped masts and the ice that stove hulls.

And, of course, there were the stories of amazing rescues.

None may have been stranger—or more wanderlust-stoking to young Nye—than the tale of a soft-spoken Japanese teen Nye saw around Fairhaven. Many called him John Mung, a crude attempt to wrap American tongues around his real name, Manijiro Nakahama. He was part of a five-member Japanese fishing crew blown into the Pacific by a storm and shipwrecked on a deserted atoll more than eight hundred miles from the Japanese mainland. The whaling ship *John Howland,* with Fairhaven Captain William H. Whitfield in command, came across the castaways in 1841. Four of the rescued Japanese were set ashore in the Sandwich Islands, now Hawaii. Nakahama, only fourteen at the time, wanted to keep going. In 1843, when Nye was nine years old, Whitfield came home with Nakahama in tow. The boy is believed by many to be one of the first

Japanese residents in the United States at a time when the Japanese emperor had hermetically sealed off Japan from the rest of the world.

Nakahama stayed for three years and studied English at a one-room schoolhouse and almost certainly picked up much more slang from the younger boys in Fairhaven. He eventually returned to Japan, but only after a stint on a whaling ship and a bit of fun in San Francisco during the Gold Rush. Back in Japan, he once again landed on his feet. When Commodore Matthew Perry arrived in 1853, Nakahama was called on as a translator because he was one of a few who spoke clear and idiomatic English. Nakahama—with his Fairhaven-honed English—played an indispensable role in the negotiations to open Japan. Some say he was something of the sartorial godfather to today's Japanese salarymen. Lore has it that the erstwhile John Mung was also responsible for introducing the necktie to Tokyo.

Thomas Nye wasn't just a bystander to tales that washed in from the sea. His own family had loads of their own tragic sea lore.

In October 1848, when Nye was fourteen, one of his uncles, a merchant named Thomas S. H. Nye, was on the clipper ship *Kelpie* sailing from Hong Kong for Shanghai. A typhoon kicked up. None of the passengers or crew was ever heard from again. But rumors persisted—probably fed by the lost Nye's influential brother, Gideon Nye Jr.—that the *Kelpie* wrecked on the shores of Formosa, now Taiwan, and that Nye and an English passenger survived and were forced into slavery by the locals.

Gideon was a powerful China trade merchant and rose to become the American vice consul in Canton. He tried to leverage the rumors of his brother's fate to push his own bit of American jingoism. In 1857, in a letter that ended up in US Senate records, he cited the disappearance of the *Kelpie* and other shipwrecks in the difficult waters off Formosa to urge American naval power to invade and colonize the island "in the interests of humanity and commerce." He didn't stop there. The letter—drawing deep from the poisoned well of Western arrogance—portrays the people living along Formosa's wild South China Sea coasts as "simply cruel, bloodthirsty savages" who would benefit from the "power of civilized governments."

Thomas Nye finally left Fairhaven as a packet ship passenger in 1854, sometime before his twentieth birthday. The vessel, most likely a mail schooner on its regular run, would have slipped down the Acushnet on the outgoing tide. New Bedford's cobblestone streets rise up a gentle hill. Across the Acushnet, Nye would have seen the flatter contours of Fairhaven pass by until the town gave way to the salt marshes around Fort Phoenix. His last sight of home, if he looked back at all, would have been the huge steeple of the First Congregational Church.

Nye was bound for New York to sign on with a packet line. He would have had his pick. Packets headed off to Liverpool or Le Havre or New Orleans just about every day.

The pay wasn't great—in fact, it was downright dismal in some cases—and the work was hard and relentless. The lowliest deck hand could make about eight dollars a month, and a first mate could pull down something in the neighborhood of thirty-five (the equivalent, in modern terms, of about a thousand dollars). A rank-and-file crew member might make more on a factory line or as a longshoreman. But the sea carried its own powerful currency. You were out in the world. You could experience things a landlubber could scarcely imagine: a shoreline fading into the ivory-white haze; the excitement of running your eyes over the delights of a new port.

In New York, Nye picked the *John Rutledge* for reasons he kept to himself. It's not hard to imagine, however, that the young man was impressed by the *Rutledge*'s size—bigger than many packets—and lured to see wild Liverpool in person. Melville once said Liverpool harbored "more sharks than at sea." That was potent advertising for a young man looking for adventure.

The trip from New York on the *Rutledge* in December 1856 was an easy run. "Fair winds and following seas" was what seamen called a nice, uneventful voyage. But on their return trip to New York that winter, Nye and the *Rutledge* crew—especially the younger ones—were getting firsthand lessons in the Atlantic's inhospitable nature.

So were any other ships unlucky enough to be out in the Atlantic that February.

∽

On February 9, the ice-damaged Cunard steamship *Persia* pulled into New York after a fifteen-day crossing from Liverpool; it had left about ten days after the *John Rutledge*.

The *Persia* ran at a good clip of eleven knots. Her captain, an old sea hand named Charles Judkins, had publicly stated in Liverpool that he would not race the Collins Line's *Pacific* across the Atlantic for the fastest time. But that was not how the public perceived it. Many expected both ships to push hard for a new record.

The *Pacific* had left Liverpool a few days before the *Persia,* so it was naturally expected in New York first to throw down its time mark. It was a huge surprise—and a stinging slap for Collins Line boosters—to see the British steamer *Persia* limping into New York harbor ahead of the *Pacific,* a pride of the American packet fleet.

Judkins's account was among the first extensive reports of the horrendous ice presence that year. It also fed worries that something very wrong had happened to the *Pacific.*

The *Persia* had run across the ice pack in the first days of February. A gale blowing from the north kicked up huge waves and constantly shifted the surface ice.

At 46 degrees north and 46 west—about forty miles southwest from where the *John Rutledge* was—the *Persia* ran headlong into a thick vein of ice. The starboard wheel took a direct hit. The paddles cracked and broke off, churning up fountains of frigid seawater instead of propelling the ship through it. Sixteen feet of metal was sheered away from the hull. Judkins, who had commanded steamships since 1840, immediately ordered the boilers turned down. He then told the crew to raise the ship's sails, which many steamers had as backup in case the pipes failed. The *Persia* was effectively trapped. For thirty-six hours, the crew kept to a southerly course, trying hour by hour to pick their way through the ice to clear seas.

Judkins was known in the States for a very different reason. In 1845, he was commander of the early Cunard steamer *Cambria* that took a delegation of antislavery activists to Ireland along with Frederick Douglass for the publication of the book *Narrative of the Life of Frederick Douglass,* which chronicled the man's experiences in the South and as a runaway slave. Judkins took a liking to Douglass and the abolitionists, including a family of singers called the Hutchinsons. At their request, the captain arranged for Douglass to give a shipboard speech. That didn't sit well with the pro-slavery passengers, who heckled Douglass and nearly touched off a mid-ocean riot that might have gone down as a most unusual setting to signal the coming schism in America.

In 1856 in the *Persia*'s mail bags was an envelope from the Liverpool agents of the *John Rutledge* addressed to the ship's owners, Messrs. Howland and Ridgway at 106 Wall Street. It contained the full passenger and crew list for that winter's crossing, 146 souls in total: 123 passengers and 23 crew.

The newspapers were filled with the developments in the Crimea after the latest clash of Europe's great powers. Westbound ships like the *Persia* carried dispatches and news of peace talks in Paris. The demand for timely Crimea news was so great that a special telegraph line—a technology just a decade old—had been linked from Europe to Balaclava, a small port on the Black Sea immortalized in 1854 as the "valley of Death" in Alfred Lord Tennyson's "The Charge of the Light Brigade."

The shipping lines didn't really give a hoot about news of the far-off Crimean war (unless there was a way to make money off it). It was the *Persia*'s report about the ice that riveted them.

It made some people in the New York shipping world very nervous.

Chapter Nine

It was especially tense at 56 Wall Street in the offices of the New York and Liverpool United States Mail Steamship Company, which everyone called the Collins Line.

There was still no word from its steamship *Pacific*—no sighting by the rival *Persia* or any other ships that had pulled in to New York or Boston.

The Collins Line staff had other ships and schedules to worry about. But it was hard to not think about the *Pacific* and what could have happened. At that stage, none of the possibilities were good. The worst, of course, was that the *Pacific* had gone down. But why give that idea credence just yet?

Though there were no sightings of the steamer, there also were no suggestions—circumstantial or otherwise—of wreckage.

Concentrate on the facts, the line's owner and overlord, Edward Knight Collins, told his staff.

It was certain the *Pacific* left Liverpool on January 23, a week after the *John Rutledge,* with about 45 passengers and more than 140 crew aboard. The *Pacific* was scheduled to steam into New York harbor in early February. But something had happened to prevent this. The question was what.

The Collins Line tried to put a hopeful spin on its comments to the shipping news reporters. Maybe there was engine trouble. They had removed the mizzenmast in 1853 in an effort to reduce drag and boost speed. That left the *Pacific* without backup sails. Any engine problem, the Collins Line spin doctors told the reporters, would mean that repairs had to be done at sea. The ship could be floating in the Atlantic waiting for the engines to be repaired before it got under way again. They left out the inconvenient fact that any foundering ship wouldn't last long in the pounding gales. And what if, perhaps, the *Pacific* was aiding another ship in distress? Anything was possible.

Still, better to be prudent, the shipping line concluded.

Another steamship, the *Alabama,* was ordered out to sea on a mission to hunt for the *Pacific*. The idea—the hope, really—was that the *Pacific* had been disabled or trapped by ice. Any rescue bid must be guided by unwavering optimism until the facts say otherwise. The *Alabama* was loaded with supplies for the possible discovery of healthy, but hungry, souls on the *Pacific:* three hundred barrels of bread, seventy barrels of salted beef, thirty of salt pork, and a whopping twenty-three hundred pounds of fresh beef and mutton.

The *Rutledge* co-owner, Williams Howland, a former clipper ship captain in his own right, wanted to contribute as well. After all, his partner, Ridgway, was on the *Pacific* along with a who's who of New York and English elite. The Collins Line was gracious to Howland, who was still lanky in his early fifties and hanging on to some of the quirks he developed at sea—such as wearing white kid gloves even in warm weather. Edward Knight Collins told Howland that no extra help was needed, but he would keep him in the loop with any urgent news they got on the fate of the ship.

Collins perhaps had extra empathy for anyone waiting on news of a missing ship. Less than eighteen months earlier, the *Pacific*'s sister ship the *Arctic* had gone down. Collins's wife and two children, a son and daughter, were among those lost at sea.

By 1856, everyone knew the story. On September 20, 1854, the *Arctic*—with its churning twin paddle wheels, each an eye-popping twenty-five feet, six inches across—left Liverpool for New York. The forty-nine-year-old captain, a Collins Line veteran named James C. Luce, brought along his sickly son William, thinking the sea air would do the boy good. The passenger list was full of luminaries: emissaries to the French Embassy in Washington, prominent scholars such as Dr. Carter Page Johnson, dean of the Medical College of Virginia, and the usual assortment of high-rollers, scions, and rich rogues.

A week later, the *Arctic* was about sixty miles southeast of Cape Race, Newfoundland, and moving through wave after wave of fog banks. So was another vessel, the French schooner *Vesta,* which was bringing nearly 150 fishermen and salters back to Normandy after a season on the windswept islands of Saint-Pierre and Miquelon, the last humble bits of France's once-huge reach in North America. The *Vesta,* under full sail, rammed into the starboard side of the *Arctic.* The *Vesta*'s iron prow pushed deep into the wooden hull of the *Arctic.* For a few confused hours, the damaged ships were locked in an awkward dance. The *Vesta* crew thought the much bigger *Arctic* was still seaworthy and would offer rescue. Captain Luce of the *Arctic* thought so, too, at first. Then it became clear his ship would not survive. He made the decision. They would leave the *Vesta* to its fate and make an all-or-nothing dash for the coast.

Soon thereafter, through the fog came the sickening sound of cracking wood and water-choked screams. The *Arctic* had plowed right into one of the few lifeboats sent from the *Vesta.* The steamer's paddle wheels turned the smaller boat into driftwood and flung bodies across the sea like playing cards. Yet the *Arctic* pressed on. Luce dared not spare a minute as water began to flood the boiler rooms. Shortly, though, the fires were washed over. The ship was sinking fast. It carried six lifeboats, the legal minimum for American ships of its size, with a capacity for about 210 people. They could squeeze in everyone in an orderly evacuation. That, sadly, did not happen. The deck of the *Arctic* fell into bedlam. It became survival of the strongest. And that left most of the women and children to fight in vain against the men and crew members who commandeered the lifeboats. In the end, few daughters, wives, or youngsters were among the survivors, even though some passengers reported seeing a few women wedged into the starboard lifeboat before it was launched. The ship's purser, John Geib, witnessed Collins's wife and children go down when their lifeboat was swamped with desperate passengers and crew clambering aboard.

The second mate on the *Arctic,* William Baahlam, offered to take Luce's son on a lifeboat. "I asked the captain what his intentions were," Baahlam wrote in a dispatch, "and he replied that the ship's fate would be his. I then asked if he would not allow his son to go with me, and he answered that he should share his fate."

A full accounting of the human toll on the *Arctic* was never clear. The best calculation of maritime historians is that more than three hundred lives were lost; some set the number dozens higher. The more than *sixty men* from the *Arctic* who did survive—more than two-thirds of them crew—reached Newfoundland on lifeboats or were picked up by passing ships. The *Vesta* lost only about a dozen men in the hours after the collision, including those torn apart by the *Arctic*'s big paddle wheels.

Initially, Captain Luce was given posthumous honors as a hero—a tragic one for the loss of his son. The public and press were inclined to put a salty halo on the masters of the great clipper ships and packets. But the mood turned as the heartlessness of the narrative sank in.

"Oh! What a manly spectacle that must have been!" wrote the *New York Express.* "Hardy, rough-handed, broad-shouldered, strong-framed men . . . men like these treacherously deserting feeble and delicate women and shutting their ears to the cries from little children."

❧

In New York in February 1856, two other ship lines waited for word of their vessels making their way from England: the clippers *Driver* and *Ocean Queen.* It was far too early for any serious concern—in a normal year. But the reports of ice were anything but routine. The clipper lines began posting watchers on the main New York docks. If anyone saw the ships, they wanted to be the first to know.

Even the self-described psychics of the era got in on the act. At four cents a copy, the popular rag *Spiritual Telegraph* offered accounts of "contacts" with the departed and various other goings-on in the phantasmagorical realm. One seer, a media-friendly figure named Harriet Porter of 109 West 24th Street, proclaimed that she had a metaphysical bead on the *Pacific.* Her news was not good. "The spirits say the *Pacific,* six days out, struck an iceberg . . . went down stern-foremost."

All this was generally scoffed at as unadulterated nonsense, of course. But the mystical stylings of Harriet Porter tapped in to the icy reality of 1856.

❧

After nightfall on February 19, the ice around the *John Rutledge* grew thicker. It was getting more difficult to find a safe path, Atkinson noted in the ship's log. The winds had fallen off sharply. The helmsman attempted to thread through the ice but was at the mercy of the currents.

The first mate kept a running account:

> At 8 saw a large field of ice ahead; tried to steer clear of it, but there being little wind it got down to the ship before we could get past it, and the wind dying away, we could not steer clear. At 11, the ship was completely wedged in with drift-ice and very large ice-bergs in all directions, and the breeze springing right aft, there was no alternative but to proceed through it. The further we got in the thicker the ice got, and the greater the number of icebergs. Midnight, light winds and the ship making very little headway through the ice. 4, morning, the same. 8, steady breeze, and the ship making more headway. Passed some very large ice-bergs. At 9, the I . . .

His log ends there. Atkinson never wrote another word.

Chapter Ten

FEBRUARY 20, 1856; ICEBERG;

THIRTY-SIX DAYS OUT OF LIVERPOOL.

Even at a light-wind crawl, the jolt of the iceberg strike rippled through every corner of the *Rutledge*. In steerage, it was like the hollow sound of a great drumroll as the ice gouged through the hull up toward the bow. In the rigging, the impact shook the sails, causing flakes of seafoam rime to rain down.

Then quiet. Everything came to a standstill. For minutes, there was only the sounds of the creaking ropes and the wind moving across the ice and the ship's ropes and rails and masts. The *Rutledge* was already sinking, but no one could sense that yet. The crew on deck stared in disbelief into the fog at the ghostly outline of the berg.

In steerage, the passengers were left guessing. What was that? The question was repeated over and over as if enough asking would produce an answer.

Sounds like we hit something, a few passengers said nervously, hoping someone else would contradict them. But once it was said and said again—yes, we must have hit something—there was only one way for the speculation to go.

Ice? You think it's ice?

What else could it be? Part of a floating wreck? Could that be it?

No, came the reply, it must be ice. It's all around us.

The fog was a dense gray curtain—brewed from the cold Arctic currents tickling the warmer Gulf Stream. But the seas had improved enough over the past day that the hatches were opened. The evening before, most steerage passengers had ventured onto deck to get some blessed fresh air after more than a week's imprisonment below. They gaped and gasped at their first sight of the blue-white cliffs and peaks of the giant bergs and the endless fields of sea ice. Some sketched in their diaries, recording a scene they might never see again.

For a while, the steerage passengers waited for word from the crew about the source of the impact. None came. Finally, a man climbed up a few steps and, popping his head from the relative warmth of crowded steerage to the sea-cold fog, looked on deck. He saw crew members peering over the edge of the boat toward the bow. An iceberg—the one that just ripped into the ship—was passing slowly just off the starboard side, almost within reach. It was pock-marked by wash from the waves but enamel smooth higher up. It loomed large enough that its edges disappeared in the fog, making it impossible to gauge its full size.

A knot of nervous steerage passengers gathered at the base of the stairs. One yelled up to the man on the steps.

Well, what's happening?

The crew is just looking over the side, he answered. Maybe it's not so bad.

Well, I'm going up, said another. I don't want to guess.

At the top of the stairs, they were stopped and told to stay below. The crew member was polite but firm. We need to have the deck free, he told them. We are looking to see if anything needs to be done.

Tell us, at least. Was it ice? the men pressed. That iceberg near the ship. Did we hit that?

I think, yes, it's ice, the crewmate answered honestly.

How bad?

I can't say anything yet, the seaman said, offering mostly the truth but trying to end the conversation before it grew too testy. We are looking now. Please stay below and stay calm. I would not worry.

That meant little. Passengers in steerage talked wildly, trading speculation and worries. Parents instinctively kept their children close.

Few, if any, of the steerage passengers knew the ship's precise location in the Atlantic. But many had picked up enough from newspapers and sailors' stories in Liverpool to make an educated calculation. Heavy ice and fog meant they were running somewhere in what mariners called the Western Ocean—basically, anywhere west of Greenland's tip.

Over the next half hour or so, the commotion on deck grew more troubling. More movement. Shouting. Heavy footfalls.

This didn't seem routine at all.

❧

Margaret Henderson gathered her youngest children, Mary and James. Stay with me, she told them. Everything will be fine. It's just busy now, and I don't want you to get lost.

All around her, other mothers were doing the same. Children were rounded up. In the women's section, Jane Black cuddled little Betty. Samuel was far too old for such comforting. He wanted to join the other lads and their fathers who gathered around the base of the stairs leading to the deck.

The men debated whether to ignore the order to stay below or make another push to get on deck and get some answers.

No, Sam, wait with us, Jane begged.

It was too late. He was already moving toward the stairs. The men were getting anxious at the lack of news and the clamor of activity on deck.

It's our lives, too, said one man. Is that not right?

A few grumbled in agreement.

We paid to be on this ship, another said. We shouldn't be pushed into a pen like sheep. What do you say, boys?

That seemed to do it. When the first man moved onto the stairs, the rest immediately followed.

William Henderson watched them. He and Margaret and the young ones were situated close to the hatch. They had gotten on board early and picked this spot, thinking the air would be better near the opening to the deck.

I'm going up, too, William told his wife. I'll take the boys. C'mon, Robert, James. Let's go.

Margaret knew it was pointless to try to stop them.

You'll come right back, then? she pleaded. Just find out what's happening. That's all. We need to stay together in case it's something serious.

The men burst through the opening and stood on deck in a tight little pack. They expected to be stopped by the crew. Instead, hardly anyone paid them attention. All the seamen worked with sharp purpose. Some were busy trimming the sails. Most, however, seemed to be gathered around the first mate near the bow, where the hull began to taper in. They couldn't hear what he was saying. It was also hard to see through the fog exactly what he was doing. He seemed to be gesturing and pointing over the bow toward the sea.

They watched Atkinson lean over the gunwale. Then he gestured for a crewmate, who took hold of Atkinson's jacket, allowing the mate to cantilever over the side of the ship.

What Atkinson could see didn't look good.

The *Rutledge* was taking on water. That was clear. When the bow rode up on a swell, Atkinson glimpsed the gouge made by the ice. Thorns of splintered wood jutted from the hull. Some smaller pieces floated away from the ship. Most of the damage would have been pushed inward, Atkinson knew. What he could see was just a hint of how bad it was. He needed to get down below quickly.

Atkinson turned toward the stern, hoping he could signal the captain. The fog was too thick. But he could hear the passengers who had defied orders to stay below. They had cornered Captain Kelley and were demanding answers.

Atkinson moved close enough to pick up the conversation. He heard the captain say that his best men were looking into the, um, issue of an, ah, encounter with ice. We don't know the extent of damage if, in fact, there is any, the captain said.

This is a strong ship, he continued. I would not be worried.

But Atkinson was. He knew what the captain did not. He moved aft and pulled Kelley aside. That berg caused major damage, he told the captain. Just below the water line. I'll go below to look and will have a full report soon.

William Henderson, meanwhile, raced back to steerage to find his wife.

He could sense this was serious no matter what the captain said. He saw the worry in Atkinson's eyes as he talked to Kelley. He'd seen that look before when railway managers were forced to confront family members after a mishap on the rails, such as a boiler explosion. Henderson scrambled below deck, elbowing his way through the others heading up.

They asked as he passed: What is it? What's wrong?

I don't know, Henderson said, keeping his panicked thoughts to himself. Ice it seems. The crew is trying to sort it.

He didn't dare say how it really seemed to him. The way the first mate raced back from the bow to converse with Captain Kelley was not a good sign.

Henderson went to their berth and shook his wife's leg. Get the children, he panted, trying to keep his voice low. We have to get up on deck now. They aren't saying anything, but it looks very serious. There's lots of talk. People are already gathered around the lifeboats. No one is saying anything. We talked to the captain and he said they were still looking into it.

But I'm worried, William went on. Let's be ready.

Lots of clothes, Maggie, he added. Wear lots of clothes. You and the children. It's very cold. Foggy and very cold.

She went from child to child, trying to layer on as much fabric as possible. It was becoming difficult to move. People were battling to get topside, lugging what they could—overcoats, umbrellas, family papers, and, of course, their money—in case they never came back.

The Hendersons finally reached the bottleneck at the stairs. Margaret had her children in tow. She had grabbed two blankets and held both tightly under her arms in case someone made a lunge for them. Sister-in-law Elizabeth was right behind with toddler Eliza in her arms. Even those who had no idea about what keeps a ship afloat instinctively knew that below deck was not the best place to be. Getting above provided, if nothing else, options. If they were going down, staying below offered none except death.

William Henderson felt the growing panic as passengers behind them shoved forward.

C'mon. Up with you! Be quick about it.

It took a few minutes for the Hendersons to reach the deck, which shimmered with sleet and frozen sea spray. It was late morning. The bow of the ship was dipping slightly but noticeably.

Margaret tried to catch the eye of a crew member. Even a reassuring look would be a relief. But nothing. The crew all seemed to be moving in different directions. One group looked as if they planned to head down to steerage. Is that a good thing or bad? she wondered.

About 325 miles to the east, the packet ship *Germania* moved into the same weather system that had rolled over the *John Rutledge* a few days earlier. "Thick and foggy," wrote the *Germania*'s first mate. "Winds S. Strong gales."

Chapter Eleven

February 20, 1856; morning; the sinking.

First Mate Atkinson ordered two sailors to the pumps.

They had anticipated the order and were already moving toward the pump station aft. They muscled through the passengers, who fanned across the deck despite the crew's efforts to keep them in a group.

A deck full of passengers was just what Captain Kelley did not need. Speed was now the only thing that mattered in checking the damage and determining whether anything could be done. Frightened passengers milling around only slowed down the works.

Some men grabbed crewmen by the sleeve. Are we sinking, man? Why is the ship tilting?

Families started to pray. They pushed their heads close together and murmured, sending up wisps of warm-breath steam that were instantly lost in the fog and winds that swirled in along the Gulf Stream.

The sailors cranked the pump's big flywheels and checked the soundings, which gauged the level of bilge water and—if the readings were off the charts—signaled that water was rising into the cargo holds. They checked the levels twice just to be sure.

Then they pushed back through the passengers to reach Atkinson, who was up at the bow trying to get a better look at the fissure in the hull.

Sir, it's not good, one crew member told Atkinson. We're filling fast. Fearfully fast.

Atkinson didn't say a word. He ran down the deck, pointing at whatever seamen he spotted.

Follow me, he shouted.

At the same time, more people emerged from the shadows of steerage, blinking at the paleness of it all. The ice, the fog, and the sea all seemed the color of watery porridge.

Panic fed panic. Passengers crowded around the winches holding the ship's five lifeboats. The simplest of craft, each lifeboat was about twenty-five feet long and without any kind of cabin or nook for shelter. If the order was given to abandon ship, these little tubs were passengers' only hope. It made the most sense to be near them. It was sure to be a madhouse if the ship was going down, and they strived to stake out a spot.

There were about 120 people in steerage. At least two dozen crew. That was about 30 people per lifeboat. Could the boats handle that number?

No matter, one passenger said wryly. They would have to.

The bow had slipped another degree or two toward the sea. The tilt was noticeable now.

A cry arose. For God's sake, launch the boats before it's too late!

Save us! Why are you waiting?

Captain Kelley expected this. He moved to center deck and signaled the passengers to assemble as best they could. The fog allowed him to see the faces of only the closest. The rest were gray outlines.

He called for quiet.

For those who don't know, I'm Captain Alexander Kelley. Now listen well. The first thing here is to remain calm.

Yes, we have hit ice, Kelley told them truthfully. We just don't know any more than that right now, he lied.

Please, Kelley continued, let us do our work. We need to get the pumps going. We must inspect the damage.

So you are saying there is damage? a passenger chimed in.

Kelley took a breath and carefully weighed his words. What I mean to say is that we are looking at whether the ice *did* damage. Like I said before, there is no reason for alarm. Let us do our work and I will tell you what we learn very soon.

He headed off, leaving the passengers to chew on his words. What they couldn't know was that his speech was designed to buy time.

Kelley and crew were well aware that they could do nothing if the passengers ran amok. Mob psychology could shift in a blink. Right now, deference to the captain's authority still held. For how long he knew not.

If they made a run for the lifeboats, there was not much to be done to stop them.

An idea struck Kelley. The crew would certainly need extra hands to deal with the damage if he could keep the ship afloat. This was the time to bring the passengers into the effort, a time-tested way to calm the mood even if it meant showing them the extent of the damage. Anyway, Kelley thought, they would know soon enough.

He returned to the spot on deck where he had addressed the crowd just minutes before. The passengers—at least those who could see Kelley through the fog—immediately gathered again.

I have a request, Kelley shouted. We need men. They will help the crew and allow us to more quickly determine what—if anything—we need to do.

Kelley looked toward the men closest to him, trying to pick the ones who looked the strongest but also still had their heads. How about you? Or you? I need you to help the crew. It's important—very important— that you follow their orders. Move lively now.

Kelley quickly set up teams. A few seamen were put in charge of a larger cohort of passengers. One group was told to head down into the hold.

Haul up anything you can carry. We need to cast off extra weight. But mostly we have to clear a path to get to the broken timbers.

It's our best chance, Kelley urged. Go smartly. Every minute is precious.

Two other groups—twelve men each, passengers and crew—were assigned to man the twin pumps in shifts. Don't stop, the first mate told them, until you hear from me or the captain. Understood? The passengers nodded. The angle of the deck shifted further. The bow was riding lower now.

Some of the lucky passengers had heavy winter coats, long wool frock coats bought with a mind toward cutting a respectable figure in America. But many others who had saved every penny to book a ticket aboard the *Rutledge* had little more than a town coat and thin scarf.

William Henderson buttoned his jacket high against his neck. He was on the pumps. It was an obvious choice. He had the muscles from working the rail lines.

Margaret and Elizabeth took the children toward the stern, which was crowding with others. It was pure danger-driven instinct—move to the highest point on a sinking ship—even if it meant being farther from the lifeboats. Margaret held tight to her youngest, five-year-old James, pulling his face into her waist. Elizabeth held her one-year-old Eliza in her arms. The older Henderson children, led by sixteen-year-old Robert, huddled together off to the side. Robert tried to convince his two younger sisters that this would all be a great adventure story to tell someday. You'll see, he said, trying to keep his voice from betraying his worry. We'll be fine.

Nearby, Jane Black gripped little Betty's hand. She didn't want the girl to wander off in search of Samuel, who had joined a group of young men that pressed closer to one of the lifeboats.

The first group on the pumps got to work. They threw themselves at the brass handles, which cranked a pulley system that drew up seawater from the lowest point in the hull. It was hard enough to stay ahead of normal leaks and the unavoidable seepage, known as the weep, that came through worn-out caulking and hairline gaps between planks. They could do nothing against the torrent pouring into the ship's gaping wound.

No one yet had a full picture of the damage.

The first mate Atkinson was only sure it was bad. He still held out hope to somehow keep the ship afloat and make a run for any port in Newfoundland, at least four hundred miles away.

He grabbed a lantern and went below, passing the steerage level and moving down into the cargo bowels. The in-rushing seawater lapped over his ankles. It was so cold it made his breath ragged. Keep moving, he told himself. There is not much time.

Wriggling like a cave explorer, he finally worked his way through the rope-lashed crates and reached the crushed section of the hull. He carried a lamp in one hand and a whistle in the other to signal for help if the crates came loose and pinned him down.

Peering between piles of boxes and sacks, he came face to face with the devastation the iceberg had carved.

A long gash at the water line smashed through all seven inches of copper-lined Southern yellow pine of the *Rutledge*'s hull. The icy water—a life-sapping 40 degrees or colder—swirled around stores of English iron and crates of crockery.

He didn't spend too much time looking over the damage. It was clear they had to work fast if there was any chance left to save the ship. Atkinson hurried back to the others waiting by the stairs and then back to the deck.

I cannot lie. This is critical, men, said Atkinson to his team of crewmates. A knot of scared passengers could not take their eyes off Atkinson's soaked trousers.

Quickly, form a line. Like firemen. We need to clear the hold. We are carrying too much weight, and we need to raise the ship's water line above the damage and get at that broken hull.

Within minutes, boxes of crock ware, sacks of salt, coils of rope—anything they could grab—were passed along and heaved overboard. Some cargo sank with a deep gulping sound. The current snatched away other boxes and they disappeared into the chilled fog. Those on deck couldn't help but wonder whether it would be the same on a lifeboat—at the mercy of the currents and enveloped in a white shroud.

The water was near shin level in the cargo area by the time it was cleared enough to show the full extent of the buckled timbers. The men were dangerously close to hypothermia from standing in the North Atlantic churn mixed with the foul-smelling bilge water. Legs turned numb, words started to slur.

Bring the carpenter below, came a cry. A journeyman sailor from Gloucester named Alexander Hobbs clomped down the ten steps from steerage into the cargo level.

Hell, he growled as he took the last steps and plunked into the rising water. With his hammer and tool box, he splashed ahead toward the bow, knocking aside the flotsam of rope and wood—and the occasional rat swimming for its life. The only natural light came from the open hatches. As he moved deeper, that light faded. His lantern cast a milky wash. The burlap sacks atop the cargo smelled something like the old root cellar back home, he thought. Earthy and yeasty. He breathed it in deeply. Even this vague hint of dry land was comforting.

Hobbs could tell already that this was way beyond anything he could fix at sea.

The speed the water was gushing in, spinning in eddies around poles and barrels, told him all he needed to know. He'd left home as a teenager and grew up on the sea. Though he had the woodworking skills to make a good living ashore, the pull of sea life was too strong. It was that way for many Gloucestermen, just like in Nye's Fairhaven, Kelley's Center-ville, and all along the New England coast. They knew the dangers of a life at sea, but the thought of staying put on land was not to be consid-ered. Before signing aboard the *John Rutledge,* Hobbs had found a bed in a German-run flophouse in New York's Bowery. Anyone handy with wood had his pick of ships. He tried to choose well. He could sense the condition of a vessel just by the way it sat in port or from the groan of the rigging in a big blow. He didn't want some shabby bucket that would need constant repairs. When the *Rutledge* advertised for a carpenter, he jumped at the chance.

He liked the *John Rutledge*. It had the solid lines of a ship from good stock. Anyone who knew ships had heard of the J. J. Abrahams yard in Baltimore. If the *Rutledge* was one of theirs, that was good enough for Hobbs. He also liked the Atlantic packet trade in general. It was all busi-ness: get into port, swap out cargo, get passengers on board, and weigh anchor for the other side of the ocean.

Now the ship that Hobbs admired was in deep trouble. He knew it would take nothing short of a miracle to keep the *Rutledge* afloat.

The damage was well beyond the reach of repair by hammer and nails. Water surged in from dozens of holes. The timbers were wrenched inward farther than any makeshift brace or jack could straighten.

The best we can do is try to plug it. Hobbs shouted to be heard over the sounds of rushing and splashing water.

If nothing else, it could give us some extra time, he continued. Tell the captain that the ship is going down. It's now just a matter of when.

Pillows, blankets, oilcloths, rags, clothes, mattresses—all was passed to the men in the bow in a last-chance effort to win back some time. They jammed things into the fracture as best they could. It did little good. The force of the water's surge was too great. The pressure spit out the plugs and spurted geysers through any crack.

This is futile, said Hobbs. We aren't doing a damn thing.

Word reached Kelley on deck within minutes. He called over the first mate, trying hard to keep at least an outward semblance of business as usual.

Mr. Atkinson, the captain said in a low voice, collect the ship's log and gather what you can. Tell your wife, but no one else just yet. Make haste. You have five minutes before I order that we abandon ship.

I understand, said Atkinson before hurrying off.

Kelley was rattled to his core. He couldn't show it. Not even a furrowed brow.

He knew well an old seafaring adage passed from one generation to the next: There is no need to worry until the captain looks worried.

If he gave off even a hint of fear, it would be bedlam in seconds, with the passengers and crew in a free-for-all for the lifeboats. His mind raced. This was really happening. And we are going out in the open Atlantic on boats no bigger than dinghies. It always lurked there in the back of the mind of anyone who put out to sea—this roulette wheel chance. Your number might just come up on the wrong ship at the wrong time.

In that age, every sailor paid attention to the great merchant wrecks in the Atlantic, just as airplane pilots later would keep mental notes on the planes that went down on the routes they flew. Even the most superstitious of the ship's crew—the ones who refused to utter the names of lost ships for fear of jinxing a voyage—knew the names by heart.

The British paddle-wheel steamer SS *President* in 1841; lost in a gale after passing Nantucket on a New York–Liverpool run; all 136 aboard lost.

The American ship *Stephen Whitney* in 1847; slammed into rocks in heavy fog off Ireland; nearly all of the 110 aboard lost.

The American bark *Ocean Monarch* in 1848; caught on fire shortly after leaving Liverpool en route to Boston; 178 lost.

The fancy British White Star clipper RMS *Tayleur* in 1854; ran aground and sunk just outside Dublin Bay on her maiden voyage from Liverpool; more than half of the 652 aboard lost.

The British steamship *City of Glasgow* in 1854; sunk somewhere between Liverpool and Philadelphia; 480 passengers and crew lost.

The list was still not complete for that wretched year of 1854: the American ships *Powhattan* in the spring and *New Era* in the fall ran aground and foundered off New Jersey, with more than 500 combined deaths. And, of course, there was the Collins Line's *Arctic* tragedy.

On the *Rutledge,* another hard-won lesson from the *Arctic* was unfolding before their eyes.

The Collins Line steamer had flooded within hours because of its design: an open-hull plan undivided into water-blocking compartments. This was the scheme for nearly every American ship of the day, including for the *John Rutledge*. An open hull had added space and lower costs but also increased risks. The French-built *Vesta*—the other vessel in the *Arctic* tragedy—had watertight compartments, as did many French vessels. Maritime scholars believe this design allowed the *Vesta* to reach port safely.

The New Bedford *Mercury* would point out the dangers of the American open-hull design in a short but impassioned blurb in March 1856. "Water-tight compartments as a protection against casualties sustained to that of the ship *John Rutledge* should be applied if not to all sailing ships at least to the ocean steamers. They can do no harm certainly, and might as in the case of the collision of the *Vesta,* save the vessel."

On the *John Rutledge,* First Mate Atkinson tried not to look at the frightened faces of the passengers, who just yesterday had been swapping happily improbable dreams about life in America.

He walked quickly past the pumps, choosing not to tell the men that they were fighting a losing battle. That is the captain's duty, he thought.

It was Kelley's ship—a fine one at that, just five years old and once the pride of Baltimore shipwrights.

And now he was about to lose it.

Chapter Twelve

Thomas Nye was told to stay with the dozen or so crew members assembled near the lifeboats. The first mate Atkinson made a public display of telling them their job was to be ready to help the passengers file onto the boats if—and he stressed the word *if* for the benefit of the passengers listening—the abandon ship order was given. The crew listened and aye-ayed at all the right moments.

It was a show. Captain Kelley had not yet given the orders to leave the *Rutledge*.

But Nye and the other crew suspected it was coming. Why else would Atkinson be keeping his wife close to his side? The crew also knew why they were placed in front of the lifeboats. They were a line of last defense in case things got ugly.

It happened on other ships, and there was no reason to think the *John Rutledge* would be an exception. Seamen routinely told cautionary tales about frightened passengers devolving into desperate and violent mobs when it was time to clear a sinking ship. The scandalous breakdown of order on the steamship *Arctic*—when women and children were left behind to die—only heightened the sense that passengers would not sit back passively as a tragedy unfolded. An outraged letter writer in 1854 said shipping lines needed to recognize that the life of the lowliest steerage passenger who wore patched clothing was just "as dear as if clad in broadcloth and velvet."

Captain Kelley had quietly conveyed to the crew the need to immediately quash any flare-up among the passengers. He didn't care how it was done. If a crewman felt order was in danger, then he was free to act as he saw fit, Kelley said.

Nye and the others took Kelley's warning to heart. It was clear the passengers could easily overwhelm them and make a mad run for the lifeboats if it came to that. So they tried a mix of empathy and encouragement—with a giant infusion of outright lying—to keep the situation in hand.

We understand your worry, ma'am, but the water you saw below is much worse than it seems. The leaks are relatively small.

Of course, sir, we are working on the repairs right now. We know you are cold. Just a little while longer. Please stay calm.

Oh, yes, this ship has grazed many icebergs before and all was well. The captain will be along presently to give you a full appraisal.

Is there enough room on the boats for everyone? Indeed there is. More than enough.

Nye knew the last statement was the biggest stretch of all.

Each lifeboat—essentially an open dinghy with a deep keel line for added stability—could wedge in up to 50 people in optimum conditions. That would be something like a glass-flat sea with prospects of near-immediate rescue and people packed in knee against knee. There were just fewer than 150 people on the *Rutledge*. Fine, Nye thought, we could in theory clear the ship if everything went like clockwork.

But that clearly was not going to happen.

He squinted out past the ship's lifeboats, some already hooked to the pulleys to send them down and others stowed on deck. The iceberg that hit the *Rutledge* had passed the stern but was still close. The marks of the collision on it could be seen even through the fog. Shards of timber and a black tar smudge ran across part of the iceberg just above the sea line. The sea's surface, what Nye could see through the fog, was dotted with rafts of breakaway ice. The sailors called them growlers, little innocent-looking bergs that barely poked above the surface. But they could surround a boat and, if thick, do lethal damage to the hull. No vessels, no matter how well built in that age, could withstand the immense forces of tons of ice driven by tons of water. Under the current conditions, it would be suicidal to launch the lifeboats with any more than twenty people apiece. Each would have to cram in about ten more. We may get everyone off, Nye thought. But none of us will last long unless—in a blinding stroke of luck—a passing ship crosses our path very, very soon.

To his left, toward the stern, he noticed his crewmates had stopped tossing over cargo.

A moment later—a few minutes after midday—the other sailors came back up from below. They moved up the steps in such close ranks that one man's heels just missed the nose of the fellow behind. Their trousers were wet past the knees.

Anyone with a knowledge of ships would know what that meant. The water was near the point when it would exceed the displacement of the ship—the point when, in simple terms, the weight of the ship exceeded the upward buoyancy of the water. The *John Rutledge,* in other words, was doomed.

Thomas Nye was about to yell out to the soaked crewmates mingling around the hatch. Then he saw the captain striding across the deck from the bow—walking uphill, careful not to lose his balance as the *Rutledge* dipped lower into the sea. Kelley spoke a few quick words to the first mate.

It took just a minute for the order to trickle down the ship's chain of command.

Atkinson told the second mate, who told the third mate, who told the boatswain William Ryan, who turned the news loose on the crew and passengers. The captain had ordered all passengers and all hands to abandon ship. At once.

You watch, one of the crew members near Nye hissed. This will turn bad very quickly.

The passengers fell into a stunned silence as they absorbed the news. The ship that carried them from Liverpool was dead. It was no longer a question of whether they would have to leave the *Rutledge*. It was how quickly they could get off and whether there was enough room on the five lifeboats. Everything that had dominated their lives for the past months was suddenly meaningless. There was no America getting closer with each day. No job on the other end. No imminent reunion with a spouse waiting in New York or, in Captain Kelley's case, back in Liverpool.

There was just the lifeboats and the few yards separating them from a spot on one. Fail to make it onto a lifeboat, and the rest is written. Your life would be measured in hours. Or however long it took for the *John Rutledge* to disappear.

The silence among the passengers ended as abruptly as it began. They surged toward the lifeboats, letting loose what Nye could only describe as some kind of primal howl.

Some of the crew abandoned their posts and joined the rush toward the boats, throwing elbows and curses.

Out of the way, Paddy. Keep a hold on yer kids. Move aside. You need someone who can handle a boat? Right. Let me through.

The crew quickly freed the lashings holding one of the lifeboats to the ship. It swung free, hanging by two ropes fed through metal davits that were part of the pulley system used to raise and lower it. The *Rutledge* listed to the side. The ship had started its slide into the sea.

It was important to deploy the lifeboats on the high side of the tilting deck first. Too acute of an angle and the lifeboat could scrape against the ship's hull and cant over.

Passengers and a few crew members crowded into the boat. More than thirty people, but no one was counting. A few passengers had blankets. But that was all they had against the weather.

Four crew members took the pulleys.

Now, shouted one.

He counted off a cadence. It was crucial that the ropes holding the lifeboat at its bow and stern were lowered at the same pace. Too fast or too slow on either and the boat would hit the water unevenly and in high danger of swamping or spilling people into the sea.

This time it went well.

Boat one was away.

The second lifeboat was on its way down the side of the *Rutledge*.

Boat two away.

Twenty-five or so more were off the ship. Nye was astonished at how quickly they vanished in the fog—just like the floating cargo heaved overboard a few hours earlier in the last-gasp effort to save the ship. Seven, eight strokes of the oars and they were gone.

The Hendersons had decided to split up to improve their chances of all getting off. It could be difficult, they reasoned, to pack all eight of them on the same boat. William and Margaret would take the two boys. William's sister, Elizabeth, would take her baby daughter and the two other Henderson girls.

Elizabeth and the girls managed to get aboard the next boat. As it was lowered, Margaret yelled out to her daughters. It will be fine, she assured them. We will be off soon and find you. Everything will be fine.

The boat splashed into the water and was soon swallowed by the fog.

Number three away, someone cried.

∞

Under the deck, the force of the water rushing into the hold snapped the ropes securing the crates. The cargo rode the currents inside the ship, which swept the wooden boxes and other debris to one side of the vessel. That forced the *John Rutledge* to list even more.

The water had almost reached the roof beams in steerage and could be heard sloshing through the open deck hatch. The masts groaned and crackled as they angled toward the sea. Most of the sails had been hauled in and secured shortly after the *Rutledge* hit the iceberg.

Some crew members fingered a personal talisman or a religious medal dedicated to a friendly saint of the sea: Saint Nicholas, the patron saint of calm waters, or Saint Erasmus, known as Saint Elmo, the patron saint of sailors. Some touched their collars without really knowing why. Their fathers—and their father's fathers and on back—had done the same out of some long-forgotten lore to bring good fortune.

Just two lifeboats were left. The *Rutledge* was so low in the water that ice-blue waves washed over the bow. More than fifty people huddled in the stern. Some, Nye noticed, were so frightened they couldn't move. Sobbing children were pulled close by mothers.

Jane Black looked everywhere.

Samuel! she yelled. Samuel!

Have you seen him? The boy with me? she asked anyone who looked up.

She squeezed Betty's hand. They were separated from Samuel when the passengers streamed on deck. He was nowhere to be found. Jane cursed herself for letting him go up on deck with the men. He must have found a spot on a lifeboat, she told herself.

That must be it, she decided. Clearly, he was no longer on the ship. And she knew he wasn't below deck. She couldn't waste any more time. There were two lifeboats left and, it seemed to her, too many people still on board.

You, seaman.

Nye turned. It was the captain calling him.

Me, sir?

Yes, you there, Kelley said. You are Nye, right? You join Mr. Atkinson in that boat. Kelley pointed to one of the two on the seaward-sloping deck. They were no longer lashed to the ship and were snapping hard against the davit lines and swinging away from the deck.

Mr. Atkinson will be on this boat, the captain repeated. I will take the other. Now go.

Nye started to move.

No, wait, Nye heard. It was Kelley again.

Take this, he said. He handed Nye a bottle of brandy, probably from his personal supply. Nye had no idea why he was singled out for the gesture. Maybe Kelley was swayed by the Nye family name.

Thank you, sir. Good luck.

But Kelley had already turned away.

Nye shoved the bottle under his sweater and peacoat, with its hallmark twin rows of buttons. He had turned the coat's wide collar up over his ears. He was careful to stow the bottle securely because he needed his hands free. And the sight of any provision—especially a bottle of brandy—could set off a brawl.

Nye found Atkinson, who was leading his wife toward the lifeboat.

I was told to get in the boat with you, Nye said.

Then get in. What are you waiting for?

Eleven were already aboard. Nye recognized a few as crew. There was the Irish boatswain Ryan and the new seaman from Scotland, John Daley. How many children? Nye counted quickly. Two boys, who look like they are with their parents. And a girl. She seemed to be with her mother. That's good. For some reason, he was relieved that someone else would be responsible for the young ones.

The lifeboat swayed wildly on its ropes. Nye waited until it swung closer. Then he took a big stride off the deck and landed in the lifeboat.

There was plenty of room left for others. Nye noticed a compass sitting in the open. That was good, too. Atkinson must have left it. But why was he still on deck with his wife? Dozens of passengers crowded behind them.

The captain's boat—lifeboat number four—was already gone. They had simply cut the davit ropes and let the boat splash into the sea. That boat had the lone cabin passenger Gale and the ship stewardess and her young son and mother, whom Kelley had agreed to bring along on the crossing. The stewards were the ship's domestic help who took care of the first-class cabins and catered to the captain. Also on the captain's lifeboat were at least three children from an emigrant family named Grundy.

From his place in the last lifeboat, Nye looked up at those still on the ship. He knew he was looking upon people who would never see the next dawn. There just wasn't room for them all in this boat. Ten more could fit at the most. But there was close to thirty jostling and screaming on deck.

The first mate Samuel Atkinson appeared at the ship's edge. He tossed something in Nye's direction. The ship's log.

Keep it, said Atkinson. I'll be right back. Hobbs and I will go back to sound the pumps. You help others get aboard.

As Nye stashed the logbook, he yelled after Atkinson. What? Are you mad? There is no reason for that. The ship is going down. For God's sake, man, come back!

Why the devil would Atkinson and the carpenter go back to check the pumps on a ship that was clearly beyond hope? It made no sense. The ship would be gone in a matter of minutes. The bow and jib rigging were already gone from view. If they didn't cast off soon, the suction created by the sinking *Rutledge* could pull the lifeboat down with the ship.

Atkinson's wife approached the lifeboat.

Here I come, she said.

Before Nye had a chance to ease her aboard, she jumped.

Then came the sound of breaking glass.

She had landed on the compass. It was shattered, but no one paid much mind amid the screams and the crushing realization on board the ship that not all would get off. Mrs. Atkinson brushed away the broken glass and took her place on the boat.

The lifeboat rose again on a swell. Nye could hear the davit arms creaking under the strain. They could give way at any moment. Other passengers on deck waited for the right moment to jump. It was maybe a yard-long leap from the *Rutledge* to the lifeboat. Enough to make people pause for crucial seconds as they tried to catch their balance or muster their courage.

Do it now, Nye yelled. Now! Jump!

Still, they waited. Perhaps hoping the lifeboat would swing closer. There was no chance of that. The ship listed even more, putting the lifeboat a few more inches farther out.

Where is Atkinson? Nye thought. He is running out of time.

Just then, a big swell washed over the *Rutledge*. It rolled up the sunken bow and along the sides still above water. It was big enough to pick the lifeboat up, which then sledded backward down the other side of the swell.

Nye heard a snap. The lines were gone. The lifeboat pulley system was shredded.

The boat floated back toward the *Rutledge*. This was the last chance for someone to make a leap. No one did. Perhaps they waited even then for a better shot. It would never come. Seconds later, the lifeboat spun twenty feet away from the sinking ship. Then another great swell. They were forty feet from the ship. Then fifty.

Come back, people on the ship pleaded. You can't leave us. For God's sake, help us. You can't leave us.

Mrs. Atkinson reached back as if she had the powers to haul in the *Rutledge*.

Sam! Sam! she moaned. No. Please.

We need to go back! she demanded. We can't leave them there! That's my husband. Go back!

She was beyond reason. She slammed her hands on the cold wood of the lifeboat, which pitched so violently that any second of not holding onto something was a second that you could be tossed overboard.

We have to go back, she wailed. We have to go back.

The boatswain Ryan spoke up. He was, at least in his mind, now the leader of this last band off the *Rutledge*. It was his job at sea to keep the ship tidy and in good order. Now, he was the highest-ranking castaway on the little boat.

Ma'am, said Ryan quietly, trying to calm her down, we cannot do anything in these seas. You think we can row back? We would be swamped. We can't take them all. Stop it now.

But just go back for my husband. He's the first officer. You know that. How can you leave him?

We cannot go back, Ryan repeated. They are in God's hands now. Either we try to live, or we all die if we go back to the ship. I have made my choice. The rest in this boat have made it, too.

Some of the others looked as if they wanted to say something. Ryan silenced them with a hard look.

The *John Rutledge* was a gray silhouette in the late afternoon fog. The figures on deck—about thirty people, maybe more—clustered into one moving mass of waving arms. The water was already over the base of the mizzen mast, which rose aft of the midpoint on deck. Two-thirds of the ship was under and it was slipping away fast.

"Souls were left upon the broad Atlantic to shift as best they could," said an account of the *Rutledge* in the *US Nautical Magazine and Naval Journal*, "with nothing but the slender hope furnished by fragile boats, to encounter still greater dangers than had already befallen them . . . exchanging that noble ship for an open boat, a mere cockle shell, amid the chilling embrace of icebergs."

❧

Ahoy, there, came a call through the fog. It was the captain.

Everyone on Nye's boat shouted at once. Here! Over here, Captain!

In the fog, it was impossible to tell the distance to Kelley's lifeboat. His voice was clear, though. Maybe a hundred feet away, Nye guessed. Sounds on the sea sometimes played tricks. Cold water—especially the icy North Atlantic—can have a confusing effect on sound waves passing over.

Kelley yelled back. Who is there? How many with you?

The boatswain was the first to respond. It's Ryan, sir. The bos'n, sir. We have two other crew. Ten others. Mrs. Atkinson among them, sir. Some children. Thirteen in all. Mr. Atkinson is still on board, sir.

Silence.

Then Kelley again, more faint. Row this way. We have a full boat here.

Which way, sir? answered Ryan. We can't see you in the fog.

More silence.

Then Kelley again: This way, this way. His voice was fading. It was hard to make out.

Then, no more voices came from the fog.

Another swell caught the lifeboat. Then the boat slid down into a trough. When they hit the top of the next swell, their heads pivoted side to side, hoping to catch the outline of the *Rutledge* or to hear something—anything—from the other lifeboats.

Nothing.

The boat dropped again into a valley of ice and water.

On the next swell, the thirteen bellowed as best they could. Ryan grabbed the broken compass and rapped it on the lifeboat's metal oarlocks.

They waited for a reply. None came. Swell after swell carried them. Without the compass, they couldn't be sure of the direction.

Sam, Sam, sobbed Mrs. Atkinson. But quieter now.

Everyone fell silent.

They were alone. They were thirteen adrift.

Chapter Thirteen

DAY ONE.

They took stock of what they had.

It wasn't much.

A glass demijohn with about a gallon of water in it. A bag of palm-sized disks known as ship's biscuits, a simple mix of flour and water baked rock hard. Some sailors generously called them seabiscuits. More often, they were scorned with names far more accurate, such as molar breakers. On land, soldiers called them hard tack. About six pounds of them, Nye guessed, maybe a little less. Nye decided to keep his stash of brandy a secret for the time being.

What else?

There was the compass, which was now worthless. The first mate had also tossed in the ship's log before going back to the pumps in some kind of pointless mission to save the ship. But a logbook meant nothing for their survival. It almost seemed a bad sign, if you believed in that sort of thing. Nye didn't. But he could understand how others might look askew at the ledger, as if they were carrying the last testament of the *John Rutledge* in their little ark in case no one was saved to tell of it.

There was no mast for a sail on the lifeboat. Just four oars to try to keep its bow pointing into the waves. This was crucial. Drifting crossways to the waves was just asking to be capsized. After that, the cold sea would kill you mercifully fast.

After running through the meager list of supplies, they took a hard look at themselves.

Nye and the other two crew members—the boatswain William Ryan and the greenhorn John Daley—were dressed warmly enough. They had been put on duty as the ship was going down and wore their normal deck gear. Nye had gloves, a waterproof hat with a wide brim, and his peacoat over a heavy sweater. He had on a pair of vulcanized rubber boots, which were superb at keeping his feet dry but did little to hold off the cold.

With them were ten passengers: the first mate's wife, Mrs. Atkinson;* the Hendersons and their two sons, Robert and James; Jane Black and Betty; and three others—an Irish couple and a man—whose names have been lost to time.

Some of the passengers were already shivering. They had tumbled up on deck with whatever they were wearing down in steerage or with the few things they could grab. Margaret Henderson said a silent thanks that she managed to get some extra clothes on her children. In the last chaotic moment, she was also happy she pulled down two blankets. She wrapped them around her shoulders. Mrs. Atkinson also had bundled herself in a heavy coat and hat. Her husband knew the ship was doomed before the passengers were told, and that had given her some extra time to prepare. Her long skirt—like that of all the women and girls—went down to her ankles, just above leather shoes that offered no barrier to the cold. The women tried to cocoon their legs by pulling their skirts tight under them.

The temperature was just above freezing, but steady winds made it seem far colder. That kind of sea chill is hard to keep at bay for long. It snaked down open collars and slipped up the hems of skirts. Jane Black nuzzled Betty, quietly reminding her that the boy Samuel was fine.

Nye thought about the broken compass. It seemed a major setback the moment he heard the glass breaking. But it was now clear that it would not have been much help. The oars were effectively useless in the open ocean without a specific target within reach. It was senseless to waste energy rowing even if they knew the direction of Newfoundland, the closest point of dry land. The distance was just too great without a sail to help.

---

*Nye's accounts did not mention the given name of First Mate Atkinson's wife, and other documents could not point conclusively to her name. This was complicated by variants in the spelling of *Atkinson* in recordkeeping in the first half of the nineteenth century. With the goal of being as accurate as possible, and to avoid making an incorrect guess on her first name from incomplete records, she is called Mrs. Atkinson.

They were at the whims of the currents. About the only benefit the compass would have brought was knowing which way they were drifting.

It grew dark. In late February off the Grand Banks, the sun slipped away around five thirty.

The passengers looked at Nye and the crew in whatever light was left. The crew looked at each other. Everyone was waiting for someone to step up and take charge. A plan—any plan, from anyone—seemed preferable to being set loose on the cold seas just to wait.

And for what? Maybe they could link up with the other lifeboats. But how would they be in any better position? Possibly more supplies, yes, but those boats were filled with twice as many people, if not more. A scramble for the remaining rations of food and water could get messy.

Their only real hope was that a ship would find them sometime after daybreak. They would have to make it through at least one night. It was far too much to hope that a ship picking its way through the ice in the dark would chance upon them.

One small element was on their side. They were not alone. Four other lifeboats made it off the *Rutledge*. That multiplied their chances of a ship coming across one of them and then mounting a search for the rest.

Nye expected the boatswain to have exerted some authority by now. Ryan had no problem lording his position over the other crew on board the *Rutledge*, casting a haughty eye over the rigging, looking for any problems he could report. But Ryan's job also included helping keep track of the supplies. That might be the difference between life and death now.

Instead, he seemed to be struggling with Mrs. Atkinson over something.

What is that? Nye wondered.

The water! someone yelled. They have the water!

Every crisis exposes some truths.

It works like a mason's hammer, knocking away whatever façade was there. What was once a moral certainty suddenly is up for question. Perceptions of social rank and gender roles are tossed on their head. Those who are selfish or cowardly show their colors even more. Those with the ability to lead may have their moment.

How it all stacks up in a group—unity versus anarchy, calm versus hysteria—comes to define many survival struggles. Psychologists, military planners, and others pick apart these stories to see what went right and what went wrong. For generations, classroom exercises have tried to game it out. Shipwrecks are a standard crisis setting. First, there are questions about what supplies to bring or leave behind. Then, it gets more interesting because castaways bring unique personalities and inclinations.

It might strike some that diversity is a problem—in other words, the more castaways are alike, the better they will do, avoiding conflicts and agreeing on ideas. But experts suggest there is the danger of "groupthink." A hive mentality drowns out dissenting voices even, in the case of castaways, if wild ideas have the potential to improve the chances of survival. The straitjacket conformity of groupthink has been blamed for countless tragedies.

But sometimes a far more powerful—and unpredictable—crisis occurs when diversity overcomes groupthink, when people with vastly different experiences, expectations, and motivations are thrown together by tragedy or happenstance. Within this volatile mix, anything can happen when survivors turn against each other.

The *John Rutledge* castaways seemed to be careening dangerously in that direction.

Gimme that, Ryan growled, trying to grab the demijohn of water from Mrs. Atkinson, who had already taken charge of the ship biscuits.

She was not a small woman and had no trouble fending off the sailor. She popped the cork and gulped down a few quick mouthfuls.

The others on the boat began yelling.

What are you doing? Stop! Ma'am, put it down.

Nye tried to reach her but was blocked by the others also moving in her direction. He didn't want to risk unbalancing the boat and getting hit by a wave at just the wrong moment. Nothing—not even their water being drained away—could be worse than plunging everyone into the sea.

Stop it! Nye yelled. That is our only water.

She didn't stop. She took a few more drinks from the demijohn until Ryan finally wrestled it away.

But something had changed in those few seconds. Ryan clutched the jug tightly to his chest.

Hand it over, Nye urged. We will put it in a safe place.

Ryan didn't budge. He gave a suspicious glare.

If I give the water to you, you have it all to yourself, he said. I see. Is that yer plan?

No, said Nye. Be reasonable. This is all we have. Please, hand it over.

Ryan looked scared. If there was to be a breakdown on the boat, then he wouldn't be the stupid one. He hoisted the water jug and drank deeply. At the same time, he held out a hand to keep Mrs. Atkinson from grabbing it back.

There wasn't enough room for Nye and the seaman Daley to rush their crewmate. They started crawling toward him, pawing over the others and crashing their knees painfully on the lifeboat's inside edges.

Damn it, man. Stop!

Then, as suddenly as he turned rogue, Ryan came back to his senses. Nye and the others didn't know what to make of the switch. Was he only fooling them, clever enough to fake a turnabout? But he pulled the bottle neck from his lips and put the jug down.

I, I, I'm sorry. I, I . . . Ryan said, wiping his mouth with his sleeve.

Nye grabbed away the demijohn. There was about two-thirds of a gallon left. That was something. But days of water rations had been selfishly chugged away in just their first hours off the *Rutledge*. If this keeps up, Nye thought, we have no chance.

Even as Ryan confronted his guilt, Mrs. Atkinson grew belligerent again. It went from bad to worse fast. If some order was not imposed, they might as well start thinking about the great beyond. They wouldn't last.

She turned to Nye and Daley, but made sure everyone on the boat could hear. I am the first mate's wife, she barked. You will not question me. Do not judge me. You have no right.

Whatever internal forces drove her, they were tone deaf to the moment. As incredible as it seemed, she was trying to stake out some status and deference as the self-imagined highest rank in the dire little band. No one else saw her as a leader. If anything, Nye and the others had been waiting for the boatswain Ryan to step up. But not anymore after his shameless display with the water.

My husband may be dead, Mrs. Atkinson added, with a bit less edge. My husband gave his life so we could get off the boat. Remember that.

This is our only water, Nye fired back. This *was* our only water. Do you know what you've done?

He stopped short of saying what he was thinking: this might have sealed their fate just hours after abandoning the ship. But he didn't want to scare the passengers, especially the children.

Ma'am, Nye finally said, I can say only this now: pray for rain or snow.

The demijohn was passed around to the others. Each person got a mouthful. No more.

Now what? someone asked. It was Mrs. Atkinson again.

What do you mean? Nye asked, still seething over the water robbery.

She took a deep breath.

I'm asking you, my husband's men, what is the next step? Do we try to find the other boats? Do we have some kind of signal? A whistle maybe?

What we do, the boatswain finally said, is we try to keep this boat afloat. That means—and I'm talking to everyone here—keeping an eye out for waves and ice. Keep them peeled for ships, too. But a ship does us no good if we are sunk.

The most important thing, he continued, is keeping the bow pointed into the seas. If a wave hits us broadside, we can capsize. Does everyone understand?

All nodded. Even the children.

Nye spoke up. My shipmate is right, he said. This boat is our only hope. If it goes over, we are done. Does everyone understand that?

The North Atlantic allows precious little room for error. Even close to shore, the winter waters can freeze a life away before rescuers can arrive. In January 1840, the steamboat *Lexington* was chugging up the Connecticut coast when cotton bales in the cargo hold caught fire. Lifeboats quickly sank or were sucked into the still-churning paddle wheel. Aid was immediately launched from shore. But only 3 of 143 people aboard survived, and they did that by clinging to the floating cotton bales and staying out of the water as much as possible.

That first night off the *John Rutledge* passed in almost total silence. The men—the three crew members and two others, William Henderson and one of the men in the stern—took turns at the oars trying to keep the bow of the lifeboat pointing into the weather. The other man on the boat, a bit older than the rest, was too sick and weak to row. He had only a thin jacket and huddled alone in silence during the night. They had no lanterns. The best they could do was pick up the direction of the waves from the boat's movement and steer blindly.

The others each were lost in their own thoughts until blessed sleep came. From time to time, a bit of drift ice would knock the side of the boat.

At first, the sound jarred people awake. Soon, quicker than they could have imagined, they grew accustomed to the slapping waves and the sounds of the boat: the groan of wood and howl of wind humming through the metal oarlocks.

A harsh sleet fell. It turned to snow for a while, and then a spell of cold rain.

It was miserable. Everyone tried to huddle under their coats. There was one good thing. Nye uncorked the demijohn to catch some of the rain.

Chapter Fourteen

DAY TWO.

The fog lifted.

That boosted their spirits a bit. At least they could see to the horizon. It gave a chance for them to spot the sails or stacks of a ship and, more important, a ship's crew to see them. But the wider sight lines also brought a crushing fact.

How alone they were. In every direction. There were no signs of the other lifeboats or any remnant of the *Rutledge*.

Mrs. Atkinson tried to stand in the swaying boat for a better look. Hold me, she asked the boatswain Ryan. It was a strangely intimate request after their fight over the water. Ryan hesitated. In his world—indeed, in the world of any Victorian man—the only woman you touched on the leg was either your wife or a whore.

Well? barked Mrs. Atkinson.

Ryan had grown quiet since his dark moment hoarding the water. He seemed in no mood to reopen an argument with Mrs. Atkinson.

Fine, he said softly.

He steadied her legs, gripping her skirt with both hands. He tried to keep the hold as loose and benign as possible. She panned the seas in every direction.

It's possible a lifeboat went back to pick up Samuel and the others, she said quietly, almost as if she was talking to herself. Or do you think the ship stayed afloat and they're all still sheltered on the deck? she asked.

No one answered. Why strip away her hopes? As outlandish as it seemed, she could be right. Certainly, stranger things had happened at sea.

At that moment, the ship *Sea Lark* was leaving Antwerp for New York. Weeks into its voyage, the crew spotted a wreck in the distance on the edges of the Grand Banks. Most of the ship's hull was underwater, but its masts stood straight above the waves in apparent good condition. No identifying flags were visible and no survivors were seen. The *Sea Lark* sailed on, noting in its log the estimated size of the wreck as 1,000 tons burthen—about the size of the *John Rutledge* and many other ships. The *Sea Lark* report was given some attention in the newspapers under the headline "A Mysterious Wreck" but was then quickly forgotten. Could the *Sea Lark* have come across what was left of the *Rutledge* before it was finally lost forever?

Anything? asked William Henderson, who didn't want to break away from the little nest of intertwined arms and legs of his wife and children. Do you see anything, Mrs. Atkinson?

No, she said. Just the sea and ice.

See here, if we made it, that must mean the others did, too, Henderson said—thinking only of the lifeboats, but not the *John Rutledge*.

Mrs. Atkinson looked over. The ship, she said. Tell me then. What became of the ship?

No one offered an answer.

We can only do what we can, Mrs. Atkinson, said William Henderson finally. We can conserve our water and food and keep watching the seas. A ship must be along at some point. We just have to make sure we see it.

Henderson turned to Nye, the crew member sitting closest. Isn't that right, Mr. Nye?

Thomas Nye nodded.

He had reckoned that they were drifting in a generally southwest direction, caught in a tentacle of the Labrador Current. The best place to spot a ship, he figured, was to the east-northeast, the direction the main routes from Liverpool to New York or Boston lay. The trouble was that an iceberg could look tantalizingly like a ship's sails from a distance.

A few times he had wanted to cry out: Sail, ho! But then the light shifted a fraction, and it was clear the sight was only a berg—a mirage in the cold sea.

❦

Where sea meets ice, the water can shimmer with a pastel palette. As often is in nature, beauty and peril are intertwined. The flotillas from Greenland's glaciers—barge-shaped frozen islands of sea-washed ice, huge Alp-angled peaks carrying the bluish hues of the mother glacier, and every other conceivable ice formation big and small—cast a ghostly wash underwater. Just below the surface the ice is a band of aqua and turquoise and robin's egg. Foot after foot, the candy colors dance and change until they give way to storm-cloud blue, then indigo, and, finally, the sunless depths. The cliché about the tip of the iceberg is true. The US Coast Guard uses an equation of mass density and volume to calculate the precise size of a berg below the water line. It comes out to the same result more or less every time. Approximately seven-eighths of an iceberg is underwater.

And what shape it takes below the waves is anyone's guess. The ice could be hewn into an anvil-headed battering ram, a smooth plane, or a spike sticking out like a horn.

The *John Rutledge* went down in some of the most dangerous maritime territory of the nineteenth century. As ship traffic increased, so did the number of collisions with icebergs off the Grand Banks and in the Strait of Belle Isle, the neck of water linking the southern edge of the Labrador Sea with the Gulf of Saint Lawrence.

In the 1820s, there were fewer than twenty run-ins with ice each year, including damage and sinkings. By the turn of the twentieth century, the number rose to close to a hundred.

For all the danger ice posed, passengers still felt a certain risk-taking thrill when they had a brush with a big berg. A celebrated Irish comedic actor, Tyrone Power, traveling in 1833 from Liverpool on the ship *Europe,* wrote in his diary of seeing great icebergs emerging from the fog as the New York–bound ship passed through Ice Alley. He described one berg in classic stage prose: "an extensive Gothic fortalice, or castle, not unworthy of the Ice-king himself if bent on a summer trip round the Gulf Stream."

Power later wrote, "If the weather should prove thick, and the ice swim deep, scarce showing above the surface, as is commonly the case, a ship going quickly through the water may strike before any measures can be taken to avoid the encounter." Eight years later, he was aboard the steamer *President* out of New York and headed for the ice fields en route to Liverpool. The ship was never seen again. But the name of Tyrone Power lived on through his great-grandson and namesake, who rose to stardom in the Hollywood movie mill of the 1930s as a matinee idol and later as a player in swashbuckling films such as *The Mark of Zorro*.

But gawking at passing icebergs was hardly the kind of story that made for great telling. Less plentiful, but certainly more riveting, were the tales of crewmates who battled to keep their ice-damaged vessels from going under before they reached a port. In 1879, the steamship *Arizona* plowed bow-first into a mighty berg while en route to Liverpool from New York. The front of the ship was crushed flat, but the bulkhead held. The captain decided to make a run for Newfoundland, about a hundred miles to the east, and managed to reach port as stunned onlookers marveled at the ship's mangled prow.

The rarest stories of all, however, were of salvation: abandoning an ice-crippled ship and chancing upon rescue. So uncommon were they, in fact, that every such account took on an almost spiritual aura. The lesson was: the waves and ice didn't always win. There was hope.

Look at the *Hannah,* anyone from Ireland would say.

The *Hannah* story was told and embellished and reworked so often that the firm details blurred over the years. What remained was a morality tale—a bit of homegrown succor—to carry with them to America or Canada or wherever. Almost certainly, the Irish emigrants on the last lifeboat off the *John Rutledge* had heard about the *Hannah*. They might even have wondered whether the same kind of amazing luck might shine on them.

Seven years earlier, in April 1849, the brig *Hannah* made it across the Atlantic and was moving down the Gulf of Saint Lawrence. More than 175 passengers, mostly Irish emigrants from County Armagh, were bound for Quebec City. It had been a relatively easy passage. The weather was kind, and they found ample open-water paths to navigate the ice packs. In the gulf, it all began to change. The ice closed in. A berg slammed into the *Hannah,* collapsing part of its hull. Once again—in a sad drama repeated over and over on different vessels in different places—the crew pushed aside the terrified passengers. The captain and some crewmates made it onto the lifeboats. The emigrants were largely left on their own.

The ice was the only thing separating them from certain death in the gulf waters. Without a choice, they went to the ice. First, a few clawed their way onto the biggest iceberg near the sinking brig. Then more joined them. Some slipped down the berg's face and were lost. Parents, with their hands frozen by the cold and sleet, fumbled children from their grasp.

In the end, scores of people made it onto the ice. More than a hundred lasted the night. They were found nearly eighteen hours later by the bark *Nicaragua,* which was making its way cautiously down the gulf.

"No pen can describe the pitiable situation of the poor creatures," said the *Nicaragua*'s captain, William Marshall, in the *Armagh Guardian*. "They were all but naked, cut and bruised and frost-bitten. There were parents who had lost their children, children with loss of parents. Many, in fact, were perfectly insensible."

Yet they lived.

Eighteen hours had passed since their lifeboat cast away from the *Rutledge*. Already, it was clear that some on the little boat might not last out the day.

One of the passengers, the man who was traveling alone and wearing only a light coat, appeared to be slipping away.

He had stopped speaking hours before and fell into stretches of deep sleep, with his hands and head exposed. His fingers had turned an unnatural ivory. Frost rings grew around his mouth and eyes. Sometimes he'd awake with a start and examine his fingers as if they weren't his own but rather some twigs of driftwood washed up by the sea. He would then bundle himself as best he could and tumble again into his private dream world, doubtless someplace far from the boat.

No one moved to help him or even to offer comfort. Something had changed on the boat when Ryan and Mrs. Atkinson battled over the water.

A critical bit of empathy seemed to shut down. It was clear that some were likely to die on this boat, and the most selfish among them perhaps had the best chance of cheating death. Once that idea took root, it wasn't too much of a leap to turn away as a fellow castaway—just a few feet away—fought his losing battle. It weighed heaviest on the Irish folk, especially the Hendersons. It reminded them of what happened during the famine before they left for England. Families that always had a plate to spare for someone in need suddenly closed ranks. Whatever they had was for their own survival, not others'.

The Hendersons were the only ones with blankets.

Should we give that man one? Margaret Henderson whispered to her husband.

He shook his head. We have to think of the children, he said. Who will help us if we give up a blanket?

I'm hungry, complained one of the Henderson boys.

Yes, right. Of course. Where's the biscuits? said Margaret, looking directly at Mrs. Atkinson.

Mrs. Atkinson had taken charge of the supplies. No one had asked her to be the guardian. She simply believed that her position as the first mate's wife—now, likely, widow—gave her that right.

Well? Let's have 'em. The biscuits, the boatswain snarled at Mrs. Atkinson. Who made you Queen Victoria?

Mrs. Atkinson was unmoved. Look, she said to Margaret Henderson, everyone gets a little at a time. We need to make what we have last. I know what's best.

That was precisely the wrong thing to say.

For the second time, it seemed that things would spin violently out of control. The anger from the water episode roared back. For a moment, the cold was forgotten. It was now all the survivors against one of their own.

For God sakes, woman, give us some, someone said.

Or we'll take it from you! another shouted.

Where are they? The crewmen Daley and Ryan tried to look past the folds of her long coat. Are you hiding some? You hoarding the biscuits?

Nye was furious, too. But for a different reason. He recognized that a melee on the boat could leave their few supplies scattered and spoiled by saltwater.

Stop! he yelled. Please, I beg. Stop.

For some reason, they listened. He was neither the oldest nor the most experienced seaman. He was, however, from New Bedford stock. Nye had shared as much with the others as they swapped details of their lives during those first hopeful hours. Any connection to New Bedford meant something, even to the emigrants who had never set foot on a boat before leaving Ireland.

Listen. Listen, all, Nye continued.

If Mrs. Atkinson wants to watch over the biscuits, let her. It's better to have someone minding them. If they get soaked by seawater, they are worthless and we are in more trouble than we are now.

But, he cast a stern eye toward Mrs. Atkinson, if there is any hint of you taking more than your share. Well, I will not be responsible for what happens after that. You understand?

She nodded silently.

Is everyone agreed? Nye said, looking around the boat.

Yes, fine, came the replies as the tension began to ebb. It was too cold—well below freezing—to stay mad. The warmer south wind, which had stirred the fog, had stopped. The weather now was coming in from the northwest.

Mrs. Atkinson broke off thumb-size pieces of the hard biscuits. She handed them out one by one to be passed among the dozen others. The listless man in the stern was awake again, but he waved off the bread.

I'll eat later, he said quietly.

The children got a bit more. Their parents made sure to share portions of their own ration.

That night, fresh gales blew in.

They sheltered down as best they could. The waves knocked the boat around as if it were little more than a castoff cork. There was nothing they could do. It was hopeless to man the oars at night and try to guess the direction of the waves.

Nye's toes had lost feeling earlier in the day. This worried him greatly. The North Atlantic was winning. He knew that was inevitable.

But he didn't think it would be this fast.

Chapter Fifteen

The man in the flimsy coat died.

He was alive at daybreak. They knew that much. He had raised his hands just enough to wave off a bit of biscuit and sip of water. No one remembered whether he even bothered to open his eyes one last time.

By midmorning, he was gone.

He was perhaps the most ravaged among them since the beginning. He might have been suffering even before the *Rutledge* went down, possibly weakened by fever or hit especially hard by seasickness. He was gaunt and quiet back in steerage as best as anyone could remember. He was traveling alone but didn't join the other men on the *Rutledge* as they tried to pass the days before the storms with cards, such as with the popular game of luck and trickery known as maw, and with endless talk about America. Just as well, the men thought at the time. If this thin man was sick, better he stay put in his berth.

On the lifeboat, he rarely ate and spent longer and longer spells in a twilight between sleep and wake. He mumbled names that no one knew and, in his last hours, his head bobbed so violently with the swaying of the lifeboat that his teeth clattered together.

His death was no real surprise. His clothes were grossly inadequate. His wool coat, once soaked by the sea spray and sleet, literally sucked the life from him. Cold and clammy, it drew away far more body heat than it helped retain.

Even so, his death was hard to accept. That withered little Irish chap symbolized something much bigger and more unsettling than simply a sick man giving out. Death would not pass them over in the lifeboat. It was conveniently abstract before that moment. Everyone—down to the youngest child, James Henderson—knew with certainty that the North Atlantic would eventually claim them if their luck didn't change. But there had been that pulse of hope. Maybe a ship was right over the horizon and, beyond all odds, all thirteen would pull through together. Now with one gone, a terrible question was planted. No one would acknowledge it by name. But they all knew what it asked.

Who would be next?

Now what? asked the man who was sitting with his wife closest to the dead man. We can't leave him there.

Of course not, came the reply from Mrs. Atkinson at the other end of the boat. You men, do something.

She had worked her way onto everyone's nerves with her dismissive manners and bossy ways. But no one wanted to rekindle the quarrels of the first day adrift. They also knew that, this time, she was right. Someone—the men, it seemed—would have to take care of the body.

Silently, three men rose: Nye, the Scots sailor John Daley, and the Irish man sitting next to the body. They were careful not to make the boat rock any more than it was already. The wind had shifted again. It was blowing hard from the west-southwest, kicking up white caps in between the slabs of drift ice. The ice was less today. At least the current seemed to be pulling the boat into clearer waters and away from the most dangerous bergs.

William Henderson made a move to join them. He was stopped by his wife. She wanted him to stay near the children.

They can do it, she whispered. We want you here.

Nye grimaced as he stepped into the center of the boat. The bottom was awash in frigid spillover from the waves and the intermittent rain and snow. They had tried bailing with a small pail and oars on the first day, flicking out a lick of water even as more found its way in. That was pointless. The best they could do now was pull up their feet or rest them on the gunwale to keep them as dry as possible.

Nye's feet were protected in his rubber boots, but he could feel the cold penetrating inside. He was thankful for the boots, but nothing could keep out the chill if you were standing in icy water. He noted the passengers all had leather boots, which were waterlogged and, whether they knew it or not, accelerating the inevitable drain of body heat that had begun the moment they left the *Rutledge*.

Let's get this done, men, Nye said to the others.

They splashed over to the body, trying to be gentlemanly and not kick up water on the ladies or children. Then they hesitated as they looked the man over.

Should we take his clothes? one of the men asked in a low voice.

What? We have women, children, said Nye.

Some lines of propriety were still in place. In every crisis, they fell by the wayside bit by bit. But Victorian mores were a stubborn variety. They didn't give ground easily. Life in Britain was jam-packed with rules layered upon rules. Men, as usual, bent the social order in their favor. Maybe nothing summed it up as well as Tennyson's "The Princess":

> Man for the field and woman for the hearth;
> Man for the sword, and for the needle she;
> Man with the head, and woman with the heart;
> Man to command, and woman to obey;
> All else is confusion.

But men of a certain class on both sides of the Atlantic were hemmed in, too, by codes of their own making. The conventions of Victorian manliness left little wiggle room. A litany of rules and subrules formed the foundation of polite society. Even Americans—who claimed the New World's egalitarian ideals had no room for ossified English proprieties— were not immune. Britain still set the bar for much of the world. American sailors who said goodbye to landlocked laws could not totally turn their backs on the expectations of manly decorum. Nye was not ready to surrender yet. Pillaging the dead for clothes was just too much, too soon.

Think about if it was you laying there, Nye whispered to the men. Would you want to be stripped clean in front of others? We are not like that, are we?

Neither answered.

Are we?

Daley and the other man finally shook their heads.

Good then. We agree, said Nye. We leave the poor fellow as he is. I think, though, we should take his boots. Those we may need. What do you say to that?

Yes, the men said, good idea.

One held up the dead man's legs and the other unlaced the sea-drenched leather boots and peeled off the thin socks. Everyone on the boat watched every move. Not because death was a stranger. But because each privately wondered if this would be their fate: a body liberated of its boots and about to be dumped into the sea. The Irish on the boat must have asked themselves how this was any more troubling than what they left behind. They had seen worse.

Any sailor who had spent time on the packets saw shipmates killed by any number of hazards: falling off the rigging, suffering a bad cut and succumbing to infection or gangrene. But the Irish castaways were on even more intimate terms with death. No village had been spared from the Great Hunger. In the preceding decade in County Tyrone, where the Hendersons were from, the population fell by more than 18 percent through death and emigration. Some villages in Tyrone bled nearly half their people. And Tyrone was among the better-off counties.

The man's boots were set aside.

Anything else? Nye asked quietly, hoping the others in the boat couldn't hear.

Should we take his money? asked one.

Nye was dumbstruck. He hadn't expected that. But he had never been a dirt-poor migrant looking for any scrap or leg up. In a twisted way, the idea of hunting for the man's money hinted at some optimism. They wouldn't be rummaging for coins if they assumed there was no chance of rescue.

Nye turned his head as the two rifled through the dead man's pockets. It wasn't his concern if they found anything. It seemed too unholy. He used the pause to adjust the brandy bottle under his coat. He didn't want it slipping out unannounced or, worse, smashing to pieces.

Ready, one of the men said.

Nye turned to the others in the boat. Should we say a prayer? Some kind of goodbye?

No one spoke up. A few made the sign of the cross. Then, softly, a few amens.

Nye and the two men waited for a break in the waves. They lifted the body. It slid into the sea with barely a sound. There wasn't anything to weigh it down. Instead, it floated for several minutes as water invaded the lungs. Only then did it drop away.

Sunk to rise no more, Nye said quietly. That's how many ship's logs described a burial at sea.

The men sat back down. No more words were exchanged. Everyone was lost in their own thoughts about what could come and who might follow the poor man into the deep. His name—if they knew it at all—was already drifting from their memories.

Nye tried to move his toes. Those few minutes standing in the water were enough to make his feet ache. He couldn't imagine what it was like for the poor passengers with thin boots and laces.

He did what everyone else was doing: furtively looking around to see who was in worse condition.

William Henderson looked bad. So did his wife—perhaps even worse. Both went into long coughing jags that appeared to leave them more ragged each time. The couple in the stern locked their arms until it was hard to tell where one person ended and the other began. The boatswain Ryan had retreated to a corner of the boat, no longer in league with Mrs. Atkinson as the self-appointed masters of their little floating island. Daley, young and fit, still looked in reasonably good shape. The children rarely said much now, and when they did it was mostly in private snippets to their parents.

Morality is elastic when it comes to our own fate.

It bends and stretches to fit the circumstance. Any honest philosopher or theologian will tell you that. But they often rely on trite and hypothetical examples to make their point. Such as: Is it acceptable to steal a loaf of bread to feed your starving family?

The twelve survivors in the lifeboat were watching a much more serious moral quandary play out for real. Just days before on the *John Rutledge*, they were—more or less—within the familiar moral guardrails. The stuff of Sunday school lectures and chivalry myths. Be good, be fair, be courteous, and so on. Everyone knows them. And everyone knows, of course, that re-moving boots and looting money from a corpse were far from acceptable. Yet there they were, with no one feeling too shaken about it.

At that moment, the boat passed under a new order. They were now fully governed by what some might call the morality of crisis. This was still within shouting distance of the old rules. But just a bit looser. If the boots of the poor dead man could be helpful, the reasoning went, it's better to serve the cause of survival. How can that be wrong? It makes sense, they said among themselves in self-convincing tones. Doesn't it? Well, doesn't it?

Nye didn't have a problem. In fact, he might have given in and stripped off the man's clothes if there weren't women and children aboard. But he also was aware that, in a day or two perhaps, they could be moving to a place darker still: the morality of last-chance desperation.

Nye paid attention. He read the papers. He knew what could hap-pen and how quickly they could get there. As a boy, he was fascinated by the breathless newspaper accounts of snow-bound unfortunates in the Sierras—later dubbed the Donner Party—eating, it was believed, the flesh of some of their own as a last resort. As a seaman, he may have also paid close heed to a seafaring case that probed even further into the psychology of survival.

It happened fifteen years earlier and was still picked over by drunken sailors, nautical scholars, and ethics professors trying to get their students to think. The American ship *William Brown* left Liverpool in March 1841 carrying more than sixty emigrants bound for Philadelphia. About 250 miles off Nova Scotia, the ship encountered dense fog and ice—not unlike the *John Rutledge* and countless other ships had.

And, like the *Rutledge,* the *William Brown* rammed an iceberg with catastrophic results. Here's where the tale took a chilling turn. The crew and captain took over the first of two boats, a small sailing craft known as a jolly boat, leaving an open longboat in the command of the first mate, Francis Rhodes. But it was far too small for the dozens still on the sinking ship. About forty-five people made it aboard the longboat—thirty-three passengers and twelve crew, by some counts—leaving more than thirty people to go down with the ship.

In the following days, madness took hold. One by one, the crew tossed passengers overboard to die a slow death in sight of the lifeboat.

The Liverpool docks in the mid-nineteenth century. (Courtesy of the collection of Maggie Blanck.)

Image of crew working aboard nineteenth-century packet ship. (Courtesy of Mystic Seaport Collections Research Center.)

An artist's rendering in the *Illustrated London News* of emigrants departing England in 1856. (COURTESY OF THE COLLECTION OF MAGGIE BLANCK.)

Statue honoring New Bedford's whaling history in front of the city's main library. The work, by Bela Pratt, was dedicated in 1913 and includes a line from Herman Melville's *Moby-Dick:* "A Dead Whale or a Stove Boat." (PHOTO BY BRIAN MURPHY.)

The Nye homestead in East Sandwich, Massachusetts, the first American settlement of the Nye family. (PHOTO BY BRIAN MURPHY.)

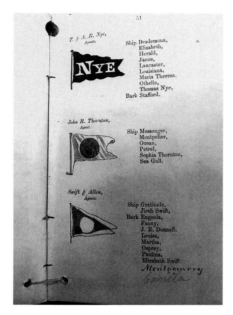

The Nye flag and some of the ships owned by the fleet in the Fairhaven and Dartmouth Signal Book from 1855. (COURTESY OF MYSTIC SEAPORT COLLECTIONS RESEARCH CENTER.)

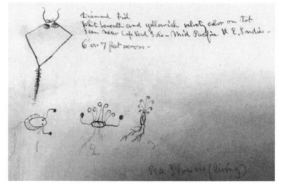

Drawings of sea creatures from the 1854–1856 log of the ship *Sea Serpent*. (COURTESY OF MYSTIC SEAPORT COLLECTIONS RESEARCH CENTER.)

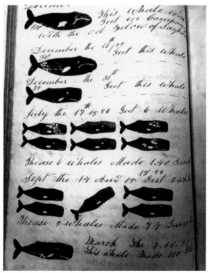

Wood block stamps of whale sightings and captures from the log of the New Bedford–based ship *Globe* during a 1855–1857 voyage. (COURTESY OF MYSTIC SEAPORT COLLECTIONS RESEARCH CENTER.)

Captain Asa Eldridge, who was lost on the steamship *Pacific* in 1856. (COURTESY OF THE HISTORICAL SOCIETY OF OLD YARMOUTH.)

Image of the steamship *Pacific,* one of the vessels lost in February 1856. The passengers included an owner of the *John Rutledge.* (COURTESY OF MYSTIC SEAPORT COLLECTIONS RESEARCH CENTER.)

Gravesite of James Lawrence Ridgway, one of the owners of the *John Rutledge.* Ridgway was lost at sea on the steamship *Pacific,* which left Liverpool a week after the *John Rutledge* in January 1856. (PHOTO COURTESY OF WALLACE G. LANE JR.)

Artist drawings in *Frank Leslie's Illustrated Newspaper* in April 1856 depicting the *John Rutledge* and the lifeboat with Thomas Nye and the other castaways. (Collection of the Library of Congress.)

The packet ship *Germania,* which rescued Thomas Nye. (COURTESY OF MYSTIC SEAPORT COLLECTIONS RESEARCH CENTER.)

MORE DISASTERS AT SEA.

FURTHER PARTICULARS OF THE JOHN RUTLEDGE.

Removal of the Survivor from the Germania.

UNKNOWN WRECK SEEN.

Brig Webster Lost near Montauk Point.

NYE'S CONDITION—FURTHER PARTICULARS OF THE LOSS OF THE JOHN RUTLEDGE.

About noon, yesterday, when Broadway was most thronged with passengers, four men were seen very carefully bearing, upon a covered couch, the body of a poor sufferer, apparently to a hospital. On inquiry, it was ascertained that the cot contained the sole known survivor from the ill-fated *John Rutledge.* His mother, his uncle, and two other of his friends were with him, and our reporter accompanied them to the vessel. At 3 o'clock yesterday afternoon, Mr. NYE was safely deposited on board the screw steamer *Potomska,* Capt. CUSHMAN, of New-Bedford, which left pier No. 11 North River, for that port, with freight and passengers.

The results of Mr. NYE's exposure to cold, wet, and hunger during nine days have not been so personally disastrous as might have been expected. He is able to converse, but for obvious reasons he was not teazed with many questions. He is about 22 years of age, and has the ordinary appearance of youths bred to the sea. He complains of pain, especially in his legs, but has not lost the control of muscular power. His limbs are swathed in poultices by direction of a medical man who saw him on board the *Germania* at the request of her Commander, Captain WOOD. He is able to eat moderately of nutritive diet. He complains of loss of sleep, but his pulse is natural, and there appears to have been neither febrile reaction, nor delirium, nor, in fact, any brain excitement such as might have been expected under the circumstances.

In conversation with his mother, a highly respectable and intelligent lady, from Fairhaven, our reporter learned that her son has always been particularly steady, abstemious and temperate. That his habits in this respect have contributed to his endurance of such horrible exposure and suffering, may be considered incontrovertible.

Article from the *New York Times* on March 27, 1856. (LIBRARY OF CONGRESS.)

Entry by the first mate Charles Townsend from the February 29, 1856, log of the packet ship *Germania* describing part of the rescue of Thomas Nye. The first line reads: "The young man's name is Thomas Nye of New Bedford." (COURTESY OF MYSTIC SEAPORT COLLECTIONS RESEARCH CENTER.)

The grave marker on Cape Cod for Captain Alexander Kelley, who was lost at sea in the wreck of the *John Rutledge*. (Photo by Kevin Murphy.)

Captain Ezra Nye, one of the most famous ship masters of the mid-19th century. (Courtesy of the Nye Family of America Association.)

Thomas Nye's uncle, Thomas Nye Jr., who traveled to New York with the seaman's mother after learning of young Nye's survival. Nye Jr. also wrote a heartfelt letter of thanks to the captain of the *Germania*. (Courtesy of the New Bedford Whaling Museum.)

The gravestone of Captain Daniel H. Wood at the Rural Cemetery in New Bedford. Wood commanded the *Germania*, which picked up Nye in the North Atlantic. (Photo courtesy of Donna J. Pimentel.)

The Fairhaven grocery store where Thomas Nye worked after deciding not to return the sea. (PHOTO COURTESY OF CHRIS RICHARDS, FAIRHAVEN OFFICE OF TOURISM.)

The home of Thomas W. Nye on Main Street in Fairhaven, Massachusetts, where he lived after his seafaring days. (PHOTO BY BRIAN MURPHY.)

Gravestone of Thomas W. Nye at Riverside Cemetery in Fairhaven, Massachusetts. (PHOTO BY BRIAN MURPHY.)

The horrible culling was staged for simple math: there were simply too many people on the boat for the rations at hand. A crewmate claimed later during trial that they first picked men traveling alone but then they also pitched a man and his two sisters. All told, between fifteen and seventeen people were shoved into the Atlantic. Two men were spared at the insistence of the first mate Rhodes because they were traveling with their wives.

Finally, a ship came along and brought the survivors to France. Authorities there had no interest in the passengers' accounts of what occurred on the lifeboat. But when the stories were later recounted in America, the Irish community grew outraged and lawyers sprang into action. A seaman named Alexander William Holmes was the only crew member found among those on the longboat. He was put on trial in Philadelphia under a charge of "manslaughter on the high seas." Holmes's lawyer tried a defense that was equal parts Machiavellian and Hobbesian. Wasn't it better, he argued, to save a few lives rather than let everyone perish? In other words, the lifeboat was outside the bounds of normal codes and was governed by "the law of nature."

"This case should be tried on a longboat," the defense lawyer was quoted as saying, according to the trial transcript, "sunk down to its very gunwale with forty-one half-naked, starved, and shivering wretches, the boat leaking from below, filling from above, a hundred leagues from land, at midnight, surrounded by ice, unmanageable from its load, and subject to certain destruction from the change of the most changeable of elements, the wind and the waves."

The prosecution countered by portraying the sailor as engaging in a God complex run amok. No one, they said, had the power to decide life or death. Holmes was found guilty but given only a six-month sentence and a modest fine. He later returned to service on whatever ship would take him.

∽

Mister Nye. Mister Nye.

One of the Henderson boys was shaking his arm. Wake up, Mister Nye. Biscuits. Time to eat biscuits.

Small pieces were passed around. Nye wasn't hungry. Neither, it seemed, were the others. Their appetites had faded to almost nothing after the second day as their bodies began drawing calories from whatever fat they had stored. Nye watched the Henderson boys nibble at the hardtack when just two days earlier they had wolfed it down. What they all wanted was water. Thirst had taken hold. It was hard to think about anything else. Nye's muscles were starting to cramp for longer stretches at a time. He thought it might be from inactivity or stress. But the first stages of dehydration were setting in.

Nye looked down at the floor of the boat, awash with rainwater and melted snow. But it was spoiled by the saltwater. If there was one lesson drilled into him as a boy roaming the Fairhaven docks, it was this: drinking seawater was like sipping from the poison chalice. You would die. It just depended on how fast and how painfully.

Water, the Scottish crewmate Daley asked. What about the water?

It's gone, said the boatswain. We had the last of it this afternoon.

The old anger toward the boatswain and Mrs. Atkinson caught hold again for a moment.

If you're holding out, boy-o, then we are in for some trouble, barked Daley.

The boatswain started to stay something, but Mrs. Atkinson touched his arm.

It's gone, she said quietly. We all drank it. We all drank it equally. I swear on my husband's soul.

That seemed good enough. Daley backed down.

This is bad, you know, he said to no one in particular. We better hope for more rain or snow now. Never thought I'd be saying that.

Look, said Nye. I have one more thing. The captain gave it to me. I've been holding it since we left the ship. I planned to let everyone know when we needed it. I think we need it now. It's brandy. We have just one bottle.

No one seemed angry at the small deception. Their spirits, in fact, rose remarkably.

Well hand it over, the boatswain said, managing a smile.

The cork slid out easily. Nye was hit by its warm, sweet smell. It made him think of drowsy afternoons and fireplaces.

Everyone take a little, he said, handing over the bottle. There is no more.

The bottle went from person to person among the dozen left. Some lingered over it a bit longer than others. The children swallowed it down with pinched faces like they would a dollop of medicine. About a quarter of the bottle was already gone when Nye pressed the cork back in. He wedged the bottle against the side of the lifeboat.

About this time in New York, agents and runners for the owners of the steamship *Pacific* hovered around the piers in growing fits of anxiety. They asked anyone on arriving ships whether they had seen the vessel or, sadly, any sign of a wreck.

It was a month since the *Pacific* had fired up its boilers on a wide stretch of the Mersey known as the Sloyne, where the big steamers could tie up on mooring buoys. The fact that there was no news on the *Pacific* from other ships cut both ways. There was no steamship wreckage along the route from Liverpool. That was hopeful. But the idea of a sinking had become harder to avoid. Steamers just didn't take a month to make a crossing even in the most battering conditions.

Day after day, no one on the arriving ships had anything to report about the *Pacific*. But they had plenty to say about the ice.

Some crews swore they had never seen the ice so dense so early. The bergs, I tell you, are as big as four main masts stacked end to end. Some added a gentle dose of exaggeration.

The papers couldn't get enough of it. Combine the stories of the ice with the search for the *Pacific,* and you got yourself some front-page copy. Plus a juicy backstory. The Collins Line was still trying to rebuild its image after the terrible disaster of the *Arctic* two years earlier.

"The conclusion is nearly universally held that she has struck an iceberg and gone down," said a syndicated dispatch on the *Pacific* that ran in papers from Maine to Chicago. "Hopes for her safety or escape are held by very few. Yet this is far from impossible."

No reporters yet had made the same conclusions for the *John Rutledge*.

There was no real worry for a sailing ship. A month or more was nothing for a westbound winter crossing. No one started to get edgy until after forty-five days—the mark that Captain Kelley had hoped against hope he could make. And ships were arriving this year with record-slow crossings because of storms and ice.

On February 9, the Philadelphia-bound packet *Nonpareil* cleared the Delaware breakwater after a brutal crossing from Liverpool of seventy-two days. The captain, when asked to explain the slow passage, cited relentless gales and almost-unprecedented ice before noting, with a broad smile, that he was just happy to be safely in port.

Take a deep breath, the *Rutledge* co-owner Williams Howland told himself. Give it one more week before we start getting ourselves worked up.

That didn't stop him from going into mental knots over the *Pacific* and his partner, James Ridgway. If something awful had happened—and there was a growing likelihood that it had—then he had some preparations to make.

It wouldn't hurt, Howland decided, to double-check the insurance papers to make sure everything was in order. The policies were always about the ships and the cargo. Lives of those aboard had no actuarial value for Victorian-age underwriters. The *John Rutledge* was insured for $64,000. The mail freight, such as packages and other posted items, as well as the passengers' passage money were covered for an additional $6,000. The cargo had a policy that covered up to $100,000. If the ship was lost, Howland knew, his pockets were at least protected to some extent.

Though captains ran ships at sea, lawyers were often at the helm on land. Howland sent a boy down Wall Street to the East River piers to see if he could scare up any more news on the *John Rutledge* or the *Pacific*.

Howland tried to take his mind off the ships with the other stories in the newspapers. They didn't help. The country was stumbling closer to fratricide and there was scant good news being reported.

The rest of the front page was about a new political party called the Republicans and the skirmishes out west in Kansas territory over which way it fell on the slavery question. A few days earlier, a shipment of fresh firepower—twenty cannons and more than two thousand rifles—arrived via Iowa and Nebraska for the antislavery free-soilers in Kansas, whose

ranks included a steely-eyed zealot named John Brown. In a North Carolina newspaper, a commentary on the Kansas crisis was eerily prescient of
the great Civil War to come: "A collision is imminent," wrote the *Char-
lotte Democrat*, "and most likely the destiny of the present United States
hangs on the result of the contest."

On the other side of the Atlantic, the steamer *Edinburgh* was loading
up in Glasgow for its next run to New York. The captain mentioned to
reporters that on the way over the crew had spotted some curious mid-
ocean debris on February 9. At 41 degrees north, 45 degrees west, roughly
midway between Cape Cod and the Azores, floated some bits of what
appeared to be broken furniture with handles, maybe cut glass, and maple wood cabin doors. Oh, yes, and what was described as a "lady's work
box," a small carrier for sewing and embroidery supplies.

Like the sighting of the ghost ship by the *Sea Lark* that may have been
a last look at the *Rutledge,* a similar question was asked about what was
seen from the *Edinburgh.*

Could this have been a chance encounter with the remains of the
Pacific?

❦

In Nye's lifeboat, they stowed the oars and gave up trying to fight the sea.
The boat was now fully in the grip of whichever current had it. The sky
cleared and the temperatures fell well below freezing. Tiny icicles lined the
rim of the lifeboat like the gingerbread frou-frou that decorated the finer
homes back in Fairhaven.

At dawn, they saw something out at sea.

This time it wasn't an iceberg.

Chapter Sixteen

DAY FOUR.

Ship!

There it is. Look, look. A ship! Ship, ho!

There was no mistake. A brig, running on a long tack in a light wind, was just a few miles off.

Raise an oar, someone yelled.

The seaman Daley took up an oar. One of the Henderson boys handed him a red handkerchief, which he tied to the handle end. He hoisted it as high as he could and began to wave it.

Help us, he bellowed. Help! We are here!

Everyone was yelling and waving wildly. It was foolish to think their voices would carry to the ship. But they weren't even considering that. Instinct took over. It was impossible not to scream out—not when they could see salvation cleanly breaking through the waves right in front of them. They flailed their arms and banged on the lifeboat.

The sea did not help. The winds had picked up again and the waves made the lifeboat pop in and out of the brig's sight lines.

But all they needed was to get the attention of one—just *one*—crew member working on deck or taking a morning watch. William Henderson held up his youngest son, James, who took off his knit cap and flapped it around like a flag.

That's it, James, signal them, his father urged. They have to notice us.

Nye, too, thought they were close enough to be spotted. But the brig gave no sign of dropping its sails or changing course. By now, Nye reckoned, if the lifeboat was seen, someone on the ship would have signaled with a mirror or at least begun to adjust the sails to change course. The brig, however, was steady as she goes.

I don't think they see us, said Nye.

Damn, cursed the boatswain. Yer right. We are too far.

Ryan was both right and wrong.

The boat was well within the brig's horizon line. They could have been spotted if someone on board was looking in just the right space at just the right time, when a wave pushed the lifeboat up into view.

But for that to happen, a crewman would have to be scanning in their direction in the first place. And, even if he was, the lifeboat wouldn't be much more than a speck. Instead, all hands were most likely focused dead ahead on watch for ice.

Grab an oar, mate, the boatswain yelled. We can get there. Look, she's doing no more than five or six knots.

Nye took the other oar.

Ryan pointed to William Henderson and Daley. We need you. Now! Take the oars.

They moved forward, slapping into the water that had pooled in the bottom of the boat.

They set a course to try to intercept the brig, or at least to get close enough to have a better chance of their cries being heard.

Now heave, said the boatswain.

The cold was forgotten. There was nothing but the boat, the oars, and the water. And, of course, the distance between them and the brig. The boatswain swiveled his head for a moment. You there, he said to the older Henderson boy, Robert. Keep watch for any ice ahead.

The bow of the lifeboat cut through the water nicely, but frigid wash spilled over the sides with each wave they breached. A well-built dory could hit close to ten knots in bursts with strong rowers and optimum conditions. These were far from it. The North Atlantic swells made it as if the boat had to travel twice the distance: slowly up the front of a swell and then faster down the other side.

Still, they seemed to be on the right course and making progress. The brig, at least, wasn't pulling away.

Heave, heave, Ryan said, trying to keep time with Nye as they pulled with all their strength.

We're gaining, said Henderson. We're gaining. Good, men, good. Henderson yelled over to his wife: We are going to be fine. Don't worry now. The ship will see us.

Nye, too, was already imaging himself safely aboard the brig. He pictured the crew wrapping them in blankets and bringing mugs of steaming tea. He envisioned a right hearty welcome by the brig's captain and crew.

Ryan urged: Keep it up, lads. Pull, pull.

But their muscles were burning. It felt like trying to row through molasses.

Just then the winds rose. They could see it billow the sails on the brig. The ship picked up speed.

No, no, cried Ryan. Pull, men, pull!

The brig's bow kicked up white water as it drove harder into the waves.

Don't give up, Ryan yelled. Pull.

But it was too late. They were beaten.

The brig got farther away by the minute. Finally, they stopped rowing. The four oar heads skimmed the water as Nye and the others hung their heads, panting and each silently wondering whether they had just missed their last chance.

Soon, the brig was the size of a nailhead. Then a cat's-eye sliver. Then it was gone.

No one could quite believe it. They had been within sight of salvation, blankets, warm food. Oh, God, and the sweetest thing of all: fresh water. Hunger had faded, but thirst was pressing down hard on everyone. They could cover themselves from the weather as best they could. But thirst did not let up.

Mrs. Atkinson wept softly.

Another ship will come, Nye said hopefully. This shows we are in the right position, doesn't it, mates? Isn't that right? Ships sail generally the same course. One ship means others.

He's right, you know, the boatswain said. We need to keep watch. Everyone listening? Keep your eyes open.

Nye slumped down in the lifeboat. It was hard to believe how just a tiny change in their luck could have made all the difference. If they had been just one mile closer to the ship—one insignificant mile in the huge ocean—they might have been seen.

He tried to remind himself that anything was possible. If they saw a ship today, why not also tomorrow? He took some comfort in old family stories. One of them he replayed over and over in his mind.

Eight years earlier, in 1848, one of the many seamen from the Nye family's Cape Cod branch, Ebenezer Franklin Nye, was working as a mate on the New Bedford whaling ship *George and Susan*. Ebenezer was in one of the harpoon boats launched after a pod of whales was spotted in the mid-Pacific grounds. The boat became caught in a current and lost contact with the ship. Ebenezer and the others on the boat decided to make for one of the Marquesas Islands, a cluster south of the equator, navigating by a makeshift sextant Ebenezer fashioned from parts of the boat. They rode the steady mid-Pacific winds using a jerry-rigged sail. They sailed for seventeen days, catching what rainwater they could. When one crewmate died, they decided they would eat some of his flesh the next day if they didn't see land. That night, a jumping porpoise landed in the boat, the story went, and saved them from the horrible choice of cannibalism.

They finally reached the Marquesas, and Ebenezer later sailed a native boat nearly twenty-four hundred miles to the Sandwich Islands. From there, he took command of a schooner bound for the West Coast, but the vessel was stricken in a storm. Ebenezer Nye once again took to a lifeboat—this time alone. And once again, fortune was on his side. A passing ship rescued him and brought him back to New Bedford, even as the *George and Susan* continued whaling in the Pacific.

Thomas Nye liked to think that maybe he had inherited some of Uncle Ebenezer's luck and resolve.

The wind grew stronger throughout the day. It had shifted direction, now pushing down from the north. It was the type of blow both reviled and welcomed by the North Atlantic fleet. The foul side was that it helped push down the Arctic ice. The favorable part was that it could bring clearer weather, usually a high-pressure system that pushed away the clouds but pulled down the temperature.

Everyone in the lifeboat could feel the difference. The southerly winds came soggy. The west winds seemed angry and full of punch. A northerly blow felt menacing and foreign. The ice-locked north was as alien to the nineteenth-century mind as the outer cosmos.

The wind that pushed the brig away from the lifeboat continued to build. By afternoon, it grew into another full-blown gale bearing down from the north. Nye felt for the brandy bottle, thinking it was time to pass it around if for no other reason than to pick up spirits. Where was it? He ran his hand over the spot where he had wedged the bottle.

You looking for this? said the boatswain, tapping the bottle.

We took a wee nip—me and Mrs. Atkinson, that is, he said. Just a little bit. Don't worry. We have it safely over here.

Nye had no reason to argue. The captain surely intended the brandy for everyone on the lifeboat. He was just the one entrusted to bring it aboard.

Fine, shouted Nye over the gale, which whistled and hissed as it spun around the edges of the boat. We need to be careful with it. We have no idea when the next ship will come by.

Right, right, said the boatswain, trying to sound positive.

Just then everyone turned.

The woman in the stern was holding her hands to her face, sobbing hard enough to be heard over the storm.

No, no, she wailed. Her husband was shaking violently. Neither had a hat or gloves. They had attempted to tent themselves with their coats, but the woman had dropped everything in the seawater wash in the bottom of the boat when her husband went into spasms.

What is happening? she asked. What? Tell me.

All anyone could do was watch the end. The man's eyes rolled back as if he was in great pain. With one last shudder, he grew still.

Shhhh. Shhhh, she moaned. I'm here. It will be all right.

Is he dead? little Betty asked Jane Black. Is that man dead?

I don't know. Perhaps. If not now, soon, said Jane, too weak to try to concoct a clever lie. Besides, the girl had witnessed death the day before. No sense being coy.

For nearly an hour, the woman in the stern tried to wake her dead husband. She pulled his head tight to her chest.

His hands hung limply in his lap. He was dead. There was no doubt. They simply had to wait until his wife came around to understanding.

Soon she did. She looked over the rest in the boat.

He's dead, she said simply. She began to fix his hair. This is what you do before a burial.

Nye and his two crewmates once again formed a sad little funeral party. They gently pried the man from his wife's embrace.

Is there anything he had? Papers, money? Anything you need? Nye asked as tenderly as he could with the boat rocking hard in the gale-tossed sea.

No, no, she replied. We have nothing. We left it all on the ship. Everything was on the ship.

Do you want to say anything, ma'am? A prayer for him?

She was looking at the others now. She didn't answer.

Nye and the others left on the man's boots. It seemed an unnecessary indignity to splay his legs in front of his wife.

Like yesterday, the man's body slid cleanly into the sea. It wavered a few feet below the surface and then was lost from sight.

They were now eleven.

The gale did not let up. One huge swell and then another carried the boat wherever it chose. The ice was back, too. The north wind saw to that. It was clear from the direction of the ice that the lifeboat must be drifting south. This confirmed Nye's earlier guess that they were caught in the Labrador Current, which bends around Newfoundland and parallels the coast as part of a massive churn of ocean flow known as the North Atlantic Gyre. Just on the other side of the south-flowing Labrador was the eastward-rolling Gulf Stream, which moves up the Atlantic seaboard and veers toward Europe. The two ocean rivers rubbed so close in places that it was very possible some of the other lifeboats from the *John Rutledge* were caught in the Gulf's grip and drifting in the opposite direction from Nye's boat.

Eventually, the winds tailed off. The eleven left on the boat came out from under their coats.

A short while later, Nye noticed the boatswain leaning over the side. He had the empty demijohn in one hand.

Wait, Nye said.

What on earth are you doing?

Chapter Seventeen

DAY FIVE.

The boatswain didn't look up when Nye yelled. He filled half the bottle with seawater, drawing it out from the North Atlantic before his hand became too cold.

Wait, Nye implored. Ryan, this is wrong. You are making a mistake.

Ryan put it to his lips and drank. He passed it to Mrs. Atkinson. She did the same.

They coughed and sputtered, but each then took another swig.

Nye was dumbfounded. Have you lost your minds? he called over to them. Do you want to die? Do you? Because this will do it surely.

Ryan, you of all people should know that, Nye continued. Please. Put down the bottle.

Others in the boat, however, were already reaching for it. Ceaseless thirst blinded them to any risk. Just a sip, they thought. How can that hurt?

Over here, said William Henderson.

The bottle was passed. Thirst was clouding all reason.

Think of your children, Nye pleaded to Henderson. It will rain or snow again. Look up. The clouds are building. It was a lie, of course. The northern gales brought cold and dry Arctic air.

We just need to wait.

No appeals worked. Everyone in the boat took some. The three children sipped a little but didn't have the willpower to push past their reflexes. They spit out the salty water.

Nye knew they had just turned a tragic corner.

Death was stalking their boat. There was sad evidence of that with the poor fellow in the stern just a few hours before. Now, though, it was as if the end was scripted and being hastened. The passing of the brig seemed to have broken Ryan's will. He took it harder than the others. This was our last chance, he grumbled, and all we could do was watch it sail away.

Even the most ignorant sailor had heard dozens of stories about the agony and delirium brought on by drinking seawater. Every schoolboy within a seagull's call of the coast had memorized at least the stirring parts of Coleridge's "Rime of the Ancient Mariner"—the curse of killing the albatross and the cautionary lines: "Water, water every where / Nor any drop to drink."

The biology behind Coleridge's timeless irony is not complicated.

Seawater has more salt and nonabsorbable minerals than can be processed by the kidneys and expelled in urine. So the body pulls water from organs to dilute the salty concentration to manageable levels. This leads to greater thirst, fast-track dehydration, and, in some cases, a cascade of organ failure as each system is essentially squeezed dry. At more than 10 percent dehydration, delirium sets in and the senses become warped, often triggering episodes of violent and irrational rages. Dehydration of about 25 percent is in the black zone, a progression of misery before listlessness, unconsciousness, and, finally, death, which can include frothing at the mouth. A modern-day British expert on maritime survival, neurologist MacDonald Critchley, cautions: "Seawater poisoning must be accounted, after cold, the commonest cause of death in shipwrecked sailors."

Seawater can be used for survival if sufficiently diluted with fresh water. On the lifeboat, there was no such option.

The bottle was refilled and passed around again. Nye would take only enough to rinse his mouth and then spit it back into the sea. It did, he had to admit, help take the edge off his thirst for a moment.

Throughout the day, the others took more seawater. Nye gave up trying to dissuade them. He spent his time hunting for small icicles that formed on the leeward side of the boat, where the wind couldn't swipe those left from the sleet.

The bits of ice were no bigger than pebbles and melted immediately in his gloves, but they were infinitely better than the dead-end course of drinking from the sea. He offered some of the ice bites to the three children. Nye tried not to look at them too closely. It was heartbreaking. They wouldn't last more than a few days if they continued to drink the seawater. Neither would their parents.

The children took the ice gladly. It tasted faintly salty, but so did everything at sea that wasn't canned or wrapped up tight.

Nye had no idea how long he could hold out. A storm would be a huge help. He could catch raindrops or snowflakes in the bailing bucket.

Toward evening, he noticed that the boatswain Ryan and Mrs. Atkinson had opened the brandy. The bottle was dry before Nye could even call them out.

You have a problem, boy-o? Ryan slurred.

Nye shook his head. He could tell that Ryan was seriously unstable.

What's going on? asked Jane Black, looking out from the hood she fashioned with her coat.

Nothing, Nye assured her. Just a bit of words.

But this was different. Ryan was swaying. And not because of the boat. He snapped at flying objects that weren't there and snarled under his breath at enemies that only he knew.

Steady, man, said Nye. We are all here. We're all waiting to be rescued together. Nothing has changed.

Mrs. Atkinson reached out to touch his arm. That, it turned out, was the spark.

Ryan turned on her like a wild dog. He ripped at her coat and drove his fists into her gut. She doubled over.

Help me! she cried. He is out of his head.

Ryan kept up the attack, slapping and punching at Mrs. Atkinson and pawing at her clothes. He was fighting something. But it was no longer Mrs. Atkinson on the other end of his fists. It was some kind of private horror pieced together in his mind. What he saw no one could tell. Only that he was intent on fighting it with all the strength he had left.

Do something, Mrs. Atkinson sobbed, doubled over to try to avoid his blows.

Nye and the other crewmate Daley came at Ryan together. They tried to hold him back. Daley grabbed the back of his coat. Nye pulled at his legs.

Too late.

The boatswain had pushed up one of the sleeves of Mrs. Atkinson's coat and sunk his teeth deep into her arm. She howled and slapped at his head.

He let go finally—wild and panting—but the wound was deep and ragged.

My God, moaned Mrs. Atkinson. My God. What are you doing? What is happening?

Ryan turned on Nye and the Scots sailor Daley.

Ryan was beyond deranged. There was no talking to him. The only thing possible was to jump him and hold him down—and hope the fit passed.

Then, in a move that surprised Nye and Daley with its agility, the boatswain Ryan grabbed the bailing bucket. He let out a roar and hurled it into the sea.

Nye watched with utter dismay as it disappeared. It was not just to bail the boat. It was Nye's rain catcher. Nye's way to avoid the poison of seawater.

Ryan went for the oars. Nye and Daley were quicker this time. They managed to get hold of one end and pull them away from Ryan, who staggered and tore at his own clothes.

Now, said Nye.

They moved in together and took down Ryan.

He countered. He picked up the demijohn and gave Nye a sharp blow on the left jaw. Nye reeled back. He felt for blood. Thankfully, not much, but he worried his jaw might be fractured.

Lunatics, Nye would recall years later. "Just imagine yourself in a small boat in mid-ocean with eleven lunatics," he later told a reporter from Boston, "and you have some idea of my situation."

They both lurched again at the ranting boatswain. Something about this grab must have had an effect on Ryan. He went limp. He breathed in noisy gulps as if trying to bite at the wind.

Nye wondered for a moment whether they should use the length of rope to tie up Ryan. He didn't have the energy and worried that it could touch off another outburst.

It was the seawater doing its damage. That meant there may be more of this to come. He looked over at Ryan, who seemed utterly spent. He slumped over at the side of the lifeboat and took another sip of the salty North Atlantic.

As Nye settled back, he looked to the stern.

The widow of the man who died yesterday had herself died at some point during the melee. No one had noticed. She was lying face down in the water at the bottom of the boat. It surprised no one. She had been drifting in and out of a private delirium for more than a day. Death was just waiting to make its move.

Nye didn't ask for help this time.

He flipped the woman over the side without mention to the others or an attempt at a prayer.

At the other end of the boat, Ryan hunched down low and muttered to himself. The temperature was dropping toward freezing.

It was clear Ryan was not going to last long. But Nye feared there could be still more darkness left in Ryan before the end would come.

Chapter Eighteen

DAY SIX.

They were now ten.

The seawater was exacting its horrendous price. Ryan had slipped into a raving half-sleep since his attack on Mrs. Atkinson. At the same time, Mrs. Atkinson had withdrawn into herself. She stopped nursing her arm and gathered herself into a tight ball, her head tucked into her knees.

The other crewmember, Daley, looked bad as well.

For a while, the young Scotsman seemed capable of staving off the crippling grip of the seawater he drank. He was, like Nye, in his physical prime. He was certainly the strongest on the boat and, at least in the first days, among the most optimistic that they would pull through. He, more than any, had tried to keep the group looking ahead to rescue rather than dwelling on the possibility that the end was nipping at their heels. He was a talker. But his chatter took on a greater purpose on the boat. For a time, just hearing him prattle on about his big plans—and coaxing others to share their dreams for the future—made it seem as if destiny might be in their favor.

The boatswain Ryan, before he was lost to the dementia brought on by the seawater, had also helped prop up the mood in the first few days adrift. He seemed far too wedded to the sea to have a wife. But he said one was waiting for him amid the Irish and German enclaves in lower Manhattan.

Now this was just what the castaways wanted to hear. The Hendersons were especially keen on Ryan's stories. New York was to be their first stop on their way to Boston. And Gotham was the centerpiece of American mythology among the Irish waiting to emigrate. Boston might have had more Irish people per square mile, but New York loomed larger in the Irish imagination. And here was Ryan, a fellow Hibernian, who had already done what they set off to do: carve out a place for themselves in America. Everyone on the boat—even American-born Nye—couldn't get enough of Ryan's ramblings about New York in all its glory and gore, even if they were certain the yarns might have equal measures of fact and fable.

From Londonderry to Cork, and even the Irish exiles in England, everyone had heard of the notorious and nefarious sides of New York. Yes, of course, they were also interested in the workaday details about landing a job and finding a decent place to live. But human nature is what it is. Stories about the sordid side of things are always in demand. In the first few days adrift, Ryan didn't disappoint. He went on about the strange, but marvelously delicious meats at German beer gardens. He took on every question, offering up his views on the awful anti-Irish bias of some employers. He mustered his best rendition of a gruff New York accent, which brought a knowing smile from Nye who, like any good New Englander, had his superiority complex firmly in place.

City life and its struggles were nothing new to any of the emigrants left on the boat. Jane Black had confronted Glasgow as a young girl from the rocky hinterlands. The Hendersons had spent years making their way around the Irish underclass in England's smokestack belt. Just a year earlier, in February 1855, the latest bread riots had flared among the hungry Irish in Liverpool after a fierce east wind prevented ships from reaching port and bringing provisions for bakers. Baton-swinging coppers did not hesitate to bust heads to restore order. Many of the Irish emigrants on the *John Rutledge*—or aboard any packet, for that matter—were not intimidated by what awaited them. They never would have stepped foot on the *Rutledge* if that was the case. Yet New York, in their minds, was a different place altogether than the cities they knew. The Irish wouldn't be fighting just among themselves for the bottom-of-the-barrel jobs as they did in England. They had Dutch, Norwegians, Russians, Prussians, and everyone else to compete against. Any bit of advice was pure gold.

But first, please, tell us about the lurid side of the city. Ryan obliged.

The stories the Irish knew best were about the gritty Five Points neighborhood and the Irish gangs with names like Dead Rabbits and Forty Thieves. They were unpleasant characters, no doubt. The anti-immigrant

New York slang of the time called them *highbinders* and *rowdies*. But, to the Irish mind, they had a heroic side. They did the right thing, standing their ground against the nativist thugs and others too fearful or stupid to wrap their heads around the social changes wrought by mass immigration.

This kind of faction-versus-faction stuff was all too familiar to the Irish, who all seemed to know someone who had had a scrape with a Protestant. What they hoped, however, was that they would be able to breathe a bit easier in America.

Just keep your head down, said Ryan. There is a lot of fuss from various groups whining all the time about us immigrants and Catholics. You know what they call one of the parties? The Know Nothings. You know why? Because when they are asked about the party they say they know nothing.

Hah! But don't worry too much, Ryan reassured them. 'Tis no problem to stay away from all the ruckus. Just worry about work and family and you'll do fine.

William and Margaret Henderson pressed for more insights. What about finding work?

It's not a bad life in America, Ryan told them. There's plenty to eat. Jobs, too, if you're willing to put your back into it. And you, Mrs. Henderson, ladies can work as well. They want them for some of the nice houses in Gramercy Park, he said. Ah, you're going to Boston, are you? Why didn't you get a Boston packet? Never mind. Doesn't matter now. I don't know much about that city, but there's certainly no shortage of Irish there. Can you sew, Mrs. Henderson? I know plenty of ladies who take in seamstress work at home. They have mill jobs up there as well. They hire the ladies. Pays well, I think. You'll do fine, just fine.

These conversations—just two days ago—seemed like a long time past. No one on the boat was talking anymore about the future. Life unfolded in small segments now, just like how Jane Black felt when the storms pummeled the *Rutledge*. Make it through one part of the day. Move on to the next.

The four Hendersons huddled together. Robert held his little brother in his arms.

Jane Black was still alert. She drank the least of the seawater, heeding Nye's warning. The young Betty was tucked deep under her coat.

Nye kept himself busy looking for icicles.

It hadn't rained or snowed in three days. The north gale was pumping down drier Arctic air. Still, there was ice from the sea spray and drip. Nye scraped up what he could. It's doubtful he knew the chemistry that made the icicles far less harmful than seawater, but his intuition was flawless. When seawater freezes, the salt ions and other minerals can't wedge into the ice crystals. The salt takes the easier route: migrating back into the sea.

Nye let the ice melt on his tongue. It felt good. His tongue was swelling from thirst. The ice couldn't fully relieve the stranglehold need for water. It was enough, though, to keep Nye from casting aside all he knew and drinking the sea as well. It did look tempting at times: cold, clean, and just a hand scoop away. There were a few bits of hardtack biscuits left. But there was no way he could get them down.

About midday, the boatswain sat bolt upright. He looked around as if he didn't know where he was.

Ryan? What is it? croaked Nye, whose tongue was sluggish from thirst. It's one of the body's first warning signs of dehydration.

The boatswain looked once at the sea. He swayed. Then he doubled over.

That was all. No whimper. No last scream or fit of rage. Hardly a sound.

Someone in the boat gasped. But otherwise all were quiet. They knew Ryan was dead and that their decision to drink seawater may have doomed them to a similar fate.

They were now nine.

Don't look, Margaret Henderson urged her boys. But they couldn't help it. Death was no longer some distant, unimaginable specter in their boyish minds. They looked at Ryan and wondered what it was like. What was it, that last moment on this earth? It might be their turn soon. Everyone thought that now. The boys couldn't look away.

Nye debated with himself whether he had the strength to toss Ryan's body over the side. I can't just leave him there, he said to himself. It's not right. The man deserves better even if he was an animal at the end. It was not him, really, Nye rationalized. It was the seawater.

Ryan was also a crewmate, even a boss as boatswain. If he had died aboard ship, they would have sent him to the deep. Only in exceptional cases—the death of the captain close to port, maybe—would a body be kept for burial on land.

Nye struggled to his feet. Again, his boots sloshed through the spillover in the bottom of the boat. The cold ache in his feet had passed. That was not a good sign. It meant his feet were slowly freezing, inviting gangrene and whatever else was waiting. There's no chance to bail the boat now, he thought. Ryan had seen to that himself when he flung the bucket into the sea. It was even worse for the women. The bottoms of their long skirts were so soaked, making it hard for them to move.

Nye hoisted Ryan's body by the armpits. He folded it over the gunwale like some laundry set out to dry. Then he lifted Ryan's legs. He was about to give a last shove, but stopped. Wait, he decided. I can take his coat at least.

Nye pried off the peacoat. He thought about the boots, but they were no better than his.

Nye pushed. It wasn't easy. The body did a half-summersault and landed on its back. That shook Nye. He could see Ryan's face a last time before it went under. Nye was panting. He looked over at shipmate Daley, who hadn't made a move to help. Daley seemed to be slipping away, too.

Nye lumbered back to a spot in the middle of the boat. He hadn't quite given up hope, but each day made it harder to imagine another ship appearing on the horizon. He was gripped by a troubling thought. Nearly a week of southern drift might have put them far from the shipping lanes. The only possible gain was that maybe word had spread about the heavy ice and captains were setting more southerly courses to avoid the biggest bergs and thickest fog banks.

Nye tried to think of the ship schedules. He had read them closely in the papers back in Liverpool. All he knew for sure were the scheduled departures from Liverpool after the *John Rutledge*'s. Let's see, he thought. There was the *Pacific* a week later. She might have reached New York already and could even be on her return leg to Liverpool, he calculated. What about the other steamers? Yes, right, the *Arabia* was leaving even before the *Pacific*. That's no good. There was the *Persia*. She was scheduled to leave a few days after the *Pacific*. That's a chance, but only if she had some problems with ice. Otherwise, the *Persia* is also in New York.

He had no idea about the traffic from other ports. But there would be vessels somewhere in these waters coming from East Coast ports. They wouldn't be looking for the *John Rutledge* unless one of the other lifeboats was found. How long ago did they leave Liverpool? Nye counted. About forty days. Still not long enough to stir any kind of search mission. Unless—and here was that big hope again—another ship found one of the other lifeboats and they were looking for Nye and his fellow castaways right now.

From the west, the *America* had steamed out of Boston on January 30 for Liverpool, and the steamer *Fulton* out of New York was bound for Le Havre on February 9. But neither ship was on the lookout for the *Rutledge*.

About two hundred miles to the east of Nye's lifeboat, the *Germania*, the packet out of Le Havre, was moving into a line of icebergs after a day of heavy rain, which had missed soaking Nye's boat with possible life-saving water.

"No let up, west gales," wrote the first mate in the *Germania*'s logbook on February 26. "Saw a number of icebergs."

Mrs. Atkinson went next.

For hours, she had been screaming for water. She held out her hands as if waiting for some angel to descend with a pitcher. Nye tried to block out her moans. He knew it wouldn't be long before they ceased. Little Betty Black peered in horror from beneath Jane's coat. Cover her eyes, Nye thought. But Jane was too cold to bother taking out her hands.

Mrs. Atkinson begged and begged for a drink. Her eyes were glassy. She began to shake. The rest watched with a kind of dazed detachment. There was nothing they could do and—although no one would say it aloud—perhaps they wished Mrs. Atkinson would simply get on with it and die. It was going to happen anyway.

After more hours, she finally went still.

Nye waited a bit, then shifted to run his hands over her eyelids to close them. He would have to be her undertaker just like with the others.

She was bigger than the boatswain. The hem of her skirt was frozen and banged about like a bell. Nye maneuvered her first over the side of the boat. Her arms stretched toward the water in almost the same fashion as when she was howling for a drink. He pushed her forward a bit. One more nudge and her body slithered off the lifeboat. Nye hadn't thought about taking her coat. He regretted that now. It would have made a fine blanket.

For whatever reason, Mrs. Atkinson's body did not sink like the others. It floated a long while beside the boat. "As if," Nye would later say, "determined to keep us company out of spite."

They were now eight.

Before nightfall, a light rain fell. Nye knew Mrs. Atkinson was already too far gone in her final hours. But what if this rain had come just a little earlier? he thought. Could it have made a difference?

He had an idea. He found the oilcloth that had covered the supply of hardtack. He fashioned it into a crude funnel and dripped some of the rain into the demijohn. He felt a bit uplifted. At least they had a way to collect rain or snow when it came. They all turned their faces skyward, catching whatever droplets hit the target of their parched mouths.

Nye touched his jaw. It was still sore and swollen from the blow by Ryan. But thankfully it didn't seem fractured after all. His wagged his jaw back and forth. It hurt, but not too badly.

The shower was brief. Yet was important. There was enough in the demijohn for a sip each.

Next time more, Nye said softly. It was hard to get the words out. The small drink hadn't done anything to ease his swollen tongue.

Daley died quietly, too. He curled up near the bow after taking a few drops of the rainwater. No sounds, no cries from him at all. The quiet deaths seemed somehow sadder than those who offered some kind of struggle at the end.

Nye thought about leaving Daley's body where it lay. William Henderson was too weak to help and Nye didn't think it was right to ask a woman to handle the remains. It would be easy just to cover Daley's face and forget about it. Yet that bothered Nye more than the prospect of heaving a body over the side for the third time that day. Leaving Daley's body seemed a sign of surrender—that they had given up on living and were just waiting to join him in death.

Nye rose once again. His numbed feet splashed through the water at the keel line.

Without saying a word, he rolled Daley's body into the North Atlantic.

They now were seven.

Chapter Nineteen

Day seven.

All they could do was wait.
For what? The answer was sadly obvious. Death seemed more likely than rescue. At first light, they looked upward, hoping for more rain or snow to ease their thirst just for a while. Then they gazed at the horizon with a momentary lift that perhaps they would see a mast or the smoking chimneys of a steamship. The skies gave them nothing. Neither did the sea.

The temperature had dropped below freezing again. That meant ice on the boat. Nye gathered a few small chips from just under the gunwales. He offered them to the others—quickly, before the ice could melt on his gloves. They waved him off. They were letting themselves slip away.

Nye thought about giving up as well.

A week adrift suggested two depressing likelihoods. One was that no search had been mounted, that no other lifeboats were spotted, and that no one had any idea yet that the *John Rutledge* was gone. The second possibility was just as bad. Perhaps further reports of this year's unrelenting ice had come in, and captains in European and American ports plotted more southerly routes for safety. That would put any possible rescue ship well out of range of the lifeboat.

Nye was right on both counts.

The other lifeboats from the *Rutledge* had not been recovered. The boats may have capsized in rough seas or simply floated unnoticed on the currents. No one will ever know. And no search was under way.

Meanwhile, the North Atlantic ice of 1856 became bigger news day after day.

The speculation that the *Pacific* met a tragic fate helped drive the stories, which were constantly fed by sailors' wide-eyed accounts of giant bergs and frozen shipping lanes. As Nye feared, captains took notice and redrew their routes to the south to try to skirt the worst of it.

On the lifeboat, the survivors hunched in separate corners: Nye toward the bow, the four-member Henderson family on one side in the center, and Jane Black and Betty on the other side a bit closer to the stern.

Nye kept a close eye on William Henderson.

Henderson had been growing more agitated. It was not unlike the last hours of the boatswain. Nye worried about another outburst and whether that could doom them all. Henderson was grumbling low about something and wringing his hands, which were bone-white and looked close to frostbite. He didn't seem to notice.

Henderson looked up. He turned to his wife. Nye thought that was a good sign. Maybe she can calm him a bit.

The two boys were between them. For a few minutes, the husband stared silently at his wife. She tried to get him to talk, but he said nothing. Suddenly, he pushed the boys aside with a sweep of his arm, as if they were tree branches in his path. Nye watched them tumble into the seawater wash at the bottom of the lifeboat.

Father? one asked. Stop!

The rest on the boat could only watch. Nye was probably the only one with the strength left to intervene. Yet he held back, too. His scuffle with Ryan made him cautious of risking it again and possibly being pushed overboard or suffering a more serious injury than the knock on the jaw. Why take another chance?

Henderson's breathing was heavy and rapid. His eyes were fixed squarely on his wife. She looked over at the boys. They, in turn, stared at their father the way boys might gawk at a beast in a circus. No one moved.

Then William struck.

So instant and intense was his fury—driven, no doubt, by delusions brought by the seawater—that Margaret had no chance to even raise her hands in defense. Her husband lunged for her hair, the easiest target, hanging loose around her shoulders. He grabbed a handful and, in a sickening sandpaper sound, ripped it from her scalp.

Stop, William, please stop, she yelled.

She managed to grab hold of one of his arms and locked her elbows around it as if she was hugging a pole. He pulled back sharply, but she would not let go.

William, it's me, she said, bobbing her head to try to make eye contact. It's me. The boys are here. Why? Why are you doing this?

He broke free. He attacked again. He sunk his hand into his wife's hair and yanked free more clumps. She tried grabbing his wrists, but her hands were too numb to hang on. The boys were too weak or too shocked to move.

He kept at it. Pausing, as if thinking of his next move for a second or two, then striking at her hair. If William heard his wife's pleas, it never showed. He was deep in a seawater-induced hallucination.

Nye thought about ending the man's misery. A sharp blow to the head with the oar should do it. It's odd, he thought, to be thinking so tactically about killing another man, a passenger whose life, just a week ago, was in his care.

As Nye contemplated moving in, William Henderson's rage ran its course.

It was just like the boatswain. Henderson was possessed one moment, then limp as a rag the next. He slumped to the side and closed his eyes. His wife looked at the panting figure. She reached over to stroke his arm. After all, this was not her husband—the man who pounded rails in north England to save up enough money to get them passage to America. This *other* man, gasping beside her, was someone else entirely, she told herself. He was something raw and sinister, hatched in this strange claustrophobic world on a cold sea.

William never spoke again or lifted his hands. He died within the hour. He fell over, his head landing in his wife's lap.

Nye was too weak to try to push the body off the boat. It remained where it was. Let his wife figure it out, Nye thought. I no longer have the will.

Toward nightfall, a fresh storm kicked up. The boat rode over giant swells and waves that broke over the edge. One big whitecap, Nye thought, and that would be all. They would be tipped into the sea and carried away quickly by death.

Once in a while, a bit of breakaway ice knocked against the boat's hull. That was unsettling. As if the sea was sending a reminder that it was there waiting to take them.

At some point during the night, the two Henderson boys died.

Margaret must have dropped the youngest, five-year-old James, into the sea. Nye had his head buried in his peacoat at the time and didn't hear a thing over the wind. He only saw the older boy's body resting near his father's. They were covered in a light coating of snow.

Nye tried to talk to Margaret, but she was lost in her own cocoon of grief and resignation.

She pulled tightly around her neck the blankets she had taken from the *John Rutledge*. Nye didn't want to stare. But he couldn't help it. He tried to imagine that utterly heartbreaking moment. A mother, just one day a widow, dropping the body of her youngest son into the sea. Neither Nye nor anyone else from his family's long line of mariners and whalemen carried any romance about the sea. They expected to be dealt the worst at any time. But this little boy, Nye thought, didn't deserve this. It was sad beyond measure.

Jane Black said nothing about the deaths. She kept Betty wrapped in the folds of her coat. They had stopped drinking the seawater. Nye was happy about that. But he was troubled by their silence. That never seemed to end well.

Nye scooped up whatever snow he could from around the boat. The only place he avoided was where the two bodies slumped. Then he changed his mind and scraped the snow off their clothes and hands.

He tried to offer some snow to the two women. He wasn't sure how Margaret Henderson would react to snow taken off the bodies. She said nothing and took a little. So did Jane Black, but she made no attempt to give any to the girl hidden beneath her coat. Nye wondered whether the girl was still alive.

In every era, each society grapples with the definitions of common responsibility and duty to the whole. Mariners of the nineteenth century are given special attention by everyone from ethicists to clergy.

Part of the added attention rises from the built-in risks of traveling the seas. The shipping news alone offered a one-stop catalog for any moralist or preacher looking to explore the gray areas between life and death. Was it right to deny food to the dying to potentially save more of the living? What would God say about a crewmate who pushed aside a woman to reach the last lifeboat? It was all there.

Nye, and everyone else in seaport towns, lived in the thick of it. Take your pick. Hardly a month passed without some dilemma at sea putting to the test those involved.

Fairhaven had an extra element that came in the form of a doomsday preacher named Joseph Bates. He was a seaman himself. And, like any sailor, he had powerful stories to tell. One even included a collision with an iceberg during a sail from New York to Russia in 1809. This gave Bates a certain credibility among seamen in Fairhaven and New Bedford. He used it to full advantage, trying to establish a moral compass for mariners that included appeals for them to turn their back on booze and vices. That clean-living message didn't go down well with seafarers who were used to a more, say, unregulated life. Yet his sermons about doing the right thing at sea often struck a chord. Even if seamen wouldn't follow his version of the righteous life, Bates implored them to be big-hearted at sea and to think of others' lives before their own. If they had worked on a slave ship, repent. If they had hoarded provisions at the expense of crewmates, make amends.

Bates peppered his sermons and writings with the seagoing lingo of Fairhaven and New Bedford. If nothing else, he knew the shipboard patois.

"But, ah, how many professed followers of Jesus, after launching out from the shores of sin and folly, with strong determinations to pursue the voyage over life's rough sea for the heavenly Canaan of rest, have laid down their watch, and thrown by their instruments of observation, and concluded to pursue their onward course and trust alone for their destination to their dead reckoning," Bates wrote in an 1847 treatise that might have even penetrated Nye's Methodist-centric world. "But, bless the Lord, there are some that are fully determined to correct their dead reckoning, by watching every opportunity for an observation of the Sun of Righteousness."

It was heady stuff to men waiting to ship out. Nye wasn't a follower. Bates was just too out there for his mainline Protestant upbringing. Bates had once even taken it up a notch by falling in with zealots who believed the Second Coming would occur in 1844. But when the earth continued to spin, Bates was not done. He charted a new course out of the "great disappointment" and founded a new movement, the Seventh-Day Adventists.

As the lifeboat drifted, Nye thought a lot about all this religious finger wagging, sermonizing, and blame casting. It once seemed so essential to keep up with it all. Who was saved? Who was not? Have a drink or become a teetotaler? Who would burn for eternity for slavery, and who would bask in heavenly glory as reward for fighting the abolitionist? Nye, like so many others, had been caught up deeply in such side picking.

Now it was down to whether he would make it through the day off a few bits of snow scraped from the coats of a dead man and his dead son.

Chapter Twenty

Day eight.

Margaret Henderson seemed to be sleeping. That was odd, Nye thought. Why would she choose to stay near the bodies of her husband and older son?

He understood her pain as the family's last survivor. But it struck him as a bit macabre to remain beside the dead.

No matter, he thought. Who am I to judge? I did nothing but watch and fret while her husband beat her in his deranged fit. At least she had covered them with one of the blankets from the *John Rutledge*.

Nye glanced over at Margaret and Jane from time to time, drifting in and out of sleep himself. He felt a drop of cold rain. It took great effort to rouse himself, but he managed to get to his feet. He could no longer feel anything below his shins. Sometimes he thought about taking off his boots and trying to massage feeling back into his feet. But even doing that seemed too much. And why bother? If a ship didn't appear soon—very soon—it was over for all of them.

It was difficult to stand in the swaying boat. The seas had calmed a bit, but the North Atlantic was rarely still. Swells up to ten feet rolled in one after the other. Nye fumbled with his rain-catching system, finally setting the oilcloth to drain what it caught into the demijohn.

Mrs. Henderson? he whispered. Rain, ma'am. We will have some more water soon.

Her features had gone slack. She looked different.

Ma'am?

He took one of the oars and poked her gently. She offered no resistance. It's not hard to tell a dead thing from a living thing when you look closely. Margaret was gone. In one of her final acts, she made an attempt at respectability. She tried to cover over the places where her hair had been ripped away during her husband's dying fit. Nye found this touching. Margaret must have known she was dying, but wanted to face it looking her best. Or maybe she wanted to cover over the sins of her husband's mindless assault.

Nye had no strength left to move her. She would rest there with her family. He may have said a private prayer. All he could remember was that he tried to shroud Margaret Henderson with the second blanket. It slipped off during the next big swell and fell into the keel water.

In that time, death was not a remote, hushed event even in the relative prosperity of Fairhaven. Mothers died regularly in childbirth; children were lost to any number of diseases. It was not unheard of for families to make a daguerreotype of a dead child with its eyes propped open and dressed as if going to Sunday service. In the Victorian world, simply growing old enough to have white hair was no small accomplishment. Doctors had a limited tool kit. A small infection could turn lethal in the age before antibiotics. Even trying to stay healthy could kill you. Either well-meaning or outright scams, hundreds of products—miracle tonics with a touch of arsenic, cure-all pills laced with mercury, and concoctions to ease the pain of teething with a cocktail of cocaine, opium, and heroin—were often far more harmful than the cure they promised.

Nye's immediate family had been fortunate. His parents were alive. His older sister Abigail, known to all as Abbie, was tapping into the early stirrings of women's rights and thinking of a career rather than of marriage.

Nye had known death before, but never at such proximity.

❧

Nye could no longer manage to toss the dead overboard. Instead, he began to assess the bodies in ways he hadn't before. If they were to remain on the lifeboat, he thought, is there any way these poor souls could help the few who remained: himself, Jane Black, and the girl?

Nye noticed the Henderson boy had a red handkerchief wrapped around his neck. It was the one he tied to the oar when they tried to signal the passing brig days before. Nye removed it carefully, trying to avoid touching the body as much as possible. It seemed sacrilegious to pilfer even this small item from the dead. But if they had any last chance, he needed some kind of signal flag with colors that wouldn't be lost in the sea and ice. Red was perfect.

He then looked to what William Henderson's stiffening body could offer. Under his dark coat was a white woolen shirt. That wasn't the best color, of course. But it would have to do. It was certainly better than anything dark.

Nye tried peeling off the shirt, then ripped it clean from the body. He looked over at Jane Black, hoping she wouldn't have a scowl of disapproval. Far from it. She watched Nye with a blank expression as if looting a body was natural.

Nye was exhausted and his upper legs ached from the cold.

He wondered again what his feet looked like. More than frostbite he feared the opportunistic flesh robber gangrene most of all. He had seen sailors whose feet looked as if they had been shredded and chewed. He leaned low toward the edge of his boots, hoping not to catch the scent of dead skin and muscle. Thankfully, nothing yet.

He then checked the oilcloth. It was working as well as could be hoped. There was already a half inch or more of rainwater in the demijohn. That was a bit of good news.

He remembered one last thing. He turned back toward the bodies of the Hendersons. He pulled away the one dry blanket covering William and his son. Nye didn't flinch. He was only thinking of trying to hold off death for another day. If a ship didn't come tomorrow, at least he could feel he gave it his best effort.

He tried to arrange the bodies of the Hendersons in some dignified manner—and in hopes of keeping the boat as balanced as possible. He folded the arms of William over his chest. He left Margaret Henderson mostly in place. It didn't seem right to drag around a woman's body. He took the dead teenager toward the stern, and nudged his father's body closer to the bow.

When he was done, Nye moved over to Jane Black, splashing awkwardly with his rock-numb feet through the deepest water in the lifeboat.

Jane was thin and delicate but had a tough bearing that came from a life of learning how to get by. Nye knew she had made her way through the rougher corners of Glasgow. She told him that much. That, in itself, was enough to impress him. She never let on about her situation with a man, whether she was leaving one behind or heading for one in America, or setting off on her own with two young companions.

For whatever reason, Jane had taken the least seawater. Maybe she listened to Nye's warnings or perhaps she knew herself it was a death sentence. Either way, Nye admired her resolve.

Here, Mrs. Black, try this. Try this until we collect more water.

He handed her a small piece of tin he had found on the boat days before. It must have been from the shattered compass. Nye would place the tin wafer in his mouth and exhale. If it was cold enough—and it often was—a thin layer of condensation would form. It did nothing really to alleviate his thirst, but it felt good on his water-starved tongue and lips. At least, he reasoned, it was doing something rather than giving up.

Try it, he urged.

Jane did. She exhaled and licked the metal.

She gave a slight smile, but said nothing.

See? he said. Does the girl want to try?

Jane shook her head, then stared ahead, suddenly off in her own thoughts.

Nye turned around to check on the demijohn. The rain was easing. There was enough for maybe a few sips between them.

When Nye looked back, Jane had just finished adjusting her coat.

Where is . . . ? He stopped midsentence. He knew what happened. The girl was dead. Maybe had been for some time.

While Nye was looking at the oilcloth, Jane had taken the lifeless body of the girl, hesitated for a moment, and then let it fall into the sea. She now stared straight ahead, gathering her coat tightly about her the same way she did when she was holding Betty.

Nye wanted to say something. A word of comfort or something. But he stayed silent. What could he say? Instead, he huddled next to her as the last rain fell. Jane Black took one sip, then waved off the rest. Nye took a little and saved the last few drops.

He moved back to his place in the stern. Jane stayed put in the boat's midsection. They both, in their own ways, prepared for the end.

Nye slept, and Jane died. He woke to find her slumped into the seawater that had collected in the boat.

He didn't get up. There was no need for it now.

He was alone. Four bodies lay around him. And around the lifeboat, only frigid sea.

He could feel his resolve draining away. It was time to make a signal. Now or never, he thought. He might not have the ability tomorrow. It was a last act. Nye knew that. After this, there would be nothing more to do.

He first moved to the bow, stepping around the bodies of Jane Black and William Henderson.

He tied William Henderson's white woolen shirt to one of the oars, then wedged the oar upright in the bow. He checked it to make sure it could survive the lashings of a modest storm. He then took a rope and ran it from the oar back to the stern. From it, he hung the red handkerchief and another white shirt that was left in the boat. It might have been pulled off by the boatswain Ryan in one of his rages. Nye wasn't sure. It seemed so long ago.

This was his final gambit—castoff clothes of the dead waving in the North Atlantic winds.

He crawled back to the stern. He wrapped himself in the Hendersons' blanket. He pulled down his hat.

His mind drifted homeward. He thought about Fairhaven and how the Acushnet River opened to Buzzards Bay, with the tawny line of the Elizabeth Islands in the distance. As a boy, he played in the coves near old Fort Phoenix at the tip of Fairhaven and pretended he was off hunting whales or riding the decks of a powerful merchant ship. In their games, like childhood playacting everywhere, Nye and his friends always overcame every imagined obstacle and challenge. They were unbeatable.

On the lifeboat, Nye drew himself into a tight ball. He prayed to the God of his Methodist upbringing, a figure of both boundless compassion and bottomless vengeance. He prayed for a ship to find him. For some rain or snow to ease his thirst. But mostly he prayed for the Almighty to be merciful and to take him without too much suffering.

Chapter Twenty-One

Nye thought he slept. But for the past day or so, he couldn't tell. He slipped between dozing and a kind of groggy dreamscape.

In one moment, his imagination took him to Middle Street in Fairhaven. He was looking in the shop windows and then turning toward the docks, where whaling ships were loading up for another long trip. Friends called his name. Thomas, you look good. Glad you're back, boy. His father, James, was there, too. He seemed strong and healthy. Just as Thomas remembered him from before he fell ill and retreated indoors. Doctors had called it "sunstroke," which was something of a catchall diagnosis for an array of problems, such as nervous disorders and chronic fatigue.

Nye was jolted out of his haze by a wave that rocked the lifeboat.

He struggled to open his eyes. He could feel his body surrendering to cold, thirst, and hunger. The decline seemed steeper since Jane died. When the mind gives up, the body listens. Nye knew this was happening. He just couldn't muster much determination anymore to fight back.

Twelve of them were dead. He might as well get ready to join them.

There was, however, a stubborn ember in him that wouldn't be extinguished. Call it the essential life force or the spirit spark or whatever. It prompted Nye to maintain some basic routine of survival. He scanned the horizon for ships and made sure his ragged little signal rig was in place.

It was hard for him to do much else. He had trouble moving. Below the knees he felt as lifeless and cold as some beached sea creature. He tried to move his toes. They may have twitched a little. He couldn't tell. What was clear was that his toes were swollen. He could feel that in the tightness of his boots. Nye knew enough that this was an exceedingly bad sign. He'd seen old seamen limping around Fairhaven whose feet had been eaten away by the cold and wet. They called it by various names. Some sailors dubbed it coldfoot. Ship's doctors often preferred the term *immersion syndrome,* and paid close attention to sketchy reports from the Crimean front about field surgeons' efforts to stave off what, in later wars, would be known as trench foot.

Nye made another quick look to the horizon for any vessels. Always nothing.

He tried not to gaze too long on the four bodies around him. It somehow seemed disrespectful. But he couldn't help it. He was strangely drawn to the faces and how death hardened them, with mouths pried open and lifeless eyes looking past half-closed lids.

He forced himself to move. He could still do some things with his arms. He took the rain-catching oilcloth and tried to bail out the lifeboat. It felt good to have a task, even if it made matters worse. Every time he could scoop up some water, some would spill back on him. Staying as dry as possible was the key to buying time. And getting wet would certainly hasten the end.

Maybe that's a good thing, he thought morosely. The quicker the better. How long could I have? A day or two at most?

Thankfully, the weather had eased. The seas were much calmer. There were still big swells, but they were coming at regular intervals and without any ice. Light winds pushed in from the west-southwest. The breeze felt just a tad warmer on Nye's face. It also pulled up some moisture from the south. Snow started falling early in the morning. A few inches had accumulated. Nye scooped it from the gunwale and let it melt on his tongue.

He nestled himself back in the stern. He was wrapped in the coats, blankets, and scarves of his dead companions. Their last possessions will probably be my last possessions, he thought.

He turned his head once more to the east.

The horizon was broken by something.

What was that? He cupped his gloves around his eyes to shield them from the snow. Was this just another iceberg? Nye studied it closely, fully expecting disappointment. Dozens of times before, what seemed to be a ship cresting the horizon turned out to be nothing more than a berg. But this one seemed too compact and dark to be an iceberg; too well defined to be some sort of storm cloud.

No. Then what? Nye fixed on the object. An hour went by. He could hardly notice the time passing. His attention was too focused. Snow built up on his gloves. Finally, the object shifted slightly and the silhouette changed.

My God. The shape was unmistakable. It was a ship on a gentle tack.

Its course pointed straight ahead.

Nye lay directly in its path.

Chapter Twenty-Two

From the deck of the American packet ship *Germania,* first mate Charles Hervey Townsend thought it might just be a trick of the waves—making a dead man move as if he were animated by life.

He turned to Captain Daniel H. Wood, who joined him on deck.

What do you think, sir? Townsend asked. The crew believes they saw someone on the lifeboat waving. The second mate informed me without delay. I am not sure, sir. Maybe it is just the waves shaking the body.

Just minutes before, Wood had been sleeping. He needed the rest, and Townsend* was nervous about waking him for this. But the possibility of a lifeboat and survivors needed the captain's attention. Wood had to decide on any rescue operation or deviation from course. This was beyond Townsend's authority.

Wood had been up most of the previous night with the helmsman and the ice watchers. The icebergs had become more threatening and the seas were wild after nearly a full day of gale winds. But the weather loosened its grip just before dawn. Snow clouds rolled in and fat, wet flakes began to fall. Wood was taking advantage of the respite with an afternoon rest in his cabin while the *Germania* sailed through the snowfall with only spotty ice ahead.

Is that man alive? Wood said to himself.

---

*Many accounts and records identify the first mate as *Townshend,* but he signed his name as *Townsend* in the *Germania's* log as well as on letters and other documents throughout his life. Many of Townsend's papers are held in the collection of the William L. Clements Library at the University of Michigan.

He squinted one eye and took a hard look through his telescope. Thomas Nye was no bigger than a matchhead at this distance, even through the spyglass.

The figure seemed to move and wave its arms. The motion of the sea can make a body bob and twist. Townsend knew that. But it can't make a corpse's arms flail like this. Can it?

By God, Mr. Townsend, it seems to be a survivor, said the captain.

It's hard to tell from this far away, Townsend replied cautiously, letting the captain make the important call on whether to investigate or sail on. The snow doesn't help, sir.

True, said Wood. But the light is still good. A few hours later, and we would have sailed right past this boat in the dark.

By now, the news had spread through the crew. Seamen craned their necks trying to get a better look at the lifeboat. Poor devil, one of them said. Imagine being out there in a dinghy like that.

Wood pondered for a moment. Then he turned to Townsend.

We have no choice, Wood said. We must look. Even if it's just bodies, we can send them off. We can't just sail by.

I agree, sir, said Townsend, privately relieved they would investigate. He had his own reasons, but kept them to himself for the moment.

Wood gave the order. Heave to, smartly.

Townsend passed the word to the crew. Pull the sheets. Sails down. We are lying ahull. Castaway spotted. Man adrift.

Seamen wiggled up the rungs and into the rigging, forgetting for a moment the dangers of slipping on the snow-covered ropes and spars. Spotting bits of wrecked ships was nothing new. Hardly a month passed without some disaster in the North Atlantic—a ship striking a berg or capsizing in a storm or a steamer catching fire or falling victim to any of the many ways a vessel was brought down. Each catastrophe left its calling cards to drift with the currents: a beam, a bit of sail, life jackets that were never used.

But to find someone alive was extraordinary. More than extraordinary, really. The odds were staggering. It was sheer luck that the *Germania* was on this course at all. Wood had heard the early rumors reaching France of heavy ice in the Grand Banks and opted to swing slightly to the south.

Sails secure, came the cries from the rigging.

Helmsman, hard to port, cried the first mate.

Then Townsend said to the boatswain: Prepare for launch.

The commotion drew some of the passengers from steerage to deck. They chattered excitedly in a hodgepodge of German dialects. The emigrants were mostly Bavarians, but some came from the central Hesse region and from across the border in Switzerland. The French port of Le Havre, where the *Germania* had got under way, was a gateway for Swiss, Prussian, Bohemian, and other emigrants from farther east.

The ocean swells, rising higher than ten feet, were far more noticeable on deck after the sails were furled and the *Germania* began to drift. Snow started to come down harder. It was getting colder with a shift in the winds. Sea spray covered everything in a skin of ice.

Townsend looked among the crew.

He pointed at four men. Into the boat with you. We're going out.

The starboard lifeboat was readied. Captain Wood stayed on deck, watching everything from the covered veranda deck. The *Germania* was maybe five hundred yards from the lone boat. The winds came from the north-northwest. They would begin pushing the *Germania* away. They had to move fast.

Take 'er down, Townsend told the crewmen at the winches.

The boat jerked lower, foot by foot. They descended past the big white band that ran the length of the hull just above the water line, which gave the *Germania* a distinctive look. The lifeboat hit the water cleanly. Townsend used an oar to push off the *Germania,* putting sea between the lifeboat and the ship. He didn't want a wave slamming them back against the hull.

Here we go, boys, Townsend urged. Give it your all.

With snow pelting his eyes, Townsend kept a bead on the lifeboat from the top of each swell. Down in the troughs, the seas were high enough to block his view of the *Germania* behind and the lifeboat ahead. Townsend looked back occasionally to the *Germania* for directions from Wood, who kept an eye on the lifeboat with his telescope.

They came within three rods, by Townsend's estimate, or about fifteen meters. The man was no longer moving. He was staring straight ahead as if taking no notice of Townsend's craft. Townsend felt sure they had been

mistaken all along about a survivor but didn't want to openly disagree with
Captain Wood. This man is dead, frozen in place, Townsend thought.

Ahoy, there, Townsend yelled, anticipating nothing.

And that's what he got. The figure hadn't moved from the stern. A
peacoat was buttoned hard against his chin and he wore the distinctive
Gloucester-style waterproof hat with a wide back brim that sailors called
a sou'wester. Townsend noticed that both the man's legs were calf-deep
in seawater—it sloshed about the top of his boots. This boat, Townsend
figured, hasn't been properly bailed in many days.

Ahoy! Townsend tried again.

Then, to his shock, Nye raised his head and turned toward Townsend.
No sea wave can do that, Townsend thought. Remarkable. The captain
was right after all. There is at least one survivor.

Townsend asked the oarsmen to row closer.

What is your name? Townsend yelled. Your vessel?

Nye tried to shout back. The snow had helped his thirst, but his body
seemed to resist his attempts to yell. He grunted out the words as best he
could.

Nye, he said. Thomas Nye. Able-bodied seaman. *John Rutledge* out of
Liverpool. Hit an iceberg. Went down.

Townsend, who was raised along Connecticut's shore, recognized immediately the man's accent was American with a touch of New England.

He was close enough now to see Nye was having trouble moving.
When Townsend's boat tipped slightly on the crest of a swell, he could
see four other figures along with Nye. There is no way they are alive,
Townsend concluded. My word, he thought. This is a man adrift with
four dead companions.

Nye, you say. Can you move, sir? Townsend asked. How many days
since you abandoned your ship. The name again?

The *John Rutledge,* said Nye. Nine days, I think. We were thirteen in
this boat. It is just me left.

Townsend wondered how long Nye had been floating with the bodies as his only mates. This wasn't the time to ask. He needed to set a line to tow the lifeboat back to the *Germania*.

Near Nye in the stern was the body of the Henderson's eldest son, Robert, stiff and covered in a thin coating of ice and a fresh feathering of snow.

In the bow was the body of the boy's father, William, who had descended into the fit of delirium before dying. Townsend was jarred by William's wide-open eyes. "He must have died a dreadful death," Townsend later wrote. In the middle of the boat were the bodies of Margaret Henderson and Jane Black. Their hair, Townsend remembered, was "washing from side to side with every roll of the boat, eyes and mouths wide open."

Nye crawled toward the bow. He had to hang on dearly to the edge of the lifeboat, worried that he would tip into the sea if he relied on his deadened feet.

Hold tight, Mr. Nye. We are taking you back. Can you handle a rope?

I think I can, said Nye.

Good, said Townsend. Send over the painter and we will hitch it.

Townsend watched Nye grab hold of the lifeboat's painter, or bow rope. Nye pulled. He pulled again. It was snagged. He let his eyes travel down the length of the painter until he saw the problem. The line was tangled with the women's bodies.

I can't clear it, Nye said. Let me get into your boat, sir. I just want off.

Belay that, man. Hold fast there, Townsend said. We can do that, but not from the bow.

It took a few more minutes for Townsend to maneuver his boat alongside. Nye was ready. He took a step off the edge of the lifeboat and tumbled forward, striking his head as he landed among Townsend's rescue crew.

There was no blanket to toss around Nye. No one had really expected a survivor. Townsend had one of the men quickly affix a tow line to Nye's boat.

Are we secure? Townsend asked. The crewman nodded, taking one long look at the four bodies.

Townsend turned back to Nye. That is the *Germania*, he told him, pointing toward his ship. Out of Le Havre, bound for New York.

Our port, too, said Nye. *Was* our port.

Have you seen anyone else from your ship? What was the name again? Townsend asked.

John Rutledge. And no. I've seen no one since just after the ship was lost. It was very foggy. We all drifted in different directions.

Well, you will be on the *Germania* soon, Townsend said.

Townsend turned to the crew.

Here we go, mates. Now, men, pull hard.

It took longer to reach the *Germania* with Nye's boat in tow. When they were about twenty yards out, the captain cupped both hands to the sides of his mouth.

Wood yelled: You have a survivor?

One, sir, replied Townsend. From the *John Rutledge*. Packet, I think. For New York from Liverpool. Ice, sir. They hit ice.

Wood knew the *Rutledge*. It and the *Germania* sometimes docked in New York at the same time. The *Germania* was built in Portsmouth, New Hampshire, in 1850 just a year before the *Rutledge*'s first sail down the Chesapeake. Both ships were similar in size and age. He had looked over the *John Rutledge* from time to time to check the condition of the hull and sails, looking for any modifications or problems. The *John Rutledge* and *Germania* had much in common and sailed the same North Atlantic waters. It made sense to keep watch on how another ship was faring.

Townsend's boat was alongside the *Germania*. The crew used their oars to draw the two lifeboats parallel.

Townsend sent two crewmates into Nye's old boat.

Do you want to say any words? Townsend asked Nye.

Words?

Before we, ah, commit with your companions.

Nye shook his head. What could he say? They had failed to listen to him about drinking seawater and refused to work together to make at least some semblance of a common effort toward survival. They did little to help themselves, Nye thought, and that was a tragedy in itself. Nye felt worst for the two littlest ones: the youngest Henderson boy and Betty Black, just a bit older at seven. They could scarcely grasp what was going on and why the older ones were helpless to make it better. But they were both gone now, already dropped over the side of the lifeboat.

No words from me, said Nye. Just get me onto the ship.

He didn't watch as the bodies were cast into the sea. He could hear the seamen struggling to pry apart the arms of Margaret Henderson and Jane Black, which had become entangled in death. Then came four splashes— one right after the other—as the bodies slid into the sea.

Anything else before we heave off this boat? one of the seamen in Nye's lifeboat asked.

Nye was about to shake his head no, but then remembered: Yes, yes, the ship's log. It's in the bow. Under some coats.

The seaman looked. Here it is, he said. I have it.

Ropes were drawn into Townsend's boat and the other crewmates climbed back aboard. The lifeboat from the *Rutledge* was given a shove.

Townsend looked up, blinking into the falling snow. All set here. Hoist away.

Nye turned back one more time. He watched the boat that carried them from the *John Rutledge*. It stayed close for a while, bobbing alongside the *Germania*. Then it slowly began to drift away, empty. There was no way for the *Germania* to haul up Nye's lifeboat and, even if they could, no one wanted something touched so deeply by death to be among them.

Nye next felt arms wrapping around him. Gentle there, men. Gentle, urged Captain Wood.

Nye was carried onto the deck. His frozen feet wouldn't allow him to stand. He collapsed to his knees.

How are you, son? asked Wood, tossing a long wool coat over Nye's shoulders. Where do you hail from?

My feet. I don't know about my feet. I can't feel them, Nye blurted. Suddenly, he was very worried he might lose them to a surgeon's saw.

Well, if you have to take my feet or legs, make sure you cut from the neck down. I don't want to live if that is what will happen.

We will take care of you, son, said Wood. Don't worry about that. I was wondering about your home port. Where is that?

From, sir? The *John Rutledge*. We hit ice. We were out of Liverpool.

That I know, said Wood patiently. The first mate just told us that. Your home, son. Where is your home?

Fairhaven, sir. Fairhaven, Massachusetts. Next to New Bedford.

Wood raised an eyebrow and then gave a big smile. We are kin, son. I belong to New Bedford as well. This is something, isn't it? Wood said to no one in particular. A Fairhaven man. My word. I'm Captain Daniel Wood.

A great pleasure, said Nye as cordially as possible in his parched voice, even as he worried dreadfully about his feet. I am Thomas Nye.

Nye, you say! Well, I know the Nyes. New Bedford is full of them. I know the Nye ships, too. Whalers. Good ones. I remember the whaling ship *Nye* coming back with so much oil that there was no room for even a rat in that hold. To find you here. This is quite something, I must say.

Enough of that, said a woman, nudging Wood out of the way. Plenty of time for talk. Let's get a look at those feet and warm you up. What you say?

A woman stepped close to Nye. I'm Sarah Wood. The talkative one is my husband. Now here you go.

The ship's steward, a Frenchman named Papon, and a few crew members carried Nye toward the stern to Wood's private cabin, which had windows facing aft over the ship's wake. Nye was placed on the bed. It was the first time he had stretched out flat since the night before the iceberg hit.

Soon someone brought Nye a mug of hot water dressed with cayenne pepper, a brew known for ages as a mild stimulant for digestion and blood circulation. Nye gulped it down.

He fell into a sleepy haze. He felt his legs being jostled but didn't bother looking down. They must be removing my boots, he thought. I wonder how my feet look. He didn't have time to check. With his belly warmed by the hot drink, sleep overtook him.

In another part of the ship, Townsend was already back at his log. He wanted to get down every detail while it was still fresh.

Saw a boat with a man in to windward. Hove ship to. Myself and four men went to his relief. Found him to be one of the boys of ship John Rutledge bound from Liverpool to New York, which was lost in an immense

field of ice on the evening of Thurs. 19th of February. He being the only
survivor of 13 souls having buried with his own hands 8, there being four
others having died in the boat. 2 men + 2 women (consigned the dead to
the deep).

Lat. 44.11

Long. 47.34

Townsend went back on deck. He knew Captain Wood well enough
to guess what was already under way. Wood had ordered the crew to set
a course to the northeast. They could not sail on without making an attempt to see if other lifeboats from the *John Rutledge* were out there.

The crew were conflicted but followed orders.

Even Townsend wondered whether Wood was making a sound call.
The winds had shifted around to the north-northeast, perfect for making
a fast run across the main ice fields into clearer water. But in his heart
Townsend knew Captain Wood was doing what was right and proper.

But something else gnawed at Townsend. It was about that odd incident on deck a few nights earlier. He would keep it to himself. There
was work to be done and he didn't want to complicate matters with the
captain. This would have to wait.

It was dark. The night watch was told to keep vigilant for anything
that could be the cry of a castaway or a lone binnacle lamp somehow kept
burning for nine days.

Just after dawn, Townsend reopened the log. In the margins, in ant-
crawl script, he added:

The young man is Thomas Nye of N. Bedford. Reports that of other boats
left the ship after. They did not see the ship and supposes the ship sunk,
the mate and about 30 others having no room on the boats.

His feet are badly frozen, but with favorable recovery the use of them.

8 p.m.—hove to set light & rigging and kept a good lookout for the
other boats. Winds NNE. Daylight sent men aloft to lookout.

Chapter Twenty-Three

MARCH 1, 1856; THE SEARCH.

All day the *Germania* tacked north. Snow was falling fast, the first mate noted in his log. The most unlucky of the crew drew lookout duty high in the masts. No one could complain too loudly. If it was them out there adrift, they would want the same type of search.

Plus, the captain was thoroughly vested in all things about the *John Rutledge* by now. Nye had seen to that with his well-traveled last name.

Saving a New Bedford man—well, from Fairhaven, but just over the river—Wood saw as a mighty stroke of fate. It was easy to run into a fellow New Bedford seaman anywhere in the world. But how many times can you pluck one, near death, from the sea? Wood also saw this event as more than just another sea tale worth a free ale or two in the taverns back home. This would form a lifetime bond with one of the most well-connected families in New Bedford.

For goodness sake, Captain Wood told Nye in his cabin, I grew up hearing stories about the Nyes.

And who didn't in that corner of New England? The captain emeritus Ezra Nye had been drawing attention as far back as 1836, when he shocked the world with his record-breaking New York–Liverpool sail of fourteen days, twelve hours on the *Independence,* a feat regarded at the time as a marvel of speed and virtuoso seamanship.

As Wood spent time chatting with Nye, Townsend was on deck. He shouted up to the lookouts every hour or so.

Anything?

No, sir. Just sea and snow and ice, sir.

Townsend also spent time poring over the frantic last entries in the *John Rutledge* log for any possible clues. The iceberg hit the ship about a hundred miles northeast of the *Germania*'s current position, about 350 miles off Newfoundland, or a three- or four-day sail to port under favorable conditions. Assuming other lifeboats followed the same currents as Nye's, they could be out there. There was another possibility, which Nye had earlier considered. The other survivors may have struck out to the east with their oars, seeking to catch the Gulf Stream, which would tug them eastward and possibly into the path of transatlantic vessels. That would leave them far from where the *Germania* was now sailing.

The *John Rutledge* logbook, written by the first mate Atkinson, offered an impression of Captain Kelley as a capable and level-headed leader. Someone like that would probably have calculated their best chances to be the Gulf Stream, Townsend reasoned. But, then again, that was just a feeling. The castaways could have just as likely floated aimlessly out of view of passing ships, just as the brig had failed to notice Nye's boat. Or, also possible, some had been picked up and were already on their way to port. Those on the *Germania* wouldn't know anything for sure until they reached New York.

Townsend also had a secret. He had kept it to himself for a few days. But it was becoming too much of a burden to carry alone.

He sought out the captain.

Sir, I need to tell you about something that happened three nights ago. It might have something to do with the present search for the *John Rutledge* boats.

Wood spun around. Well, sir, let's have it. Fine thing to wait. Why didn't you note this earlier?

It made no sense earlier, sir. Now it does.

Spill it, man.

Remember that night? It was that terrible weather, Townsend began. The snow and hail. We were on a port tack driving into the waves. It was my watch. It was about ten p.m. We had one lookout, a man at the wheel, and one on the forward poop deck.

Go on, said Wood.

Townsend told the story step by step. How the light went out in the skylight on deck, which also served a convenient place to hang a binnacle lamp at night. Townsend went to relight it.

I was gone maybe seven minutes, sir. When I came back on deck the man at the wheel seemed frightened out of his wits. He told me he heard a man's voice trying to hail the ship. It came from the windward. The voice was close, he told me. Faint but clear. Maybe right next to the ship. He swore to me he heard the cry. Not once, but twice.

What did you make of it? Wood asked.

Well, sir, I didn't hear anything because I was below with the skylight. But, to be honest, sir, I thought it was just wind through the rigging. You know, sir, how that can sound like a voice in distress. I told the man he was just nervous. I told him it was probably just the mizzen topsail yard creaking. He didn't agree, sir. He stood his ground and told me he believed he heard a cry for help.

I relieved him, sir, Townsend went on. I brought another man to the wheel. The first man said he was sorry. He wasn't trying to deceive me, he said. He insisted he heard a voice.

And what then? Wood asked.

Nothing, sir. I thought the man was hearing things, ship's noises and the like. I didn't give it another thought until we picked up Mr. Nye yesterday. Now I believe, sir, that we heard a cry from another lifeboat from the *John Rutledge*. I truly believe that now.

Wood could only listen.

There wasn't much they could do now. No one could say where the sea would drive a lifeboat if the voice was real. But Townsend was no novice. He had been at sea since signing on with the bark *Hyperion* in 1849 and had steadily climbed the ranks since. His judgment had proved sound on many occasions. Wood wondered privately about this time, though.

I wish you would have told me this earlier, even if you thought it was nothing, said Wood. But I am not going to question your decision. Too late for that now.

We just need to keep looking, he continued. Stay the course.

Down in Captain Wood's quarters, Nye had woken a few hours earlier. For a moment he wondered why his clothes weren't wet. Then he remembered someone peeling off layer after layer. First, the sweaters and wraps taken from the dead, then he was wriggled out of what he was wearing when the *John Rutledge* went down. Finally, he was redressed in some of the captain's clothes.

Nye's feet ached. But that was encouraging, he guessed. Some feeling was returning. That was certainly better than the deadness of before. Sarah Wood and the steward had begun soaking Nye's feet in slightly heated seawater, the first step in the proper treatment to gradually rewarm the tissue. The water was only a few degrees warmer than the breath-robbing sea. Even that small difference, however, was enough to evoke the pin-prick sensations in Nye's feet.

That's a good sign, said Sarah, who had seen her share of nursing at sea. She had tended every seagoing ailment thrown at her husband, from cold feet to sun-scorched hands.

Nye was afraid to ask more about his feet. Sarah could read it in his eyes.

With some luck, Mr. Nye, we can save those feet, she said. Maybe all the toes, too. You're lucky there, Mr. Nye. I've seen worse. I've also seen better. But we'll get you through this if you do what I say.

The steward brought down another mug of hot water infused with cayenne pepper.

Drink this, she said. This is what you need.

Nye did as told.

We don't want to get too much food into you too quickly there, do we? she said. That can cause more harm than good. Tomorrow we can get you some porridge. Drink up now.

Nye finished but cupped his hands around the mug until it gave up all its warmth.

Good, she said. Now we are going to wrap up those feet. Lay back. That's good. Now here we go.

She first slathered on a thick poultice of warm, cooked bran. It was an old horse treatment for leg abscesses and boils. Many country doctors swore by it for humans, too, as a healing salve. Sarah coated both feet until Nye could no longer see his cold-ravaged skin, which was a distressing color etched with veins of broken capillaries such that it reminded him of scrimshaw.

Now we'll wrap it so it stays in place, she said. We'll be doing this for a while, Mr. Nye, so get accustomed to it. All you have to do is lay back.

The door opened.

How is our patient? asked the captain.

Steady as she goes. His wife smiled.

Captain Wood pulled up a stool at the bedside. He gave Sarah a nod of admiration. A captain's wife was often more than just a companion at sea. She would pitch in when and where needed—for something as mundane as mending an officer's coat or for real seafaring duties such as offering a hand on deck in a pinch. It took some doing to crack the macho bravado of life on deck, but it happened under the right conditions. The wives of some captains even achieved a level of fame. None perhaps more than Eleanor Creesy, a first-rate navigator, who became an international sensation in 1851 when her observations were credited with helping her husband, Captain Josiah Creesy, demolish the speed record between New York and San Francisco. They made a run of eighty-nine days, twenty-one hours on the famed clipper *Flying Cloud*—a sail almost twice as fast as it took for the standard trip around the tip of South America.

And in seagoing places such as Cape Cod or New Bedford, the women learned to be strong and resourceful out of necessity, despite the romanticized tales of women pacing rooftop widows' walks waiting for their man to return. Their husbands and brothers were off sometimes for years at sea. Some, of course, never returned. Cemeteries were dotted with markers for lost seamen. It was a built-in hazard of the trade, like black lung for coalminers and deadly blizzards for the Great Lakes boatsmen. Society adapts. So many men were at sea—or claimed by it—that an informal matriarchy took hold. Debts and crops and home repairs couldn't wait for the men to return. Women took on roles that, in other landlocked burgs, seemed positively scandalous in the context of the day. Louisa May Alcott put a playful spin on the proto-feminism that was given a chance to test its wings. "The female population exceeds the male, you know, especially in New England," one of the characters in *Jo's Boys* says, "which accounts for the high state of culture we are in, perhaps."

Sarah Wood was forged against such a backdrop. She was no stranger to getting things done on her own. Her father, a ship captain, was lost at sea when she was thirteen. Her mother died six years later, leaving Sarah to make her own way until she married Daniel Wood in 1843.

Captain Wood never hesitated to bring her along even on the challenging winter crossings. Nye remembered again that Captain Kelley's wife stayed back in Liverpool, a decision that may have saved her life. Yet she probably had no idea, Nye thought, that the *Rutledge* was lost.

Now, said Wood, tell me about you, Mister Thomas Nye. What did you do at home?

First, sir, I have a question, Nye asked. Any sign of other boats from the *John Rutledge*?

Nothing yet, the captain said somberly. It's snowing rather hard now. Makes it damn difficult to see anything. But we are heading north for a while. There's always hope.

Nye sighed. He hoped that the others were safe on different ships and maybe already in port somewhere. He refused to contemplate that he could be the only survivor.

Now, Mister Nye, tell me about you and Fairhaven.

Nye told his story.

Because Wood was a fellow New Englander, Nye added details about how his family was deeply sympathetic to the cause of abolition. He was usually careful to steer clear of any talk, in port or at sea, about his views on slavery and the ever-widening national divide. It wasn't worth stirring up an argument with seamen who most likely had a knife or two stashed under their shirt and knew how to use them. By this time, just saying you were from New Bedford pretty much signaled your loyalties.

When Nye was a boy, one of his uncles brought him over to New Bedford to hear some oratory on human dignity that made more sense than anything he'd ever heard from the pulpit of his church. The speaker was Frederick Douglass, who arrived in New Bedford in 1838 under a fake name to avoid bounty hunters looking for fugitive slaves. Douglass was put up in the home of abolitionists on Seventh Street, a short walk up from New Bedford's piers. The couple urged him to adopt the name

Douglas, after one of the key figures in Sir Walter Scott's epic narrative poem, "The Lady of the Lake." Frederick Augustus Washington Bailey was the name he was given as a slave; he agreed to shorten it. But he gave the new name his own twist, adding the double *s*.

Nye soon grew tired of talking and answering questions. It was Wood's turn.

Nye already knew Wood—not personally, of course, but he knew the brand of man from New Bedford who was destined to go to sea and might very well die there. Wood was born in 1816 at the dawn of New Bedford's whaling era. It didn't take much to persuade a boy that hunting whales was a better occupation than anything he could do on land. Some in Wood's extended family were among the first New Bedford whalers striking out. One of his uncles, also named Daniel, had a whaler bearing his name, the *Daniel Wood,* which would head home in March 1856 after more than four years hunting the Pacific whaling grounds.

In those times, it was easy to find some way to line your pockets in New England. The shipbuilders were busy and always looking for skilled hands. The house builders, meanwhile, were putting up the first great homes of the newly rich captains and shipowners. The merchants were busy outfitting the boats. At the bottom of the heap were the shipmates, willing to set aside three years, maybe more, to comb the seas for whales or join the packet runs. You wouldn't get rich as a deck hand on a whaler. But it was a stepping stone up the ranks.

Make it to captain, like Wood, and the rewards came in. Wood was on the cusp of being forty. He had established himself as reliable and able to keep a schedule—the two most prized attributes for packet ship captains—in his years taking the *Germania* back and forth between New York and Le Havre.

He had curried even more favor by paying attention to innovations in rigging. He copied a French system that allowed a sailor to reef the topsail, or reduce the size of the sail by folding or rolling the canvas, without going aloft. He added the new pulleys and rope network to the

Germania and was able to cut the number of crew, to the great delight of the owners.

New Bedford and its surrounding ports were a checkerboard of family bloodlines. Get two old-line New Bedford folk gabbing—like Nye and Wood—and it was nearly impossible for them not to find connections. Wood's wife, Sarah, was of the big Howland line. Yes, the same clan that branched off to the New York shipping world and included shares in the *John Rutledge* among its holdings. Captain Wood's niece Cornelia married into the Delano family, old French Huguenots whose line would eventually merge with the Roosevelts with famous results by the initials of FDR. The Nye family knew the Delanos well and would eventually sell them land that became one of Fairhaven's most serene cemeteries.

Are you married, Mister Nye? Wood asked.

No, sir. Been at sea.

Ah, I'm lucky to have Sarah. We have two children. A young boy. He turned four this July, and a daughter. She'll be twelve in June. They are back in New York.

What he didn't say was that they lost their second child, a girl, as an infant. In those years it was hard to find a family that hadn't lowered a tiny coffin into the earth.

Get some rest now, Captain Wood finally said after they had exhausted their mutual histories. Sarah will keep watch on your feet.

You'll let me know if you see any other boats from the *John Rutledge*? Nye asked.

Of course, of course, Wood replied. I am going now to check.

Wood found the first mate Townsend bundled up on deck. The snow was still coming down at a good clip. They weren't going to find anything out there unless they bumped right into it.

Give it until nightfall, Wood said. If nothing, set a course for New York. If any passenger complains about the delay, remind them that it could have been them on a lifeboat.

The next morning, the *Germania* was off the search. Wood had weighed all the factors. It was unclear whether the other lifeboats had followed the same currents as Nye's craft. The ice was growing thicker. Wood didn't want to put his ship at any additional risk without an idea whether they were even close to the other *Rutledge* lifeboats.

Wood ordered the ship to turn course. The *Germania* headed to the southwest, trying to find a favorable wind to push it toward Sable Island off Nova Scotia, still more than four hundred miles away. No one told Nye that the search was over. But he could tell by the activity of the crew that they were back to the regular sailing routine.

Townsend updated the log. No other signs of the *John Rutledge*, he wrote.

As an aside in the March 2 entry, Townsend wrote simply: "Thomas Nye better."

Chapter Twenty-Four

MARCH 5, 1856; NEW YORK.

On a leafy block in Brooklyn near the ferry docks to Manhattan, the Ridgway home had bolts of sad black crepe and bunting ready to hang.

But not just yet.

It was clear that something was gravely amiss with the *Pacific*. That was undeniable. It had been nearly seven weeks since the steamship left Liverpool. Speculation of what could have happened came from all directions. Many of the top newspaper reporters covering shipping were clear on where they stood. Very likely, they wrote, something terrible befell the *Pacific*.

Still, it was not time to accept the worst and make an open display of mourning. There were too many prominent New Yorkers and others on the steamer. Many of their families and friends were holding out hope— or at least making a public show of it.

The *Pacific* had a passenger manifest replete with top Knickerbocker money and influence. There was Joseph Kershaw, a prominent Manhattan lawyer who was in the Ridgways' circle of friends; Henry Dutilh, a well-known silk merchant based for years in New York and who had recently shifted his operations to Liverpool; George N. Cutter, a successful millinery importer who brought in some of the latest fashions from Europe; Legrand Smith, a theatrical producer who was in London looking for talent for a new Broadway production; and the Reverend Bernard O'Reilly, an Irish-born bishop of the Hartford diocese in Connecticut who had earned a reputation over the years for standing up to the Know Nothings and other anti-Catholic thugs.

If that wasn't enough, the new captain of the *Pacific,* Asa Eldridge, was on friendly terms with one of the world's richest men. Three years earlier, Eldridge had commanded the *North Star,* the steam-powered luxury yacht of uber-tycoon Cornelius Vanderbilt, on a cruise through Europe, a seagoing twist on the Grand Tour that the *Chicago Tribune* gushed over as "princely and magnificent." On board were Vanderbilt, his family, and a swanky entourage. Eldridge did not disappoint. His command was masterful, and the crew, discreet. Vanderbilt and the others held Eldridge in such high regard that they presented him with a silver tea service at the end of the spare-no-expense voyage. At the stop in Le Havre, a chance encounter occurred. The *North Star,* a masterpiece of gleaming white metal and dark rosewood and maple, pulled into port as the packet *Germania* was preparing for another Atlantic crossing. Vanderbilt took notice of the American ship. In short order, Captain Wood, his wife, Sarah, and their daughter, Elizabeth, were hosted as honored guests aboard Vanderbilt's yacht.

The family of James Lawrence Ridgway knew it would be in horribly bad form to start the public grieving when others—especially the powerful Vanderbilts—were still grasping for bits of good news from the ships arriving in New York.

Yet the crews from every vessel out of Liverpool had nothing to offer except shrugs.

The blank reports piled up. No sightings of the *Pacific* or wreckage that would fit the bill. Nothing from steamships *Baltic* and *Africa* after their Atlantic crossings. No sign of anything from the packet ship *New York.* The Prussian bark *Fifth of May* finally made it to New York from Newcastle after a calamitous 106-day crossing in which gales tore away sails and ice crushed part of the hull, but it had seen no sign of the *Pacific.* And nothing, too, from the ship *Onward,* which arrived in New York from London in early March.

On the other hand, there was no obvious evidence of a wreck either. That was enough to keep alive a wisp of an idea that the *Pacific* could be laid up in some far-flung Canadian port or drifting in the North Atlantic, far off the normal shipping routes, just waiting for a vessel to cross her path.

In the meantime, the rumor mill churned on and on. In Boston, the captain of the steamship *America* had to publicly deny spurious reports out of Halifax that crew members on his ship had spotted the *Pacific* heading back to Liverpool.

Reconnaissance missions turned up nothing as well. The steamer *Alabama,* which was sent out February 24 on a search for the *Pacific,* was back in port in New York with nothing to report but lots of ice. It had forayed as far north as Cape Race on the southeast corner of Newfoundland before encountering impassable ice fields. The ship then took the zigzag path down the Canadian Maritimes favored by Collins Line steamship captains when ice was thick, surmising that perhaps the *Pacific* took this route as well. The *Alabama* first steamed around Sable Island, a wind-blown crescent about 180 miles off Nova Scotia. Then it weaved back and forth through the waters off Halifax. The *Alabama* encountered about thirty other vessels. None had any word of the *Pacific*.

Out of Halifax, the propeller steamer *USS Arctic*—the namesake of the Collins Line ship lost two years earlier—also joined the hunt. The captain vowed to cruise the waters off Sable until at least April. The British government did its part, sending a search ship to scan waters close to Ireland.

Among those waiting for the *Pacific,* some took solace in the axiom that no news was good news. The gloomy ones, meanwhile, sunk deeper into apprehension.

❧

Edward Collins was thinking ahead.

He knew well the mentality and moods of the type of people who could afford luxury steamers. They had money. That meant options. Twin tragedies—the *Arctic* in 1854 and now likely the *Pacific*—would be a massive blow to the Collins Line, especially when rival Cunard ships offered as much luxury and the added peace of mind of construction using watertight compartments, which were becoming common among European ship designers but were still rare in America.

The newspapers had pretty much written the obituary for the *Pacific,* and those reading between the lines might have heard a death knell for the

Collins Line as well. "Not the slightest intelligence, report or rumor," said a March 20 item in the *Times-Picayune* of New Orleans. The conclusion that the steamship was lost at sea "can no longer be doubted with reason," it added with grave finality.

Even Ezra Nye, the *Pacific*'s former commander, couldn't keep silent. It was considered bad form for one captain to publicly speculate on the abilities of another or question the decisions of a shipping line. But Nye broke protocol. He offered a gloomy theory, which eventually made its way into the *New York Courier and Enquirer*. Ezra Nye postulated that the *Pacific* could have been cursed by the crews' lack of familiarity with the steamer. Nye noted that the top echelon on the vessel—from Captain Eldridge down to the officers and key crew members—were all new and generally unacquainted with the *Pacific*. Could this combination of inexperience have led to decisions that put it in danger amid the ice? Ezra Nye seemed to think so.

Casting blame, even obliquely, on a shipmaster of Eldridge's stature could probably be carried off only by someone of Ezra Nye's renown. Eldridge was just as famous as Nye for his record-breaking Atlantic runs. Perhaps Eldridge had even a bit more glow because of his association with the Vanderbilts.

At the corner of Old King's Highway and Vesper Lane in Yarmouth Port, on the north shore of Cape Cod and less than fifteen miles from Captain Kelley's Centerville home, well-wishers stopped by the home of Captain Eldridge to visit his wife, Eliza. This kind of neighborly mourning was familiar to all in Yarmouth Port. More than a dozen ship captains lived within a few minutes' walk of the Eldridge home. At some point each home had shed tears for a loved one lost at sea.

In New York, William Howland, co-owner of the *John Rutledge*, was caught between two unthinkable outcomes.

If his partner Ridgway was lost on the *Pacific*, that would be a huge blow to their shipping venture. Ridgway was the one who had the connections. He hobnobbed with the people necessary for the revolving door of paperwork, permits, and stamps to keep a shipping enterprise in motion. Ridgway knew Manhattan bankers, judges, lawyers, and, most important, fixers and midlevel port bureaucrats who could always get things done for the right price or right favor.

Thinking of Ridgway gone was devastating enough. But Howland also feared a double tragedy—that something awful had happened to their latest investment, the *John Rutledge*.

There would be insurance money. Howland was glad that he checked the policy. That at least brought some reassurance. But most of any insurance payout would go to cover creditors and the merchants who lost their goods at sea. Howland and Ridgway, if he was still alive, would be on the hook for the rest. And other costs were piling up for the partnership. They had commissioned the famous Boole shipyard in East Boston to build another packet, this one bigger than the *John Rutledge*. The Boole shipwrights planned to finish work on the *Plutarch* early that summer. Then the bill would come due.

As March unfolded, Howland grew increasingly uneasy. He started to make his own visits to the East River piers seeking any scrap of news on either ship. At the same time, Howland boosted his information network. He hired more boys to quiz the crews of incoming ships for possible sightings of the *John Rutledge*.

No one had to tiptoe around James Ridgway's wife, Sarah Maria Ridgway. She was no novice when it came to the sea. She was all too aware that the waves were greedy for lives. Who was picked was often a matter of pure happenstance. Mercifully, her own family had been spared any major tragedies, until perhaps now.

Sarah Maria's father, illustrious ship captain and naval hero Hubbard Skidmore, cut his teeth as a teenage shipmate serving under his father, Zophar, in the Revolutionary War. In 1805, Hubbard Skidmore returned from Nantes, France, on the *Mississippi*, a ship he both owned and commanded. Among his passengers was Robert R. Livingston, the chief

American envoy to France for President Thomas Jefferson. Livingston was coming home after helping hammer out a treaty with Napoleon that included a stunning land deal later known as the Louisiana Purchase.

Livingston also dabbled in the budding technology of steam engines. In Paris, he befriended and collaborated with steam pioneer Robert Fulton, who was conducting experiments with steam-powered vessels on the Seine. As the story goes, Livingston urged Fulton to return to the States to work on his steamships, which, generations later, finally buried the age of the tall ships.

Sarah Maria's children, all grown now, never strayed far from her side during the vigil for the *Pacific*. They had enjoyed nearly every privilege that 1850s New York could offer: good schooling, opportunities, and the money to make choices. Two sons would become lawyers in Manhattan; her daughters found more interest in staying unmarried and helping manage the family affairs.

The Ridgway clan kept the fireplace tended round the clock as visitors came and went at their brownstone. It had been an unforgiving cold season in the Northeast. One Arctic blast after another rolled over New York—perhaps the same weather systems that helped push the ice south in the Labrador Sea. In early January, the city came to a standstill after a blizzard left drifts up to fifteen feet deep in some places along the New York–New Haven rail line. That was followed by days of subzero misery. The cycles of snow and cold wouldn't ease up until spring.

Out in the Atlantic, it was far worse.

The *Germania* was battered as it struggled toward New York.

At times, Nye had to grip the bed to keep from tumbling off as waves slammed into the ship. Some strength was returning to his hands. His feet, however, continued to trouble him.

Sarah Wood reapplied the wraps of warm bran several times a day. They seemed to help greatly to restore some circulation and color. Sarah had other tricks. She concocted a soothing balm for the cut on Nye's jaw where the boatswain Ryan had smacked him. She also brought him his first real meals, some soft vegetables from a can and a few bites of oatmeal. Sarah wouldn't let up with the cayenne water. She believed deeply in its curative powers.

In the rare stretches of calm weather, Nye tried to take a step or two. That was discouraging. His feet still couldn't handle the pressure and his knees buckled. Give it time, he assured himself. At least you seem to have escaped the fate of amputation.

In those quiet days alone in Wood's cabin, Nye had time to think about Captain Kelley, his shipmates, and the terrified faces of the passengers as they gathered one last time on deck. It was a private mourning. No one on either side of the Atlantic had any idea that the *Rutledge* was lost, although Howland's worried visits to the docks in New York were starting to stir curiosity about why the ship was so late.

On March 5, a Liverpool paper, unaware of the misfortune at sea, dutifully published the standing notice for the next scheduled packet ship departures. The *John Rutledge* would set sail May 11 for New York, and cargo needed to be stowed two days in advance, the announcement said. Irene Kelley might have seen the notice and jotted down the day, calculating that her husband should be back in Liverpool by late April to make a May 11 return to New York.

A special notice was added to the packet ship announcements in response to the mounting stories of extreme ice that worried prospective passengers: "To avoid danger from Ice," the ships "will not cross the Banks of Newfoundland north of 43 [degrees latitude] until after the last August next." Had that rule taken effect earlier, the *Germania* would have been more than seventy miles south of Nye's lifeboat and the two would not have crossed paths.

On the *Germania,* First Mate Townsend kept his log brief. It was too hard to keep the pen from dancing off the page in the storms.

March 4: "Tremendous seas."
March 8: "Gales return. Lat. 44 Long. 57.22."

They were nearing Nova Scotia, and about six hundred miles due west of where they picked up Nye.

March 11: "Barometer falling. Tremendous heavy gales and heavy sea."

But the *Germania* was lucky to be moving toward the coast. An even bigger tempest was brewing behind them, out past the Grand Banks. It was bearing down on vessels, including the British bark *Blake,* which was bringing a load of pitch pine from Mississippi to Ireland.

The *Blake* eventually lost that battle. The bark capsized, tossing at least seven sailors to their death before righting itself, but its masts had snapped and its cargo hold folded. The dozen or so survivors had no provisions left and no water. They managed to capture rainwater, which poured down in the storm, and trap a half-drowned rat on the seventh day. "It was a delicious morsel," said a statement from the captain, Edward Rudolf. He also admitted the unthinkable. On the thirteenth day, the men began to cut away small pieces from a dead crewmate. The men ate the flesh "very sparingly indeed," Rudolf insisted, trying his best to downplay the notoriety and stigma, "for the thought of it were almost as bad as death itself." The survivors were eventually picked up by a schooner after seventeen days adrift.

Townsend continued his log as the *Germania* kept its southwest course.

March 18: "New squalls. 48 days out. Lat 41.06 Long 62.26."

The *Germania* was about five hundred miles east of Cape Cod.

March 21: "Saw a number of fishing vessels."

❧

Three days later, the *Germania* slipped past Neversink, the name some called the highlands on the south end of New Jersey's Sandy Hook.

The ship—under a pilot's hand—passed through the narrows separating Staten Island and Brooklyn. It tied up at the South Street piers on March 24, making its crossing sixty-two days long, counting the time spent looking for *John Rutledge* survivors. Even in port, the weather stayed grim. "Mingled snow and rain . . . all squally and squashy," read an unusually whimsical observation in the *New York Times* that day.

Captain Wood signed the passenger manifest, a standard Port of New York document that required the ship's master to faithfully account for every passenger on board and those who may have died en route. "So help me God," the declaration ended. In his looping script, the captain signed "DH Wood."

Nye was not mentioned in these papers. He also wasn't noted on the passenger list. A rescued seaman was something that had to be dealt with separately and with some tact. Finding a lone person adrift suggests that many others—perhaps everyone else—did not make it. It was up to the *John Rutledge*'s owner and shipping line to inform the families.

By now the shipping news press pack was asking more questions about the missing *John Rutledge*. Reports of extreme ice and huge bergs in the North Atlantic came in nearly every day from awestruck captains and crew. Nature had thrown a baffling twist. Normally, the ice didn't drift south from Greenland until the spring thaws. This year, it came early and in staggering amounts.

"In the month of January, a vast portion of the Atlantic Ocean, always open to navigation at that season of the year, was taken possession of by an icy continent with its mountains and plains," wrote the *New York Courier and Enquirer*.

The *Pacific* was pretty much written off as gone. Could there be a second ship? The newspaper items on the *Rutledge* all took the same tone: draw your own conclusions, but it doesn't look good.

Then came grapevine chatter, likely started by the gossip-loving crews and dockhands. Did you hear? A young sailor was plucked from the sea by the *Germania*?

It got juicier. Someone heard this lucky soul was found in a lifeboat surrounded by bodies. This was too good a story to let sit. The shipping news reporters fanned out looking for a *Germania* crew member to try to get access to the ship. This survivor was from where? they asked. The *John Rutledge*, you say?

Wood was eventually found. Then there was no holding back the story hounds. Nye was tracked down on the *Germania,* where he was being treated. For the first time on shore, Nye told the story in full.

The headlines were front and center on page one. "Terrible Catastrophe at Sea" capped the story in Baltimore's *Sun*. "Appalling Catastrophe at Sea" echoed the *New York Herald* headline over the lines: "The ship *John Rutledge* Sunk by Ramming into an Iceberg—One Person Rescued—Probable Loss of the Remainder of the Ship's Company."

The news spread fast by telegraph.

In seen-it-all New Bedford, the editors of the *Mercury* newspaper first reported Nye's rescue in classic understatement for readers who had heard every type of sea story both genuine and invented. "The foundered ship," headlined a short piece on Nye's rescue, noting without fanfare that he was a Fairhaven neighbor. That was all it took for word to spread across the Acushnet. Nye's family reread every word, making sure there was no mistake. This was their Thomas they were talking about.

Two days later, as Nye's account was transcribed and hyped by New York reporters, the *Mercury's* tune had changed. If New York papers considered it a big story, the *Mercury's* editors decided they better get with the program.

"Thrilling narrative," the *Mercury* wrote.

Nye's mother and his uncle didn't read it. They were already on their way to New York.

Meanwhile, steamships bound for England carried American newspapers that recounted Nye's story and the loss of the *John Rutledge*.

In early April, perhaps April 7 to be exact, the captain's wife, Irene Kelley, finally learned she was most likely a widow.

On that morning, *Lloyd's List,* the London journal widely viewed as the archive for shipping, ran the one-paragraph notice on the *John Rutledge* filed by Lloyd's New York office. The item was accurate in every detail except the date of Nye's rescue, which was February 29:

> The *JOHN RUTLEDGE*, Kelley, of and for this port, from Liverpool, fell
> in with ice 18th Feb. in the lat. 46 N. lon 47 W, and the next day got into
> field ice; worked clear, but subsequently ran into an iceberg, stove a hole

in her bow, and was abandoned the same evening; mate and several others drowned; five boats left the vessel; on the 28th of Feb. one of them was fallen in with by the *Germania,* from Havre, and one man only, the survivor of 13 persons, who were in the boat, picked up, alive and landed here.

It was in a long rundown of grim news.

Entry after entry tallied the dangers, deaths, and near misses across the North Atlantic. The *Harvest Queen* reported passing the wreck of a ship with just stumps instead of masts at latitude 44 north, longitude 38 west. The crew of the foundering Swedish bark *Petrus* was saved by the ship *Sparkling Wave* off Ireland and brought to London. The *Onward,* recently arrived in New York, passed a "quantity of wrecked spars and boards" hundreds of miles off Newfoundland. The steamship *Edinburgh,* bound from New York to Glasgow, had to redirect its course 350 miles to the south to avoid ice.

For Thomas Nye, it was time to get back on a ship and leave New York.

Chapter Twenty-Five

The crowds on Broadway parted just enough to give room for the odd little procession. Some people leaned in for a closer look at the man being carried through the Wednesday morning bustle. Who is that? came time after time. Well, he cannot be dead, someone whispered. Look, his face is not covered.

Four men held the corners of a simple canvas cot cradling the frail form of Thomas Nye, a minor celebrity for a day or two as the stories of his rescue played out in newspapers. His mother and uncle, who had hurried down from Fairhaven on the fastest trains they could find, were at his side. Nye's father stayed behind because his health remained uncertain and Harriet Nye thought the trip would be too taxing for him. The men carrying Nye turned onto Rector Street toward the North River Piers, which stuck out like teeth on a comb from Manhattan's Lower West Side.

It had been just two days since the *Germania* reached port. But so much had happened, Nye could barely keep it all straight.

He was surprised—pleasantly, but still taken aback—to see his mother sweep on board the *Germania*. Nye hadn't quite figured out his next move. Harriet Nye took care of that detail. They would return to New Bedford by packet. It was all arranged. Nye also absorbed the troubling news that no vessel bound in either direction across the North Atlantic had spotted any sign of the *John Rutledge*. In all likelihood, Nye was told, he was the only survivor. Captain Kelley was probably gone. So was the first mate Samuel Atkinson, who made the reckless and unfathomable decision to check the pumps one last time. Everyone was lost. Nye thought of the faces of his crewmates and the passengers he remembered best. He couldn't stop thinking about the clump of a few dozen people—Atkinson, the carpenter Hobbs, and the passengers—left on deck knowing the *John Rutledge* would sink into the waves within hours.

Nye also learned about the *Pacific,* missing and presumed lost. Imagine, he thought, about ten weeks ago I was in Liverpool admiring that same steamship and wondering if someday I could take the same ship once commanded by Ezra Nye.

Any other ships missing? Nye asked, knowing the ice and storms were likely to take more vessels.

Yes, they said. At least two remained unaccounted for: the clippers *Ocean Queen* and *Driver* out of London and Liverpool, respectively.

Nye had a lot of time to wonder whether they met their fate the same as the *John Rutledge,* in a foggy, fatal collision in Ice Alley.

His only duty now was to listen to the doctors. The medics had done all they could for his feet. Two toes were beyond saving and were amputated while Nye was in a chloroform stupor. Just two toes gone was better than they had hoped for after their first look at him. Both feet still had a bluish cast and, in places, were covered by a wrinkled coat of dead skin. But Sarah Wood's warm bran poultices had stopped the worst of it and may have saved his feet.

The best treatment from now on, one doctor said, is to get rest and good food.

Nye was all for that. He was eager to leave New York. He had grown tired of the pressures of talking to reporters and—even more stressful— fielding the incessant questions of the shipowner Howland and his insurance minions. They were keen to learn that the captain's wife, Irene Kelley, did not make the trip. Nye didn't care about the ins and outs of the *Rutledge* ownership. But he did pick up enough to know that Captain Kelley must have had some minority stake in the ship. Otherwise, there wouldn't have been so many inquiries about Irene, who probably stood to inherit all of her husband's holdings and some insurance money, too.

∽

Nye was happy to be back on the streets, even if he was being carried along like an ailing potentate. It took his mind off the sadness of the *Rutledge* and the domino of deaths on the lifeboat. The cold would have claimed some of them no matter what. Yet he was bothered wondering whether he could have done more to prevent them from drinking the seawater. Especially the children. He tried his best to look forward, not back. Luck had shone on him for some reason. Be grateful, he thought. There was no real logic to why he was the only one left. He might have gotten on any of the other lifeboats. You'll twist yourself into knots if you try to make sense of it all, he decided. Not everything has an answer.

And heading home meant he'd soon be among people who wouldn't treat him like a curiosity. Nye chuckled thinking about the condescending tone some of the newspaper hacks had taken and their surprise when he could string together two thoughts. One account in the *New York Courier and Enquirer* added an observation that was possibly intended as a compliment but that came across as pompous conceit: "A sailor before the mast cannot know many things of interest in connection with an event of this character, and yet the statement of Mr. Nye is full, concise and intelligent."

I guess they expected a tattooed dullard to fit their stereotype of the rank-and-file sailor, he joked with his mother.

Nye tilted his head a bit to catch a glimpse of the ships on the North River, which would later become universally known as the Hudson. Seamen stopped work and poked each other. Look there, one would say. What do you make of that?

Hey, you there! someone yelled to a fellow sailor on the *Potomska*, a sturdy, screw-prop steamer that bounced between ports on the East Coast. Who's that there?

That's Nye, came the sailor's reply. Thomas Nye. You read about the *John Rutledge*? Ship that went down after hitting the berg. This is the one who made it. Only one. We're taking him home.

At about three in the afternoon, the cot bearers gently placed Nye in the cabin of the *Potomska*'s captain, Frederick Cushman, a New Bedford man who knew some of Nye's relatives. Nye's legs were swaddled in poultices similar to the ones Sarah Wood threw together on the *Germania*.

Nye complained of leg pain, but he was slowly regaining muscle control and, without any setbacks, could try a few steps before spring was out. "There appears to have been," wrote the *New York Times* reporter who followed Nye's little caravan down to the pier, "neither febrile reaction or delirium nor in fact any brain excitement such as might have been expected under the circumstances."

Before nightfall, the *Potomska* slipped around the tip of Manhattan and set a course for New Bedford.

About the same time, more ships were being piloted toward New York docks after crossing the ice-riddled Atlantic. Among them was the sailing ship *Caravan*, under command of the former *John Rutledge* captain William Sands, with its steerage full of a new crop of Mormon immigrants. Shipping news reporters, hungry for any word on ice, besieged Sands. He told them nothing was getting better that devastating winter. He described day after day of heavy pack floes and lines of icebergs.

Just behind the *Caravan* was the British packet *Northumberland,* which had left London on January 27, eleven days after the *Rutledge* cleared the Mersey. Its logs recounted "tremendous seas" and ice as well as one gale so strong it ripped away some of its sails.

"Ships have been out forty, fifty, sixty, even one hundred days," the *New York Times* chimed in the day after Nye left the city. "And many, many hearts are throbbing with the keenest anxiety, at the moment the reader is perusing this paragraph, for the fate of beloved friends who consigned themselves this last winter to the perils of the ocean."

Little *Potomska* pulled into port in New Bedford about half past ten on March 27.

Word had spread that Nye was arriving that morning. Since sunrise, crowds had gathered along the wharfs, trying to stay out of the way of the dock haulers, whaleboat outfitters, and sailors, who were not pleased that New Bedford's hoi polloi had invaded their domain.

But the seamen were just as curious as any about Nye. Perhaps more so. Each one had looked out on the sea from the deck of a ship and wondered how long they could last out there adrift. Especially this winter, which dealt out storm after storm with hardly a break. Even in late March, stubborn north winds pinned the temperatures near freezing and held spring at bay. As far south as Georgia, the *Atlanta Republican* bemoaned winter's jealous grip. "Scarcely a peach bloom is to be seen," someone wrote, "and the forest now looks like bleak winter."

By the time the *Potomska* tied up, hundreds of people were waiting.

There he is! came the cries. From the proper angle, Nye could be seen lying in the captain's cabin. Volunteers came forward to carry his cot. He waved as he was placed in a horse carriage. It clopped over the Acushnet River on the bridge to Fairhaven. Someone chipped in the few cents for the bridge toll.

Nye took it all in. He had crossed that bridge countless times, but never paid more than passing attention to the vista: brick-and-brown New Bedford, the white clapboard homes of Fairhaven arranged under the needle-sharp spire of the Congregational Church, the dozens of ships coming and going on either side of the Acushnet.

On this morning, Nye memorized every detail. He had tried to convince himself on the lifeboat that a rescue and homecoming was possible. At least that is what he kept telling the others even as the madness from the seawater took hold. He was never sure he believed it, though. Just before the *Germania* came into view, he had felt an unusual sense of calm and clarity of mind, which he interpreted as his soul getting ready to welcome death.

The carriage turned right onto Main Street and crossed the bridge over the mouth of Mill Pond. At Washington, it swung right again onto Middle Street, a collection of tidy homes near Fairhaven's waterfront. The office of the town's main doctor, Isaac Fairchild, was number thirty-four. Fairchild was waiting and helped Nye up the four steps into the front room. Almost everyone in Fairhaven had made the same trip at some point. Fairchild's parlor with the tall windows was the one-stop emergency room. Grappling hook gashes, embedded fish hooks, broken arms, burns from a hot stove. Fairchild had seen it and treated it all.

With Nye inside, the well-wishers and others finally went on their way. Fairchild got to work. He unwrapped Nye's feet and seemed pleased with the results. It was almost a month since Nye was picked up by the *Germania*. The sores on his feet were nearly closed, but he was still weak and needed to regain his strength and to be sure there were no reversals in the healing process.

Two days later, Nye's uncle, the wealthy and well-connected Thomas Nye Jr., sat down to write a letter addressed to Captain Daniel Wood of the *Germania*.

> My dear Sir; I have been listening to the touching story of suffering, as it fell from the quivering lips of my nephew. I have followed him from the sinking ship, through the perils of cold, and hunger, through dark and stormy nights. I have seen his companions fall, one after another, until he alone is left, without food, without shelter, no living object presenting itself to him.
>
> The lifeless forms of his fellow voyagers beneath his feet, his strength exhausted, his mind fast yielding to loneliness, despondency and gloom, half dreaming, half waking, lulled by the moaning of the wind and starting at the spray of the sea. No sun, no moon, no stars, all was dark and dreary to him. Almost the last gleam of hope had passed away, when the noble ship came bearing down upon him, bringing to him a HOME. That home of which he speaks, when he tells me of the kindness of yourself and Mrs. Wood.
>
> Placed as he was in your private cabin, clothed from your own wardrobe, and nurtured from the hands of your estimable lady, watched over by yourself as a father would have watched over a suffering child; day after day, and night after night, this kindness and care, came unsolicited to him. All this, and much more, he tells me, of your unbounded kindness and many little incidents of motherly affection from Mrs. Wood, to the suffering, helpless child. But, sir, the dark cloud has passed away, and sunshine rests once more upon his heart, and he lives to thank you and yours a thousand times over, and he bids me tell you in his own words, "That you have saved his life, and that he loves you as he does his father and mother. And that he will bless you so long as he lives."

His father and mother request me to offer you their heartfelt gratitude for he has told them of your kindly care, and they, too, will in their hearts bless you, and wish you every possible happiness, for they will ever feel that you by your unremitted kindness, have brought back to them their lost child. And his sister, too, who now watches over him, listens to his tale of suffering, and treasures up in her heart every act of disinterested kindness and care, and she, too, says, "Tell them that I love them, for they have saved MY BROTHER!"

In all this, you will as a sailor feel, that you were only in the line of duty, but as related to me, it is a noble act of humanity. You have done much for this boy that the world can never know. But you will have ample reward in, the consciousness of humane and disinterested motives, and that you have placed upon record a precedent of kind and generous feelings, which will not be lost upon the world, and will ever be remembered by the friends of the suffering "Sailor Boy."

I am very truly, your friend.

Thos. Nye, Jr.

Newspapers that spring ran stories detailing the full passenger and crew list of the *John Rutledge* and a summary to remind readers of the sinking. The *Times-Picayune* of New Orleans added a bit of journalistic poetry to its coverage: "It will be seen that 123 persons, the captain, mates, stewardess and eighteen of the crew, all in the prime of life, were hurried into eternity without warning. Young Nye, one of the crew, who was picked up in an open boat, was the only survivor."

The names from the *Rutledge* often appeared above snippets about the mysterious fate of the steamer *Pacific*. There was now no doubt it was gone, but not a sign had been found of where the catastrophe happened between Liverpool and New York.

The twin tragedies supplied fresh ammunition to campaigners for shipboard safety. Nothing topped their list more than the demand for watertight compartments below decks.

One of the strongest cries for reforms came hundreds of miles inland from the sea in Buffalo, a main port of call for the Great Lakes fleet. Those vessels were in no less danger from killer storms and ice.

"No one indeed can read the graphic narrative of Mr. Nye, the sole survivor of the crew of the ill-fated *Rutledge,* without being deeply impressed with the countless horrors attendant upon a shipwreck amidst icebergs," said a front-page commentary in the *Buffalo Evening Post.*

"Is it not quite probable that the *Pacific* has experienced a catastrophe as dreadful and decisive as befell the *Rutledge*? . . . We are informed by those familiar with maritime matters that it is possible to build ships so that a collision either with an iceberg or another vessel shall not necessarily involve a shipwreck. Watertight compartments will enable steamers or ships to run afoul of, without sinking each other." The missive pointed out that shipyards in France and England routinely added water-blocking compartments. "Let this subject be agitated. Let Congress be appealed to and let a law be enacted requiring every American vessel sailing to sea with passengers on board, shall be built with watertight compartments."

On the morning that Nye left the city, a long and impassioned column on page four of the *New York Herald* begged politicians and shipping executives to realize some kind of silver lining for the *John Rutledge*'s tale by requiring watertight compartments on all American vessels. "The lesson taught by the terrible catastrophe of the *John Rutledge* should not be lost," the editorial began.

> Now we have a very simple choice laid open to us. We may either continue to run as we are now doing, with a tolerable certainty of several accidents like that of the *Arctic* and that of the *John Rutledge* every year, or we may derive means of rendering such catastrophes impossible. Anyone can judge which of the two plans is most constant with the spirit of the age, the duty of legislative authorities, the bare policy of this nation.[*]
>
> It is possible to build ships so that a collision either with an iceberg or another vessel shall not necessarily involve a shipwreck.

---

[*]American shipbuilders increasingly experimented with systems of watertight compartments throughout the second half of the nineteenth century, but it took the *Titanic*'s sinking in 1912 for stricter requirements on the use of watertight chambers to be imposed for most large vessels.

The *Rutledge* was cited in the influential *US Nautical Magazine and Naval Journal* in a call to action for American lawmakers to impose rules for bulkheads and water-blocking chambers on US vessels. Resist the pressures from shipowners and insurance underwriters, the essay urged, who "are computing the advantage in dollars and cents. . . . A few hundreds, or even a few thousand dollars, expended in adding security to human life, is of little consequence," it concluded.

❧

On April 16, the steamship *Ericsson* moved down the Mersey en route to New York. The Collins Line had made a quick deal to charter the *Ericsson* as a replacement for the *Pacific*. If anything in the shipping world was an inviolable code, it was that of not spending money needlessly. By opening up the corporate wallet for the *Ericsson,* Collins was effectively declaring the *Pacific* lost without any hope.

Sixteen first-class cabin passengers were making the crossing on the *Ericsson*. Among them was an American doctor and his wife, a South American merchant, an English grocer, and an American clergyman and his family. And Irene S. Kelley, who tried to forget that the ship would be passing over the same waters that held her husband's body and all the rest from the *John Rutledge*.

The *Ericsson* had an uneventful crossing, keeping a course below the southern edge of the ice per instructions for all vessels. It's unlikely that anyone on board knew it, but the self-styled American clairvoyant Harriet Porter—the same one who claimed to have foreseen the *Pacific* tragedy—publicly predicted that the *Ericsson* would catch fire and burn all the way to the water's edge on April 26. At the time, such prognostications were not instantly dismissed as crackpot. To many mid-nineteenth-century minds, news from the spirit realm in all its forms, including glimpses into the future, was out there just waiting to be plucked. So there was some genuine relief when the *Ericsson* steamed toward the tip of Manhattan late on April 30. Mrs. Porter had no comment and moved on blithely to other predictions.

Irene Kelley had rushed back to the States with the faintest of faint hopes that there might be some miraculous news. There also was no more reason to stay in Liverpool. If the worst had happened—and her heart told her it had—then she would have lawyers and creditors and associates to face. Her husband hadn't gotten around to writing a will. That struck everyone as a bit foolhardy given the long lost-at-sea registries for the North Atlantic.

Well, she was now one of the newest members in the growing sorority of sea captain widows. She would have to figure her next moves alone.

On May 12, Irene paid a visit to Surrogate's Court in Brooklyn and officially put to paper that her husband was gone. It was a routine document. But it had to be done. Irene could have waited a while to take care of these legal finalities. But that would not be to the liking of the lawyers and creditors and others sorting out the financial fallout from the loss of the ship. Sign now, they urged, then grieve in peace. The captain, like many shipmasters, had a small stake in the ship's complex ownership. That needed to be settled as did legal responsibility for the captain's debts and assets. They had no children. Everything of his went to Irene, who last saw her husband in Liverpool four months before when the *Rutledge* moved down the Mersey.

The last section of the document didn't even bother to acknowledge the captain's rank. It read simply: "Alexander Kelley deceased."

Chapter Twenty-Six

THE LOST.

As Thomas Nye recovered, the full extent of the North Atlantic's toll that winter took shape. Even compared with other frightful mid-nineteenth-century tallies of deaths at sea, that from the first months of 1856 was exceptional.

All told, nearly 830 passengers and crew were lost before the end of March in four main wrecks: the *John Rutledge,* the *Pacific,* and the clipper ships *Driver* and *Ocean Queen.* The North Atlantic took dozens of others on smaller vessels during the same time, pushing the death toll toward one thousand. Exact numbers are difficult to determine because passenger records on American-bound ships were often imprecise and reports to maritime authorities inconsistent.

There was no deadlier three-month stretch in the Atlantic for generations.

Every six months, the maritime insurance underwriters offered a list of the payouts for ships damaged or lost. It was a global accounting of disasters covering every route around the world. More than three hundred ships made the list for the first half of 1856.

"The amount of loss, total and partial, within a period of six months is nearly *sixteen millions of dollars,*" said the insurance underwriters report in July 1856, adding its own italics for emphasis, "and is probably without parallel in our commercial history."

That was more money than it would cost to build the Brooklyn Bridge a generation later—approaching half a billion dollars in today's money.

And of the four biggest wrecks, Nye was the only survivor to give a reckoning of the disasters.

The *Ocean Queen* out of London and the *Driver* from Liverpool were lost without a trace. The *Queen* had about 90 passengers and crew of 33; the *Driver* carried more than 340 passengers and a crew of 28.

The names of steerage passengers on the *John Rutledge* have all been forgotten, or maybe they mark a small footnote in some family histories. Each one, though, was a person who laughed, struggled, and set sail on the ocean in hopes of a better life on the far shore. These are just names on a list now. But a dry roster like that leaves out the most important part. Each person once meant a great deal to someone. A son or daughter. A father or mother. A sibling or friend.

Richard Grundy, 5.

Margaret Newhan, 32.

Sarah Ryan, 23.

James McCann, 24.

Ellen Magee, 35.

Andrew Taylor, 36.

And so on for a total of 123 entries who booked passage in steerage on the *John Rutledge*.

The *John Rutledge* tragedy was overshadowed in many ways by the loss of the more glamourous *Pacific*. It's part of the sad, inevitable—and often unconscionable—selectivity that shapes history. The *Pacific* was simply a bigger story. Its captain, Asa Eldridge, counted tycoons and taste-makers among his friends. Captain Kelley had none of that cachet. The passengers on the *Pacific* were society register types. The emigrants on the *Rutledge* were anything but, even though some American news reports, without any touch of shame, described them as a "better class of emigrants" than others setting off from Europe. The mourners for the *Pacific* presided in board rooms, law offices, cathedrals, and well-appointed brownstones. Word of the *John Rutledge* tragedy spread mostly in New York tenements, Liverpool boardinghouses, and famine-struck villages in Ireland.

"So passeth the world," wrote the *Pittsburgh Gazette*.

A handbill circulated around New York in early 1856 was written for the *Pacific*, but its stanzas could be read in a more timeless way—a farewell to all taken forever by the North Atlantic.

> Have fierce gales swept her on to her doom,
> Till, helpless, she sank 'neath the surge
> Of the billows, in ocean's vast tomb,
> And its waves chant her funeral dirge?
> Perhaps from the North's frozen sea,
> An iceberg has hastened her fate,
> And, shattered and shorn, perchance she,
> Lies low, with her thrice precious freight.

Years later, the *Pacific* gave up one last mystery.

In 1861, more than five years after the ship was last seen leaving Liverpool, a bottle with a note inside washed ashore in the Hebrides islands off Scotland's western coast. The paper, about two inches by two inches, was covered on both sides with what appeared to be a hastily scrawled message in pencil:

> On board the Pacific, from L'pool to N. York. Ship going down. Confusion on board. Icebergs around us on every side. I know I cannot escape. I write the cause of our loss, that friends may not live in suspense. The finder of this will please get it published,
> WM. GRAHAM.

Questions were immediately raised.[*]

---

[*] In 1991, divers discovered a wreck in the Irish Sea about sixty miles from Liverpool. Some believed it could be the bow section and other remains of the *Pacific*, but no conclusive evidence has been presented and many maritime experts cast serious doubt on whether the wreck is the steamship lost in 1856.

Skeptics called it a cruel hoax since there was no William Graham on the passenger or crew manifests filed with the Collins Line agent in Liverpool.

Later, however, the *New York Times* and other newspapers dug deeper. It turned out a helmsman who went by the name Robert Graham shipped out with the *Pacific*. This led many to believe that the note was authentic despite the name discrepancy. It was not unusual for names to be mangled or flat-out wrong on ships' lists. As the *Times* noted regarding the Graham note, the mismatched first name on the bottle-borne message "will not count for much with those who are acquainted with the careless manner in which seafaring people frequently give their names, and the facility for such a mistake presented by the ordinary mode of entering the names of a ship's company." The *Times* and others decided the note was possibly authentic.

Ice continued to harass North Atlantic ships for decades to come.

The British journal the *Nautilus* reminded every sea traveler to keep the memory of all those who were tossed into the ocean from an ice-crippled ship and who suffered until death kindly granted them a "merciful termination to their existence."

The shock of the *Titanic* sinking in 1912 brought important reforms aimed at improving maritime safety.

A year later, a group known as the International Ice Patrol was put into action. The patrol, first by sea vessels and then by air as plane technology improved, kept watch and compiled records from across the North Atlantic Ice Alley, reporting on ice conditions and the southern limits of the ice. Since this monitoring began, only a handful of close encounters between ships and bergs has occurred in the zone off the Grand Banks. But farther to the east, near Greenland, several ships nevertheless collided with icebergs, notably the Danish liner *Hans Hedtoft*, which was lost in 1959 with ninety-five people aboard.

Years of heavy ice come and go.

Observations tracked by the National Geographic Society show a generally cyclic pattern of iceberg density. In April 1912, the month the

Titanic went down, 395 icebergs were spotted. Yet far fewer appeared on either side of the tragedy: in April 1911, about 100; in April 1913, about 90. The greatest number—953—was spotted in April 1984. A year before that, in April 1983, slightly more than 300 floated the seas; and in April 1985, about 200. In other words, predicting ice levels in the North Atlantic one year to the next is something of a roulette spin.

But climate change poses as a potential game-changer.

Experts in glaciology predict an acceleration in the calving process of icebergs dropping off the Greenland ice sheet. Global warming is melting glacial ice. At the same time, it's speeding the pace as the immense Greenland glaciers grind their way to the sea. Stress from higher temperatures opens cracks in the ice and deep fissures—some that run down thousands of feet to where the ice meets the land. Meltwater on the surface of the glacier cascades down these gaps and acts as a kind of slickening agent. In the words of one top researcher: "It's almost like putting oil under the ice. It helps it move along."

And it's not just what's happening under the ice. Climate change works to shift prevailing winds, currents, and the howling jet stream at thirty-thousand feet and higher, which serves as a giant conveyor belt for weather. Any sustained change in the winds pushing down from the north means more ice heading south into shipping lanes. A possible sign of what's to come is visible from the shores of Newfoundland: whereas in decades past iceberg spotters used to see dozens of big bergs, now they tally them in the hundreds.

Epilogue

On a chilly day in late February—exactly thirty-eight years after Thomas Nye was cast adrift in the North Atlantic—he put on a freshly cleaned constable's uniform. He made sure the stripes were straight and aligned the polished buttons. It was a big day. He wanted to look his best. Everyone did.

A celebrity guest, none other than the writer and raconteur Mark Twain, was in Fairhaven to dedicate the new town hall, an event that had every Fairhaven official and city booster, down to the shellfish inspector, turned out in their finest outfits and widest civic pride smiles. The town hall was worth the extra effort. It was a handsome structure, designed in the French Gothic style, with a four-face clock tower, expertly crafted stained glass windows, and an auditorium lined in polished oak paneling. The three iron-barred jail cells made it one of the region's most elegant lockups.

No expense had been spared. That's because it was bankrolled by one of the country's wealthiest moguls: Henry Huttleston Rogers of Standard Oil fame—or infamy, depending on your views of the era's robber barons. Rogers could buy anything, or anyone, he wanted. But what made him most happy was breaking ground on projects in his hometown. He had already put up Fairhaven's magnificent Renaissance-style Millicent Library just across Center Street from the new town hall. He also elicited a promise from his friend Twain that the author would return years later to lay the cornerstone for the next big project: the Unitarian Memorial Church, the design of which included a 165-foot bell tower and a bevy of limestone gargoyles.

Rogers's friendship with Twain was not even a year old in early 1894, but already it was intensely important to both men. Twain was grateful to Rogers for helping him straighten out his personal finances, which had reached train-wreck status. Rogers advised Twain on how to save his copyrights and sort out a thicket of commercial ventures, partnerships, IOUs, and handshake deals. In return, Rogers found in Twain a pal who was not awed—at least, not too much—by his yachts and townhouses and power and yes-men. Rogers seemed to need a homespun character like Twain as a friend, even if the writer's countrified act was a bit staged. It may have reminded Rogers of the way he was regarded in Fairhaven. He was admired, no doubt, but not fawned over. Fairhaven had seen its share of big shots rise and fall during the whaling times. Rogers knew that preening and smugness didn't play well in those parts. Maybe that's why Rogers liked to lavish money on the place. They let him be him.

Back in 1856, when Nye returned, Rogers was a teenager living a few doors down from Dr. Fairchild. He was six years younger than Nye, but probably remembered the castaway from school or from knocking around the docks. A sea life wasn't really for Rogers. So he did what he could, working as a grocery store stock boy and on the Fairhaven Branch Railroad. Then in 1859 came word of an amazing event in Titusville in the northwest corner of Pennsylvania, where locals had for years tried but failed to pump a goop they called rock oil out of the ground. Finally, someone had done it. A test bore hit a vein and oil was flowing. Rogers had seen all the money that could be made on whale oil lubricants in the factory built by Nye's uncle. He figured this new stuff coming out of the ground in Pennsylvania could be worth something as well.

Rogers headed to Pennsylvania as a twenty-one-year-old oil rusher like tens of thousands of other young men. But he didn't see himself working the rigs. He wanted to process what came out. He founded one of the first oil refineries and turned out kerosene for lamps and other devices. Though he may not have known it at the time, he was putting the first nails in the coffin of the whaling industry back home.

Later, Rogers faced down a different sort of leviathan in the form of Standard Oil. Rockefeller's monopolist view of the world held no room for independent refiners such as Rogers. Rockefeller got his way, gobbling up or steamrolling company after company. Most of the small fries were collateral damage. Rogers, however, managed to leverage himself to a top spot at Standard Oil and eventually became Rockefeller's right-hand man.

At the town hall ceremony, Rogers stood aside proudly to let Twain do his thing. Rogers nodded at the Fairhaven dignitaries and families he knew, which was just about all of them. Some merited extra attention. The Nyes were most definitely on that short list, right up there with the town's other gentry, including the Delanos.

In the crowd, hardened seaman Joshua Slocum, fifty years old, was taking time away from his Fairhaven workshop where he was refurbishing a thirty-seven-foot sloop. He had named it the *Spray*. The following spring, Slocum would set off for an around-the-world solo sail, carrying only an old sextant and a windup alarm clock for navigation. His was hailed as the first one-man circumnavigation. Slocum's book, *Sailing Alone Around the World*, is credited with inspiring generations of adventurers for adventure's sake.

Thomas Nye stood stiffly off to one side with the rest of the town fathers. He scanned the crowd for his wife, Eliza. They had married later in life, when Thomas was fifty-two and Eliza was in her early forties. They had no children but were happy to keep space for Thomas's older sister, Abbie, who never married. Abbie stood with the staff of Millicent Library, where she was an assistant librarian, to hear Twain's speech.

Twain was in good form. He began with a folksy ramble about how the building was the real star of the day and then took some perfunctory jabs at lawyers, one of his favorite foils. Finally, he spun a classic Twain-esque vignette—probably made up, but who cared?—about stealing a watermelon from a farmer's wagon when he was a boy. But he had pangs of guilt, thinking of the example of noble George Washington and how old George would never have enjoyed the spoils of theft. So he returned the watermelon to the farmer only to find out the fruit was far from ripe. The farmer was so ashamed of being exposed for trying to sell unripe melons, he gave young Twain a free juicy watermelon as penance.

"So I forgave him," Twain said. "For when a person has done wrong and acknowledges it and is ashamed of it, that is enough for me."

Twain, of course, mentioned none of Washington's moral warts, including the fact that he had slaves. That wasn't Twain's style. The crowd was there for pure Twain, not a lecture on the uncomfortable complexities of American history.

After his speech, Twain toured Fairhaven's new library. His books were prominently displayed. Among the staff who greeted him was Abbie Nye, who was looking forward to the gala ball planned for that night, with Twain and Rogers as guests of honor.

Thomas Nye and the other Nyes in town also attended the evening's festivities. The Nye family numbers had dwindled a bit in Fairhaven from the glory days decades ago. Both of Thomas's parents were gone. So was his uncle, Thomas Nye Jr., who wrote the heartfelt letter to Captain Wood of the *Germania*. In 1882, he used a gun to take his own life. Newspaper accounts remarked on his past wealth and good standing in the community but avoided, as was custom when a prominent citizen was involved, mentioning possible motives for suicide.

Thomas W. Nye's seafaring time was long over. He spent his days working in a grocery store and doing his part for the community in the volunteer fire brigades, as one of the town's measurers of wood and bark, and as a constable, a semiceremonial position that required he suit up for action from time to time. Once, he took part in raids on illegal liquor sellers and earned prominent mention in the local press as part of the crack constabulary. But when the weather was just damp and cold enough, an old ache throbbed in the stubs of his lopped-off toes. The damage to his feet kept him out of the Civil War, though he would have been happy to go. A draft form listed him as lame.

Neither Nye nor Twain ever mentioned encountering each other that night at the soiree in Fairhaven. If they had met up, though, master storyteller Twain would have had the rare treat of hearing someone else tell a fantastical story, the one of Nye as sole survivor of the *John Rutledge* cast adrift in the frozen sea.

❧

Nine years later, in 1903, Nye did retell his story in full. A reporter from Boston heard about his remarkable ordeal and tracked him down. The journalist finally found Nye at his home, a comfortable two-story place with twin fireplaces on Main Street in Fairhaven. Nye was just a few weeks shy of seventy, and his health was erratic. Yet he still had more good days than bad. The reporter approached him on one of the good ones.

Nye settled into a chair and asked the reporter if he was ready.

I am, came the reply.

Fine, said Nye, now take this down. He began to talk and the reporter scribbled it down word for word as best he could.

"Our ship encountered stormy weather, but made fair progress until the early morning of February 19 when she struck an iceberg, which stove a hole in the starboard bow just below the water line. The pumps were put to work, but without avail."

Nye went on for an hour or so. The reporter wrote furiously to keep up. Near the end, he said:

"How much longer I could have stood this God only knows, but soon after sunrise on the 29th, the last day of February of that leap year, I brightened up. I felt as though the voyage was done. Just before noon I sighted a ship advancing from the leeward. I saw her mainsails hove up and the jibs lowered, and then I knew that I was seen and that my deliverance was at hand."

The article was syndicated and sent around the country. It ran in places where people had never even set eyes on the sea. For a day or two, Nye, Mrs. Atkinson, the Hendersons, and the others from the *John Rutledge* were mentioned by Nye one last time.

Nye died June 11, 1905. Cause of death was listed as arterial sclerosis that brought on a cerebral hemorrhage. Across the Acushnet River in New Bedford, the era of whaling was meeting its end as well. The last whaler headed out from port in 1927. Nye's wife, Eliza, had died just three years earlier, in 1924.

Nye's sister, Abbie, died in October 1914. She served for eleven years as an assistant librarian and had some stirring stories of her own to tell. In February 1866, she headed to the Deep South in the tense years of Reconstruction. She agreed to go to Columbus, Georgia, to run one of the

Freedmen's schools, which had been set up as part of a program to aid freed slaves. In a letter home in April 1866, she wrote about the crushing poverty and needs left by the war and how she tried to help a black woman who couldn't afford the ten dollars a month needed to rent a shanty. She called her students "scholars" and said each day one of them would bring her a lovely bouquet of hyacinths, jessamines, and japonicas.

During the war, the Nye family shipping fleet began its decline, pushed along by Confederate raiders and waning demand for whale oil. In 1863, the whaler *Nye* was captured and burned in the equatorial Pacific by a British ship allied with the Confederacy. In June 1865, the ship *William C. Nye* was torched by the Confederate ship *Shenandoah* in a bizarre blitz across the Arctic Ocean. The *Shenandoah*'s commander had not yet learned of Gen. Robert E. Lee's surrender. That November, the *Shenandoah* showed up in Liverpool, a city always friendly to the Confederacy because of the cotton trade. Essentially, the ship's crew sailed halfway around the world to surrender in England, fearing that a return to the States would mean trial for piracy.

Captain Daniel H. Wood died of dysentery in 1861 in Brooklyn, and his body was returned for burial in New Bedford. His wife, the former Sarah Allen Howland, died in 1890.

First mate Charles Townsend left the *Germania* to take command of the packet ship *Bavaria* but returned to his old ship as captain after Wood moved on. He led thirteen voyages on the *Germania,* making runs to Le Havre and, once, to New Orleans during the Civil War by outrunning Confederate ambush flotillas the entire way. He died in 1904.

The *Germania* outlived them all. Its ownership, homeport, and role changed several times over the decades. It eventually ended up in San Francisco as a coal barge. In March 1910, a reference in the *Seaman's Journal* said the ship was to be burned and its copper and other metals reclaimed.

The former master of the *John Rutledge,* Captain William A. Sands, died in 1863 while making a crossing from London as a cabin passenger.

Irene Kelley remarried just months after returning to New York from Liverpool. She died in 1870.

In Centerville, behind the South Congregational Church, the Kelley family put up a grave marker for Captain Alexander among the plots for his parents and siblings. His marker rests on a ridge that's a short walk from the tidal marshes that feed into Nantucket Sound. The inscription on Kelley's stone contains lines popular for nineteenth-century seamen who never returned: "He sleeps beneath the blue lone sea. He lies where pearls lie deep."

The Collins Line never recovered from the loss of the *Pacific*.

It attempted to rebound with a new steamship, the *Adriatic,* but that vessel made only two voyages before the company's financial foundation collapsed. Congress dealt a crippling blow when it cut the crucial mail-delivery subsidy to the Collins Line. In 1858—four years after Collins lost his wife and children in the *Arctic* sinking—the three remaining Collins ships were auctioned off. The *Adriatic, Baltic,* and *Atlantic* were sold for a paltry $50,000. Edward Knight Collins died in 1878.

The Cunard steamship *Persia,* which Nye had admired in Liverpool, was cut up for scrap in a London shipyard in 1872. Eleven years later, on a midsummer day in Brooklyn, Williams Howland died, years after the last Howland & Ridgway ship was sold off.

And Ebenezer Franklin Nye, the other Nye with a remarkable tale of sea rescue in the Pacific, eventually had his luck run out. He was lost at sea in 1879.

❧

In Fairhaven's Riverside Cemetery, on a small knoll, sit some of the Nye family graves. It's a pleasant little patch, a bit removed from the grand graves and tombs of Fairhaven's finest, such as the Delano family.

The granite gravestone for Thomas W. Nye occupies the highest point on that little rise. Through the pine trees you can see the slate blue Acushnet River flowing into the sea.

I visited the grave on a late winter afternoon, believing that I might be the first person in many years to pay homage there. I was not. A stone rested on the top of Thomas Nye's grave marker, a gesture showing someone cared enough to leave a remembrance. I looked it over. It hadn't been there long. It was free of the moss and lichen that grow on objects left for years in the damp sea air.

I will never know who left the stone. But that doesn't matter. Someone remembers Thomas Nye. And that keeps alive a connection to everything that happened amid the dreadful ice of 1856: Nye, the *John Rutledge,* Captain Kelley, that horrible moment of striking the ice, the thirteen adrift in a lifeboat, and the other crew and passengers lost in the North Atlantic.

I left a small stone of my own. I hoped it stays there long enough for moss to grow.

THOMAS NYE FAMILY TREE

Thomas W. Nye
1834-1905

James Sellars Nye
1806-1881
+
Harriet Stevens
1810-1886

Captain Thomas Nye
1768-1842
+
Hannah Hathaway
1769-1857

Captain Obed Nye
1736-1815
+
Mary Sellars
1739-1797

Cape Cod Branch

Peleg Nye
1817 - 1896

Ebenezer Franklin Nye
1799 - 1879

Captain Ezra Nye
1798 - 1866

Benjamin Nye
circa1620 - circa1704

Types of Vessels

PACKET SHIP

Typically a three-mast sailing vessel that is square-rigged, meaning that the sails are held by spars arranged perpendicular, or square, to the center line of the ship running bow to stern. The term "ship" can be used as generic reference for ocean vessels.

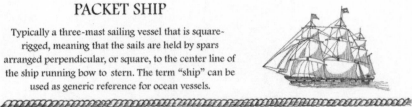

BARQUE or BARK

Similar to a ship, but with a rigging variation. The foremast and mainmast are square-rigged, but the mizzenmast is fore-and-aft-rigged. This means the sails are held by spars that run parallel with the vessel's center line rather than perpendicular.

BRIG

A two-mast vessel, square-rigged. A variation known as a brigantine has its mainmast fore-and-aft-rigged.

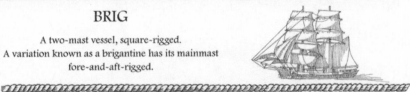

SLOOP

Single mast, fore-and-aft-rigged.

CLIPPER

A general term for a very fast sailing ship, often fitted with additional sails to increase speed. The hull design also was modified to cut through the water as cleanly as possible, including long and narrow lines and sharp-pointed bows.

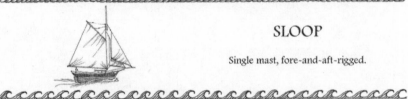

STEAMSHIP

A general term for vessels powered by steam from onboard boilers. The early vessels included paddle steamers with one sidewheel or twin paddles with one on each side.
Later, steamers were made with screws, or propellers. For decades, steamers had masts and sails as a backup in case of boiler failures or other malfunctions.

Acknowledgments

Every book is a collaboration. And every attempt at acknowledging all the assistance, inspiration, and advice is incomplete. There is always someone left out. My apologies for anyone omitted. It was purely unintentional.

To all, mentioned or not, please accept my deep gratitude.

For the fourth time, my spouse, collaborator, and muse, Toula Vlahou, has put her remarkable stamp on a book. Every page is better because of her.

I am also humbled by the enormous talents of my editor, Robert Pigeon, and artist Terry Kole. I am honored to call them friends and colleagues.

My agent extraordinaire, Russell Galen, has assisted with his expertise and impeccable judgment. His mark is everywhere throughout this project. Once the manuscript was done, project editor Amber Morris and copyeditor Christina Palaia added the finishing polish.

Let me begin the other thanks at the most logical point: the Nye family. Members and associates of the Nye Family of America Association of East Sandwich, Massachusetts, have been hugely helpful each step of the way, including John Cullity, executive director; archivist and author Nils V. Bockmann; and genealogist Julia Hendy.

Across Britain and Ireland, there are many to recognize: Captain Geoff Topp, chairman of the Liverpool Pilots' Association; Lorna Hyland, assistant curator, maritime archives at the Merseyside Maritime Museum in Liverpool; Christine Johnston, senior library assistant at the Mellon Centre for Migration Studies in Omagh, County Tyrone; Alisdair Moran and Sheena McClure in County Tyrone; Paul Keogh at the Liverpool Central Library, record office; Janet Bishop, Genealogy Scotland; journalists Karla

Adam (and her save-the-day loan of fifteen pounds) and Greg Katz in London; Jon Earle at the National Maritime Museum; and Roger Cooter for his excellent 1972 theses at Durham University, "The Irish in County Durham and Newcastle, 1840–1880."

In Fairhaven: Chris Richard, director of tourism, and Debra Charpentier, head of special collections at the Millicent Library.

In New Bedford: Jodi Goodman and Janice Hodson at the New Bedford Library's Special Collections Department; Karen De Mello at the New Bedford Historical Society; and Arthur Motta and Mark Procknik at the New Bedford Whaling Museum.

On Cape Cod: Randy Hoel and Bebe Brock at the Centerville Historical Museum; Tom Nortz and Rick Garceau at the Captain David N. Kelley B&B in Centerville; Kevin and Joan Murphy; Nadine and John Kerns; Duncan Oliver at the Historical Society of Old Yarmouth; and the staff at the Centerville Public Library.

Elsewhere around New England: Maribeth Bielinkski and Carol Mowrey at the Mystic Seaport Research Center; Doris (Deb) Townshend of New Haven, Connecticut; and Cipperly A. Good at the Penobscot Marine Museum in Searsport, Maine.

In Washington: the staff of the Reading Room at the Library of Congress.

And at other points: Jessica Pigza at the New York Public Library's Brooke Russell Astor Reading Room for Rare Books and Manuscripts; Emily Chapin at the Museum of the City of New York; Michael W. Pocock at maritimequest.com; Carey Stumm at the National Archives in New York; Nic Butler, historian with Charleston County Public Library; Kenneth J. Blume, history professor, Albany College of Pharmacy and Health Sciences; Carl Akins at the Hatch Family Association; Diana Mankowski for research with Townsend papers in Michigan; Liane Fenimore of the Townshend Society of America; Michael Mann, distinguished Professor of Atmospheric Science at Penn State University; Jeniann Neilsen at LDSGeneaology.com; Madalina Veres at the Historical Society of Pennsylvania; Maggie Blanck for her historical image collection.

Bibliography

Some of the books, periodicals, and other material used in the research for this book.

NYE FAMILY, FAIRHAVEN and NEW BEDFORD

Bockmann, Nils V. *Peleg Nye: The Jonah of Cape Cod*. North Charleston, SC: CreateSpace Independent Publishing Platform. 2014.

Carhart, Lucy Ann. *Genealogy of the Morris Family: Descendants of Thomas Morris of Connecticut*. New York: A. S. Barnes Co. 1911.

Davidson, James Wheeler. *The Island of Formosa, Past and Present*. Taipei: Southern Materials Center. 1903.

Harris, Charles A. *Old-Time Fairhaven*. New Bedford, MA: Reynolds Printing. 1947.

Hurd, D. Hamilton. *History of Bristol County, Massachusetts*. Philadelphia: J. W. Lewis & Co. 1883.

Nye, George P. *Legendary Lives: True Tales of Old Time Survivors, War Heroes, Statesman, Artists & Adventurers*. Sandwich, MA: Nye Family Association of America. 1997.

Nye Family Association of America. *Proceedings at the First Reunion in Sandwich, Massachusetts*. New Bedford: E. Anthony & Sons. 1903.

Yentsch, Anne. "Applying Concepts from Historical Archaeology to New England's Nineteenth-Century Cookbooks." *Northeast Historical Archaeology* 42 (2013).

PACKET LINES and ATLANTIC SHIPPING

Butler, Daniel Allen. *The Age of Cunard: A Transatlantic History, 1839–2003*. Annapolis, MD: Lighthouse Press. 2003.

Choules, John Overton. *The Cruise of the Steam Yacht North Star*. Boston: Gould and Lincoln. 1854.

Clark, Arthur H. *The Clipper Ship Era: An Epitome of Famous American and British Clipper Ships, Their Owners, Builders, Commanders, and Crews, 1843–1869*. New York: G. P. Putnam's Sons. 1912.

Colburn's United Service Magazine and Naval and Military Journal. London: Hurst and Blackett. 1869.

Druett, Joan. *Petticoat Whalers: Whaling Wives at Sea, 1820–1920*. Hanover, NH: University Press of New England. 2001.

Fagan, Brian. *Beyond the Blue Horizon*. New York: Bloomsbury Press. 2012.

Folsom, Burton W. *The Myth of the Robber Barons: A New Look at the Rise of Big Business in America*. Herndon, VA: Young America's Foundation. 2010.

McKay, Richard C. *Donald McKay and His Famous Sailing Ships*. New York: Dover Publications. 2011.

Miles, Vincent. *The Lost Hero of Cape Cod: Captain Asa Eldridge and the Maritime Trade That Shaped America*. Yarmouth Port, MA: Historical Society of Old Yarmouth. 2015.

Sawtell, Clement Cleveland. *Captain Nash DeCost and the Liverpool Packets*. Mystic, CT: Marine Historical Association. 1955.

Shaw, David W. *The Sea Shall Embrace Them: The Tragic Story of the Steamship Arctic*. New York: Free Press. 2002.

Simpson, A. W. Brian. *Cannibalism and the Common Law: The Story of the Tragic Last Voyage of the Mignonette and the Strange Legal Proceedings to Which It Gave Rise*. London: Hambledon Press. 1994.

Staff, Frank. *The Transatlantic Mail*. London: Adlard Coles Nautical. 1956.

US Nautical Magazine and Naval Journal 4 (March–October 1856). New York: Griffiths, Bates & Co.

LIVERPOOL and IRISH EMIGRATION

Anbinder, Tyler. *Five Points: The 19th-Century New York City Neighborhood That Invented Tap Dance, Stole Elections, and Became the World's Most Notorious Slum*. New York: Free Press. 2001.

Belchem, John. *The Irish, Catholic and Scouse: The History of the Liverpool-Irish, 1800–1939*. Liverpool: Liverpool University Press. 2007.

Conliffe, Tom. *Pilots: The World of Pilots Under Sail and Oar. Vol. 1, Pilot Schooners of North America and Great Britain*. Brooklin, ME: Wooden Boat Publications. 2001.

Coogan, Tim Pat. *The Famine Plot: England's Role in Ireland's Greatest Tragedy*. London: Palgrave Macmillan. 2013.

Gallman, J. Matthew. *Receiving Erin's Children: Philadelphia, Liverpool, and the Irish Famine Migration, 1845–1855*. Chapel Hill: University of North Carolina Press. 2000.

Guillet, Edwin C. *The Great Migration: The Atlantic Crossing by Sailing Ship Since 1770.* Edinburgh: Thomas Nelson and Sons. 1937.

Hansen, Marcus Lee. *The Atlantic Migration, 1607–1850.* Cambridge, MA: Harvard University Press. 1940.

Macilwee, Michael. *The Liverpool Underworld: Crime in the City, 1750–1900.* Liverpool: Liverpool University Press. 2011.

Nautical Magazine and Naval Chronicle. London: Simpkin, Marshall and Co. 1850.

Neal, Frank. *Sectarian Violence: The Liverpool Experience, 1819–1914: An Aspect of Anglo-Irish History.* Manchester: Manchester University Press. 1998.

Ó Murchadha, Ciarán. *The Great Famine: Ireland's Agony, 1845–1852.* London: Continuum International Publishing Group. 2011.

Smith, William. *An Emigrant's Narrative: Or a Voice from the Steerage (1850).* Whitefish, MT: Kessinger Publishing. 2009.

Whyte, Robert. *The Ocean Plague, or A Voyage to Quebec in an Irish Emigrant Vessel.* Boston: Coolidge and Wiley. 1848.

Willcox, Walter F. *International Migrations, Volume II: Interpretations.* Cambridge, MA: National Bureau of Economic Research. 1931.

Winter, James H. *Secure from Rash Assault: Sustaining the Victorian Environment.* Berkeley: University of California Press. 1999.

Work Projects Administration writers. *A Maritime History of New York.* New York: Going Coastal. 2004.

ICE

Across the Atlantic in Sailing Packet Days: First Hand Accounts. Lincoln, MA: Sawtells of Somerset. 1973.

Edinger, Ray. *Love and Ice: The Tragic Obsessions of Dr. Elisha Kent Kane, Arctic Explorer.* Savannah, GA: Frederic C. Beil. 2015.

Flayhart, William Henry, III. *Perils of the Atlantic: Steamship Disasters 1850 to the Present.* New York: W. W. Norton. 2003.

Goodman, Nan. *Shifting the Blame: Literature, Law, and the Theory of Accidents in Nineteen-Century America.* New York: Routledge. 1998.

Hill, Brian. *Ship Collisions with Iceberg Database. Report to PERD [Program of Energy Research and Development]: Trends and Analysis.* Ottawa: National Research Council Canada. 2005.

Wadhams, Peter. *Ice in the Ocean.* Amsterdam: Gordon and Breach Science Publishers. 2000.

THE *JOHN RUTLEDGE* and CREW

Blume, Kenneth J. *Historical Dictionary of the U.S. Maritime Industry*. Plymouth, England: Scarecrow Press. 2012.

Bray, Mary Matthews. *A Romance of Barnstable*. Boston: Gorham Press. 1909.

Deyo, Simeon L. *History of Barnstable County, Massachusetts*. New York: H. W. Blake. 1890.

Duncan, Brad, and Martin Gibbs. *Please God Send Me a Wreck: Responses to Ship-wreck in a 19th Century Australian Community*. New York: Springer. 2015.

Hawthorne, Nathaniel. *Passages from the Note-Books of Nathaniel Hawthorne*. Boston: Houghton, Mifflin & Co. 1883.

Herberger, Charles F. *Three Centuries of Centerville Scenes*. Centerville, MA: Centerville Historical Society. 1989.

Koch, Tom. *The Wreck of the William Brown: A True Tale of Overcrowded Life-boats and Murder at Sea*. Vancouver: Douglas & McIntyre. 2003.

Learmonth, Eleanor, and Jenny Tabakoff. *No Mercy: True Stories of Disaster, Survival and Brutality*. Melbourne, Australia: Text Publishing Company. 2013.

Lindemann, Hannes. *Alone at Sea: A Doctor's Survival Experiments of Two Atlantic Crossings in a Dugout Canoe and a Folding Kayak*. New York: Random House. 1958.

Miller, Ruth Richards. *The Seven Villages of Barnstable*. Binghamton, NY: Vail-Ballou Press. 1976.

Ravenel, Henry Edmund. *Ravenel Records*. Berkeley County, SC: Franklin Publishing. 1898.

Ravenel, Rose Pringle. *Piazza Tales: A Charleston Memory*. Charleston, SC: Shaftesbury Press. 1952.

Sawtell, Clement Cleveland. *Captain Nash DeCost and the Liverpool Packets*. Mystic, CT: Marine Historical Association. 1955.

Staff, Frank. *The Transatlantic Mail*. London: Adlard Coles Nautical. 1956.

Index